BREAKING THE WATCH

BREAKING THE WATCH

THE MEANINGS OF **RETIREMENT** IN AMERICA

JOEL S. SAVISHINSKY

CORNELL UNIVERSITY PRESS

ITHACA AND LONDON

All rights reserved. Except for brief quotations in a review, this book, or parts thereof, must not be reproduced in any form without permission in writing from the publisher. For information, address Cornell University Press, Sage House, 512 East State Street, Ithaca, New York 14850.

First published 2000 by Cornell University Press

Printed in the United States of America

Library of Congress Cataloging-in-Publication Data

Savishinsky, Joel S.
  Breaking the watch : the meanings of retirement in America / Joel S. Savishinsky.
      p.   cm.
Includes bibliographical references and index.
  ISBN 0-8014-3771-7 (cloth : alk. paper)
  1. Retirement—United States. 2. Retirees—Recreation—United States. I. Title.
HQ1063.2U6 S39   2000
306.3'8'0973—d21

                                                    00-009092

Cornell University Press strives to use environmentally responsible suppliers and materials to the fullest extent possible in the publishing of its books. Such materials include vegetable-based, low-VOC inks and acid-free papers that are recycled, totally chlorine-free, or partly composed of nonwood fibers. Books that bear the logo of the FSC (Forest Stewardship Council) use paper taken from forests that have been inspected and certified as meeting the highest standards for environmental and social responsibility. For further information, visit our website at www.cornellpress.cornell.edu.

Cloth printing   10 9 8 7 6 5 4 3 2 1

*For Janet Fitchen and Barbara Prud'homme,
who showed us how to live
and how to die*

CONTENTS

ACKNOWLEDGMENTS

Virtually every person who participated in this project had a favorite joke about aging and memory. One of the best one-liners belonged to Ed Trayvor, a retired fund-raiser from Taylor County, who liked to observe that "by the time you reach 80 you've learned all there is to know. You just have to be able to remember it."

In trying to recall all those who helped me in this endeavor, I am fortunate here in being able to remember more people than I can acknowledge or name. Those who participated directly, including Ed, his wife Harriet, and 24 other retirees of Shelby, New York, have each been given a pseudonym in this work. The same is true for the county in which they live, the community of Shelby itself, and its coffee shops, schools, factories, churches, and streets. Though private and public details have been altered to protect identities, the town, its people, and its institutions are nevertheless real, and I owe the community's citizens a great measure of respect and gratitude for their cooperation, humor, patience, and honesty.

The opportunity and encouragement to carry out this work were provided by several other individuals and organizations. Research and writing were supported by a sabbatic and a leave of absence from Ithaca College; by foundation grants to that college's "Pathways to Life Quality" study, its Gerontology Institute, and its Dana Professors program; and by a fellowship from the National Endowment for the Humanities in 1997. During the tenure of the NEH fellowship, I had the chance to learn about the aging experience in Asia while lecturing at Lady Doak College and Appasamy College in Tamil Nadu, South India. Earlier, in 1994, I had had the privilege of sailing around the world with a group of retired people while serving on the faculty of the University of Pittsburgh's Semester at Sea program; the senior passengers there were wonderful teachers as well as students, showing me a great deal about the ongoing passion for learning and growth in later life.

Several chapters in this work are based on articles of mine which first appeared in other formats. I thank the editors and publishers of the following periodicals for permission to utilize material that first appeared in their pages: Sage Publications for "The Unbearable Lightness of Retirement: Ritual and Support in a Modern Life Passage," *Research on Aging* 17(3): 243–59 (1995) (Chapter 1); the American Anthropological Association for "Mastering the Art of Retirement," *Anthropology Newsletter* 3(7): 15 (1998) (Chapter 2); and the Society for the Anthropology of North America for "At Work, at Home, at Large: The Sense of Person and Place in Retirement," *North American Dialogue* 3(1): 16–18 (1998) (Chapter 3).

Last, there is my indebtedness to people close to home. A number of my American students actively collaborated in collecting, transcribing, and analyzing original materials, most notably Stephanie Block, Joseph Braitsch, Leigh Chapman, Keri Dackow, Mollie Dusinberre, Andrew Eigenrauch, Deborah Horman, Nicole Kochenash, Janice Lindsley, Kristin Maloney, Amy Mullen, Sarah Raleigh, Alison Riley, Jacob Savishinsky, Eric Trum, Abigail Unger, and Meredith Zaslowe. In addition, several colleagues and friends were particularly generous with their ideas, encouragement, and experiences, including Nancy Bereano, Jules Burgevin, Janet Fitchen, Bea Goldman, Ann Halpern, Paul Hamill, Janet Kalinowski, and John Krout. I am also very grateful to Maria Vesperi and David J. Ekerdt for thoughtful readings of the manuscript; to Joel Ray and Kay Scheuer for their careful editing; and to Sydelle Kramer of Frances Goldin Literary Agency, and Fran Benson of Cornell University Press, for their advocacy and guidance; their support for this project helped bring it to completion and the light of day. Finally, a special word of thanks is due to my wife, Susan, and my sons, Max and Jacob, who have borne with my obsessions while I worked on this as well as my previous books, and who have given my own life, well before retirement, a full measure of meaning.

JOEL S. SAVISHINSKY

A NOTE ON SOURCES

References and explanations for materials that are cited or quoted in the text are provided in notes following the last chapter. Complete citations are given in the References. All quotes from the people of Shelby are based either on taped interviews or on fieldnotes in which conversations were recorded or reconstructed within a few hours after they took place.

Remember the days of old,
consider the years of many generations;
ask your father, and he will show you;
your elders, and they will tell you.

Deuteronomy 32:7

BREAKING THE WATCH

INTRODUCTION

THE POIGNANCY AND POETRY OF
THE EVERYDAY

American Voices: Reflections on Retirement

"The key questions change every decade or two of life. You wonder at 10: Is there life after death? At 20: Is there work after college? At 40: Is there sex after marriage? At 60: Is there life after work?"

"Oren and I went off camping for three weeks after I retired. I took a pile of novels, worked through my insecurities, the nostalgia, the blues, doubts, mourning for people. I saw that happiness was a route, not a destination. My last day at work I slipped off my watch and I haven't put it on since. And since then I've been able to do what I want to *when* I want to."

"I do this competitive planning, asking myself, Are the Joneses or Smiths doing it better than we are? Because I want to make sure I have at least as good a retirement as the others. I don't want to be pointed to, an example of how *not* to do it. Is there *one* best way to do it? No, I know that. Still, you think, Did I screw up? Did I get it right?"

"My father, from the 'old school,' the labor-union Jewish radical from New York, he never retired. He keeled over at his sewing machine on Rivington Street. So did I deserve retirement? All I'd figured out was that I'd finally be able to buy and read the Sunday *New York Times*. Otherwise, I was floating toward it. Not aimlessly, you understand. I just wasn't sure which of the things I enjoyed most was going to be primary for me: Reading? Studying Spanish? Perfecting . . . ha! . . . my golf?"

"You can have a positive outlook on retirement, but don't fool yourself into thinking that at 65 you can actually live out the dreams that were vivid when you were 30 years younger. Retirement *now* is not as thrilling as it might have been two or three decades ago. When you've lived that much more of your life, it's difficult, or at least different, because there are a lot of memories, a lot of history. You carry all that with you. Thank God I still have my family, and this home, and my friends. Believe me, just having hobbies wouldn't be sufficient to build a life around. If that's all you can do, you might as well have stayed at work."

"You need to have a *plan*; otherwise life gets away from you. What did I do? I counted the months backwards from 65, to where my Medicare and COBRA could start, and that fixed the date so that I wouldn't lose money, or coverage, or time. If you don't plan it out, you wake up and hours, days, a whole week is gone, and you don't know what happened. It's the way weekends disappear for working people. Laundry. Errands. Shopping. Bills. Repairs. . . . Anyway, we've waited too long to do too many things to let that happen in *our* retirement."

"What particularly excited me about retirement was when I began to see it as a new chapter with empty pages, ones that I was free to fill in any way I wanted to. . . . I'm so glad I didn't plan anything specific for it, because my plans would only have been based on my past experiences, whereas everything that's happened to me since retiring has been new."

"I'm totally skeptical of folks who boast they'll make radical changes in their retirement. I think most of us tend to stick to the patterns we've always had. It's the rare person who goes from being, say, a corporate executive to a portrait painter."

"For me, this is what retirement has meant: an unexpected invitation. Something like the childhood dream of walking through a hidden door and stepping into—what? Some strange, magic land."

"I object to it when I hear people say, 'When you retire, you'll get to do all the things you always wanted to.' If they were so important, you would have made time for them before. For me it's more of a chance to do more of the things I've been doing all along."

"The best part about . . . work in retirement . . . is that I don't have a feeling of compulsion—that I have to do everything right away, or perfectly, or else my world will crash. There was this constant tension at the conservatory, and I used to squeeze all the other things in my life around that sense of obligation. Now, I'm as conscientious as before, but the feeling is 180° different. I feel in control. . . . It's work without the feeling of work. It's play."

"At the start I was insecure, and I'd make dates to make my calendar and life look full. But now days open that are no longer just marked with errands and lunches. I have three or four things on my calendar most weeks, which is good, but what I really welcome is a blank day when I do my own things, or let them discover me. Retirement's different from a vacation, which is a break *from* work so that you can go back *to* work. No. This is a break *with* work. And for me the goal has been one of balance: finding the way to feed my spirit, my intellect, my ties to the people I care about."

"The toughest, or the most perilous thing about retirement, is that you have time to slow down and reflect. If you view your life negatively, that's pretty serious. I run hot and cold on that; the thermostat keeps flipping over. You certainly can't change the past, or who you are. I've been lucky—and I've been cursed. I never thought I'd make it this far, and still there's an underlying dissatisfaction with what I've done."

"Retirement is like a progressive illness—*and* a spiritual experience. There's a loss of efficacy, but the moral side grows. This is what allows you to give up control over a lot of this other stuff. Now I'm making choices on the basis of values, which I didn't do so much in my youth. I have the freedom to decide how to live and what to live for, and I'll sink or swim on the basis of my decisions. . . . Retirement is the gift of time, but its real burden is the rediscovery of choice, the responsibility for making up your own life."

"In retirement, it's not the watches that get broken, it's the promises. No one who talked to me about a job came through. I came to feel you can't rely on anyone, and I'd never felt that way before. Society tells you if you want to be an adult, then be productive. Then at work they say, Hey, make way for these others, and be happy about it and don't complain. You're told retirement's going to be great, but then the money's not there . . ."

Beyond the stereotypical gold watch and the handshake, what are the promises of retirement? In the United States today retirement is the last of life's major active phases, and perhaps the one most mystifying to those who have yet to reach it. The hopes and fears it invites are both fundamental and contradictory. It evokes ideas of freedom and frailty, loss and opportunity, and a sense of time that is either pregnant with possibility or else weighs heavily on the soul. For some, retirement is the promise to fulfill dreams deferred, for others the face of dread. Some people expect from it new forms of life, liberty, and the pursuit of happiness where others envision a failed landscape populated by the workless and worthless.

In every culture, such images and stereotypes of the life course can take on a life of their own. Whether people's naive notions are about class or sex, race or retirement, they become part of "the definition of the situation," the reality that those individuals inhabit.[1] But in the end they are only one part of that "real" world. There is always the other reality of actual experience. The challenge for any serious student or citizen of society is to put the two together, to make sense of both experience and expectation. A deeper understanding of retirement and aging in modern culture demands that same level of attention—to actions as well as ideas, to both the real and the ideal in the human condition.

In modern culture, the broadly universal and age-old pattern of distinct life stages, each marked by role transitions and appropriate rites of passage, has developed some remarkable new features. First, industrial life and political upheavals have made people extremely mobile; migration and immigration have often separated them from the circle of kin and community within which, in the past, the life cycle would have been lived out. Second, life expectancy has increased dramatically. An American child born in 1900 could expect to live till 47. Her great-grandchild, entering the world in 1998, could enjoy the prospect of a 76-year life span. During the first nine decades of the twentieth century, life expectancy increased more than it had over the preceding two millennia. Larger numbers of people are living longer lives, with the result that elders constitute a progressively greater percentage of the populace. At the turn into the twentieth century, only 4 percent of Americans reached what is now normal retirement age. In the year 2000, their numbers will have risen to 13 percent. By 2030, people 65 or older will account for some 22 percent of our populace.[2]

This "graying" of the population has been accompanied by a third feature, namely, the creation of "retirement" itself as a new stage in later life, a largely uncharted territory. In the past, as in other societies, older men and women had of course always withdrawn from work as age and health required. But this had never happened to such large numbers as those involved in what scholars have come to call "the demographic transition." Most members of our present population can anticipate spending up to a quarter of their lives as retirees. And we are now not just living longer but retiring earlier. Whereas 60 percent of men over 65 were still working in 1900, under 20 percent were doing so in 1990.

This book began as a study of how real people deal with retirement and its contradictions. But it also soon became a journey into the poignancy of everyday life and the poetry of everyday speech. In late 1992, I identified a group of 26 people from Shelby, a small town in Taylor County in upstate New York, who were expecting to retire within the next 12 months. Though the names of this community, its residents, and its institutions have been changed to protect people's privacy, the lives I describe here are real. My intent was to follow these 13 women and 13 men over the following years to see how their lives were affected by the approach and the beginning of retirement. What emerged from their stories was a set of unexpected lessons about people coping with deep and conflicting values in their own culture. These included the tensions between creativity and duty, work and leisure, material and moral fulfillment, a sense of place and a sense of adventure, altruism and self-realization, and prudence and spontaneity. Underlying all these was the basic challenge of balancing freedom with responsibility.

The impetus for this project was simple and, in at least one sense, obvious. In all cultures, the human life cycle involves a series of transitions. At certain junctures in time, as individuals move through infancy and childhood on to adolescence, adulthood, and old age, they alter their social roles, their identities, and sometimes their names. Societies mark and dramatize these changes with rites of passage—baptisms, initiations, and weddings among them—designed to help the maturing individual move from one phase of existence to the next.

But though aging and its rites of passage are universal, around the world responses to the old and to retirement vary greatly. The very concept of "retirement" is not universally recognized. Among tribal peoples, one encounters groups that treat the aged with respect and give them security, and those that find them a burden and hasten their deaths.[3] Only some cultures expect people to stop their adult work entirely as they grow old. Even in those societies where withdrawal from labor does eventually occur, its meaning, timing, and consequences can be quite varied. The ideas of both old age and retirement, then—in the language of gerontology and anthropology—are "culturally constructed." Consider just a handful of current and historical cases from Europe, the Americas, Africa, and Asia.[4]

A Cross-cultural Framework

In the traditional culture of rural Ireland, right up to the Second World War, inactivity was equated with immorality, and retirement seen as a precursor of death. Elderly couples held onto and worked their farmland for as long as they could before age and social pressure compelled them to pass it on to their oldest son. The parents then retired to the honored West Room of their home and limited their farming to a nearby small plot of land—what people referred to as a field as large as "the grass of a cow": from there they supervised and advised, but were in most respects supported and cared for in their remaining years. By delaying their retirement for as long as possible, men and women were able to hold on to their power and influence until a considerable age. But this also earned them the resentment of the younger generation, whose own maturity and marriages were postponed until they could finally succeed to the family farm. Here, retirement came late, it came with security, but it carried a cost for both the old and the young.

The people of Abkhasia in the Caucasus Mountains had no such concepts as "retirement" and "old age." Even in the decades after the Russian Revolution, women and men who reached the century mark were simply called *dolgozhiteli* or "long-living," and they continued to work at whatever tasks, and at whatever pace, their abilities allowed. They remained with their families and communities, advising the latter through the council of elders, and allowing younger generations to move into more central roles in a smooth and seamless transition.

In several tribes of northeast Africa, successful retirement historically hinged on the proper relationship between timing and social structure. Well into the colonial period, young males from the cattle-herding Korongo and Mesakin of the Sudan were still organized into a series of age classes. Boys born just a few years apart formed a cohesive age grade with its own name; the group's members engaged in sporting contests, formed cooperative age-villages and, bound by a mystical interdependence, moved together through the stages of the life cycle. Upon entering the last of these phases, senior men were expected to transfer their cattle, and their authority, to one of their sisters' sons in the next age class. Among the Korongo, who divided life and communities into six age levels, the older men were quite mature in years by the time they agreed to retire in this way. They were even allowed to postpone giving their gift of cattle, but when this event finally took place, the ritual transfer of wealth and power to their chosen nephews worked well. The Mesakin, on the other hand, had only three age grades, and no system for deferring the bestowal of their herds. Being chronologically still young, their "senior" men often felt vigorous enough to resist retirement and its ceremonies when the time for these came. The resulting struggle over succession sometimes expressed itself in accusations of witchcraft, which the younger males directed against their resentful elders and supposed benefactors.

Perhaps the most stereotypic cultural image of the end of work, and life itself, has been that of the Eskimo (Inuit) elder left to die on an ice floe. The larger world has both overstated and misunderstood this practice. In their aboriginal way of life, older Inuit men and women tried to remain productive for as long as they were physically able by participating in such activities as making tools and clothing, minding children, and performing rituals. The rare solitary death took place only under conditions of great adversity and starvation, and when it did happen, it was as likely to be an act of altruistic suicide by the old as one of abandonment by the young. Furthermore, believing in reincarnation, and in the identity of a person's soul with his or her name, Inuit elders faced death with the knowledge that they would soon be reborn in the person of the next child to carry their name.

Unlike the Inuit, traditional elders in China sought the rewards of retirement in *this* life, not the next. If life went as the culture prescribed, decades of hard work and duty to kin were repaid with filial respect, material comfort, and the company of grandchildren in one's later years. In the era before industrialization, Communism, and the "one-child policy," married sons would take in and care for their retired parents, bestow namesakes and heirs on their fathers, and thus fulfill the patriarchal dreams of succession and security. The ideal of retirement then was to live in a large extended family home. If elders of either gender lacked the children and grandchildren required by such a vision, they feared they would pass through retirement and death to an unsettled and haunting eternity as "hungry ghosts."

Time binds generations together, but it can also pull them apart. In the Bahamas, modern tourism and its effect on the region's economy have impacted families in both these ways. Among the isolated communities of Cat Island, for example, older people have come to constitute a disproportionately large percentage of the adult population; many of their grown children have had to leave home to seek work at the hotels, casinos, and resorts that have sprung up on Nassau and other islands. But when these mature sons and daughters have their own sons and daughters, they usually decide to send the offspring back to Cat Island so that the grandparents can raise them in that more familiar and more wholesome environment. In the Bahamas, then, older generations, left in charge of their own farms, homes, and churches, and doing the kind of family caregiving that anthropologists call "kinwork," never really retire. Instead, at a speed and rhythm that fit their age, the senior men fish the waters, build boats, and minister to people's souls; older women weave baskets, grind corn, and boil up "bush medicines"; and elders of both genders raise crops of corn and grandchildren. The rural parts of Cat Island are thus largely a world of the old and the young, who are bound together by love, duty, and work.

Whereas the duty of age has doubled back on itself in the Bahamas, in India it has released people from all their ties. Retirement there has ideally taken on a religious rather than a social or a material focus. In the ancient Hindu model of the life course, which persists as a model in the modern world, people pass through three *shramas* or stages of existence before becoming elders: first that of a celibate student developing discipline and preparing for mature responsibilities; next a householder with obligations to spouse, children, and community; and then a hermit, giving up material possessions and retreating to the forest for contemplation. The fourth and final phase, the true retirement, is that of the *sannyasin*—the elder who renounces all bonds to people, places, and possessions, and becomes a wandering ascetic seeking spiritual enlightenment. Equipped with just a staff and begging bowl, even the *sannyasin* is not devoid of meaning or modeling for others, however. At holy rites such a person bestows *darshan* or grace on those who enter his presence, and his very existence in the world is itself a constant reminder of the rewards of retirement that await those who have fulfilled life's other duties. Even those *sannyasins* whose religious efforts are insufficient to end all rebirths and achieve *moksha*, or liberation, will have another chance in their next reincarnation to pursue their spiritual development.

In each of these non-Western societies, the nature of retirement—or its absence—reveals some of the most basic features and dilemmas of later life.

- *Work* and *pace*. In some cultures, such as China and India, people have completely retired from productive work, while in others such as Abkhasia, their economic role has been reduced but not terminated. The pace at which elders perform their responsibilities may also slow, with the contemporary Bahamas and Abkhasia being especially accepting of this change.
- *Timing*. The time in life when a person expects or is expected to retire is shaped by each culture's model of the life course and by the ceremonies that signal this transition. Among the Korongo, and traditional peoples in India, there have been clear rites or markers for this passage. But as the Mesakin and the Irish examples show, personal and community expectations may not always coincide. When retirement has been a reluctant or involuntary process, considerable stress between the generations may develop.
- *Power*. At retirement, a person may have to give up some of the tempo-

ral and spiritual powers that he or she has exercised in life. In Ireland, China, the Bahamas, and Abkhasia, however, elders have retained some of these functions well into their later years.

- *Succession.* When wealth, power, and other forms of adult privilege must be transferred at retirement, older persons in cultures such as the Korongo and Ireland have had strong feelings, and some measure of control, over how, and when, and to whom, this succession will occur.
- *Gender.* Throughout the life course of all societies, women and men participate in distinct work patterns and social roles. But whereas later life may stereotypically be viewed as "sexless" in some cultures, traditional Chinese and Bahamian patterns have shown that older people's domestic and community roles are not likely to be "genderless"; whether or not men and women retire, they continue to engage in distinct activities.
- *Social ties.* As demonstrated by elder Cat Islanders, Irish, Abkhasians, Inuit, and Korongo, altering life's tempo and focus in retirement can also transform older people's social bonds, including their personal commitments, their place in their culture's system of caregiving, and their role in intergenerational relations.
- *Place.* Whereas retired people in most traditional societies have remained in the same homes and communities they had previously lived in, the nomadic existence of *sannyasins* in India has redefined their sense of place, as well as their connections to possessions, personal networks, and spiritual pathways.
- *Health and material security.* As the Irish, Abkhasian, Mesakin, and Inuit cases suggest, the impetus *for* retirement, and men's and women's actual experience *of* it, have been rooted in their levels of health and material well-being. If cultures expect elders to withdraw, or to remain active and alert, those very models of aging can become a self-fulfilling prophecy.
- *Meaning.* Finally, the meaningful roles of older men and women have been diverse: Abkhasians worked, the Irish advised, Bahamians still minister and doctor, and retirees from all cultures grandparent. But in some societies, elders such as India's *sannyasins* have also been challenged to make sense, to render an account for themselves, and others, and God, of what they have so far done in life, and what they conceive to be the purpose of the life stage they are about to begin. For Indians

and Inuit who continue to believe in reincarnation, even the end of this life is but a time of transition into the life to come.

The American Context

Retirement in the United States confronts elders with the very same factors and dilemmas found in these other societies. Time and place, meaning and work, success and succession, gender and family, power and control, fulfillment and responsibility, security and well-being—all must be dealt with in some fashion.

The rise of retirement as a district stage of life has come about from the confluence of demography with economics, politics, and cultural change.[5] Starting in the latter half of the nineteenth century, governments and corporations began to introduce social security and pension systems. They did so primarily to reduce the number of older workers in the labor force. In one of the first such public programs, Bismarck's Germany set a precedent in 1889 by selecting 70 as the age of retirement. This was a safe bet financially, since few workers were likely to live long enough to collect their pensions. This figure was reduced to 65 just before the First World War, and that age was later adopted for Social Security benefits in the United States when this nation's system was created in 1935. Growing industrial economies in the twentieth century supported public and private pension systems, which served a dual function: First, that of easing older and presumably less efficient workers out of the labor force to make way for younger, more productive ones; and second, simultaneously providing elders with the financial security that eases their later lives, and makes their exit from work possible. More recently, as labor market demands have contracted and then expanded, legislative changes in 1962 lowered the age for Social Security eligibility to 62 and then, in 1983, raised the age for it in stages to be phased in during the first decades of the twenty-first century.

Pensions plans and welfare state policies have thus been products of modern ideas about efficiency, preferred employment patterns, and social justice. They continue to influence and constrain people's retirement decisions. Though stereotypes of unproductive older workers have been proved wrong, they too have contributed to a changed model of the life course.

Since the late nineteenth century, Americans have been retiring less because of ill health or unemployment than in response to "new economic and cultural opportunities." When they could afford it, they have left full-time work because—in the view of some historians—"retirement itself was attractive." This pattern has prevailed in the midst of such recent labor market forces as decreases in overt age discrimination and in the tendency to hold lifetime jobs, and increases in plant closings, mergers, early retirement incentives and "windows," and corporate downsizing. And consumerism and advertising have also played a major role: retirement itself is now aggressively marketed by the housing, financial, clothing, travel, leisure, and publishing industries.[6]

The American shift to viewing retirement as a norm, an expectation, and a right is now unmistakable. And along with the baby boomers, it has "boomed" since the Second World War. Though the percentage of older people at work has been rising again for both genders since 1985, the basic trend to full- or at least part-time retirement still remains clear.[7] Another development, the recent invention of planned "retirement communities"—which have much in common with boarding schools, summer camps, army barracks, and college campuses—is an intriguing if unintended parallel to the generationally segregated, age-villages of traditional Africa.

Although it is a relatively new phenomenon, retirement and its prelude have not suffered from the benign neglect of researchers. Scholars have established, for example, that despite all our labor-saving devices and conveniences, working Americans actually have far less leisure time than they or the popular imagination has assumed. By the dawn of the 1990s, employed men and women were putting in more hours of labor per year than at any time since the Second World War. Though long years of work could certainly serve as an inducement to retire, some experts argue that Americans as a whole have also been unable or unwilling to save adequate money for this phase of their lives, and that they worry about having an adequate retirement income. In addition, many people are having trouble collecting the private pensions they are entitled to from employers as companies merge, rules shift, and eligibility gets redefined.[8]

There have been various portraits of retirees cast in the languages of social science, journalism, and literature.[9] A number of projects have described the nature of specific retirement communities in the United States and other countries, often bearing such tell-tale titles as *Fun City, The Unexpected Community, City of Green Benches,* and *Old People, New Lives.*[10] But, although Sun Belt states, specialized housing, and planned developments have received a lot of popular and media attention, the evidence shows that seniors are five times more likely to "age in place" in their own homes and hometowns, turning many of the latter into what are now referred to as NORCs—"naturally occurring retirement communities."[11]

Other studies have been prompted by quality-of-life issues. Some early research focused on "Disengagement Theory," which argued that older people and society undergo a natural, voluntary, and mutual process of disengagement from one another. The concept of "Differential" or "Selective Disengagement" qualified this by noting that people disengage from different roles at different rates. They may drop out of their jobs but not their families. In contrast to these approaches, "Activity Theory," along with the evidence from other cultures, has suggested that elders choose to remain actively engaged in life by substituting or following other pursuits and responsibilities when work ends. The idea of "Consolidation" has refined this insight by focusing on how people cope with retirement through a process of reorganizing their involvement in the roles they already play, rather than seeking out new ones. This view reinforces the theory that retirement is not a "crisis" but rather a process in which individuals seek to sustain a sense of personal identity and "continuity" as they adapt to later life.[12]

Collectively, these different concepts suggest that people respond to retirement in a variety of ways. One size—and one theory—does not fit all. This diversity is borne out by still other research that documents the characteristics of retirees in an aggregate sense.

Though numbers can be numbing, the surveys and statistics available on retirement do clarify some of what we understand, and still need to learn, about this experience. Findings reveal the ways in which retirement affects and reflects health and finances, race and class, marriage and gender, attitudes toward work and leisure, and well-being and morale. The following facts map out some of what is known and unknown about this social landscape.

- Nine out of ten people plan to retire, with some taking "bridge jobs" between full-time work and full retirement. Those who do work in retirement come from the economic extremes: people at the top are able to hold onto jobs, and those at the bottom may need to. Also, engaging in paid or volunteer labor after retiring enhances many people's feelings of self-esteem. While most forms of mandatory retirement were eliminated by Congress in 1986, few workers choose to stay at their jobs past 65. Though professionals with strong career attachment—those who believe in "staying the course"—may feel negative about retiring, many working people show both a high level of job commitment and a positive retirement orientation. They suffer little loss of identity after leaving work. In essence, retirement at normal ages is commonly encouraged by the expectations of employers, fellow workers, and family, and most people retire because they want to and can afford to.[13]

- The acceptance of this pattern means that health and finances, though still important matters of concern, now play a less critical role in people's decisions to retire than was true in earlier periods. Instead, prospective retirees' feelings about their work commitment and work history may be becoming more influential and decisive for them. Declines in health among older individuals have, in fact, been found to be the result of age, not retirement itself. As gerontologists sum this up, "Deterioration in health is more likely to cause the retirement than vice versa." Contrary to conventional wisdom, depression and dissatisfaction with life are not caused by a withdrawal from work, and the great majority of people do not find retirement stressful. On average, retirees retain between 60 and 75 percent of their preretirement income, though there are repeated warnings that Americans do not save enough for retirement and are anxious about "outliving their money."[14]

- How factors of race, class, and gender influence people's quality of life in retirement has also been the subject of much research. The working poor may actually experience an improved economic situation after retiring because they become eligible for additional benefit programs. Women and minorities, however, are particularly vulnerable to economic distress because of their often discontinuous work histories, their late-starting careers, their lower access to pensions, and their modest assets. Such vulnerability is likely to remain true for females and people of color from the baby boom generation, especially if they enter retirement as single individuals who do not own homes, and have had low incomes and education levels. Currently, for example, women get only about 60 percent of what men do in their pensions, and they are far more likely to be widowed. Furthermore, it is not as common for black women to retire as white because of their economic needs and even greater chance of widowhood. When blacks of both sexes do take retirement, they commonly experience fewer negative effects than whites, but this is because they already tend to be at lower socioeconomic levels, and have usually been engaged in less satisfying work. Yet they also enter and go through retirement in poorer health, and with Social Security checks that average only about 80 percent of what whites receive. Compared to professionals, managers, and salespeople, blue-collar workers are more inclined to retire because their jobs are less fulfilling, though their adjustment may be more difficult because of their lower levels of schooling and financial leverage. Top managers and executives, on the other hand, can find retirement hard because of the loss of power and prestige it entails. And white-collar workers, in contrast to their bosses, tend to adjust well because of the interests and resources they bring with them to retirement.[15]

• Among American workers there is a low level of participation in formal planning programs for retirement, but most people adjust well to this transition even without formal preparation. Despite the traumas pictured in popular folklore, retired people's morale and satisfaction with life are generally as high as those of people who have chosen not to retire.[16]

• Experts have distinguished several phases and routes to retirement. People pass through these in different ways and often discover that what they experience in the early, as opposed to the later stages, can be quite disparate. Most have grown up expecting to retire, and they may go through "mental dress rehearsals" for it, or a process of "anticipatory socialization," as they approach this brave new world. As described by the sociologist Robert Atchley, the major stages in this process include a preretirement period during which individuals commonly fantasize about what their new life will be like. People then begin their actual retirement with one of three distinct approaches. Some start off by following a "honeymoon" path, intensely enjoying their freedom from work by enthusiastically engaging in such activities as hobbies and travel. Others establish an immediate retirement routine, especially if they have already been leading full lives before leaving full-time work. A third approach is taken by those who enter an initial period of rest and relaxation as a respite from years of labor.[17]

These opening pathways usually lead to other phases. The frantic honeymoon pace generally yields to a more measured schedule and the establishment of a routine. Those who start by relaxing eventually grow restless and become more involved in selected activities. There are also people who never establish a routine. Some do not need routine to be content, but others do and in the absence of one may not adjust well to retirement, instead experiencing a phase of disenchantment. Others may have their plans upset by a reversal to their health, or the loss of a spouse, either of which can lead to a period of depression and disappointment. At some point in retirement, women and men may also go through a time of reorientation. They question the lifestyle they have so far chosen, and then follow new priorities as a result of these reflections. Finally, for most people, the aging process eventually brings changes in physical or mental health. Though still retired, their diminished abilities may limit the activities they had been pursuing in their first years after work, and thus effectively terminate that earlier lifestyle. While there is no word comparable to "retirement" to label this period of frailty, its onset shows how inseparable the aging and retirement processes ultimately are.

- Some researchers have argued that the retired person occupies a "normless" or "roleless" role with "no vital function to perform," but others note that being a retired person has real rights and duties. These include the rights to economic support, to respect without stigma, to autonomy, and to health insurance and other benefits, and the duties to manage one's own life, to offer one's knowledge and skills to the community, to meet one's responsibilities to family and friends, and to care for one's health and resources so as not to become unnecessarily dependent on others.[18]

- For many retired people, leaving full-time employment means trading in the "work ethic" for what gerontologist David Ekerdt calls the "busy ethic," that is, keeping responsibly active by pursuing hobbies, talents, interests, the maintenance of one's house and possessions, family commitments, or community and volunteer roles. The pursuit of such worthwhile goals gives retirement a moral dimension; it justifies leisure, promotes health, and demonstrates that retirees are still capable and productive. Retirees who stay actively engaged in volunteering, for example, have been shown to have less depression and to enjoy higher degrees of self-esteem, energy levels, and physical well-being than those who do not volunteer.[19]

- Most retired people do not relocate; even most of those who move to smaller or easier-to-maintain houses or apartments stay in the same area. And, regardless of where they reside, they maintain ample social contacts. It is a myth that retirement means migration, or that retired people become isolated. Among those who do move, factors of security, comfort, and closeness to family and friends are far more important than climate. Couples account for the majority of those who relocate to have better amenities; single individuals are more likely to change residence to be near kin.[20]

- Several factors have been shown to enhance, or at least predict, good cognitive and intellectual functioning in retirement: a long-term, intact marriage to a well-educated and intelligent spouse; a high level of education; a history of high occupational status and workplace complexity; and exposure to stimulating environments and cultural resources.[21] Participation in leisure is at least as great in retirement as it was before, and the central activities of the past continue to be important. However, leisure rarely dominates later life. There is a gradual shift to social rather than physical pursuits, and the amount of leisure is less dramatic than commonly assumed; caregiving, housekeeping, and other activities and responsibilities persist, and consume a substantial proportion of retirees' time.[22] And more people are now entering retirement with responsibilities for some elder. Seventy-five percent of America's caregivers are women and 20 percent of them are 65 or older. Females are more likely than males to retire because of caregiving responsibilities.[23]

- Most retired persons are married, and couples are likely to plan retirement together, choose to enter it together, and make this transition with relative ease. Retirement is thus increasingly a "couple experience." When differences in the timing of retirement do occur, these do not usually affect couples' life satisfaction significantly. The desire of men to retire early may, however, conflict with their wives' occupational aspirations. Still, retirement generally tends to maintain or increase marital satisfaction, even though some researchers have noted that this may be less common in working-class couples. For women of all socioeconomic backgrounds, having a husband's pension to depend on has been found to yield a more positive attitude toward retirement.[24]

- In summary, retirement at the normal age has minimal effects on the average retiree's health, activities, and attitudes. Even considering differences in age, class, race, gender, and occupation, people generally look forward to retirement and adjust well to it without much formal preparation. The basic trends in retirement indicate that incomes drop, but remain adequate; that physical and mental health does not deteriorate when work stops; that the content of activities changes, but not their level; that marital satisfaction generally tends to be high; that most people age in place; that retirees rarely become isolated as a result of the termination of work; and that contrary to older views, people do not experience this life change as a major crisis. The negatives often associated with retirement—depression, declining health, and loneliness—if they occur, are actually products of the long-term effects of aging, not exit from full-time labor. Retirement itself generally proves to be a positive experience, and retirees are as satisfied with their lives as those their age who are still working.

Retiring as a Process

These insights into retirement are all valuable, but they have their limits. One of the most serious is that the studies they come from rarely allow us to hear the voices of the retirees themselves, or the details of their adjustment to this new life stage. Furthermore, general statements may predict little about particular people. In effect, trends, probabilities, and percentages describe the contours of retirement but do not tell its story in human terms. Nor do they show how real women and men deal, day to day and year to year, with *the transition into retirement as a process*. Specifically, we lack humanistic accounts of how individuals actually prepare for, move through, and look back upon this crucial life passage.

It was the better-read among Shelby's older women and men who were especially sensitive to these deficiencies. They felt that the large gap between what we know and what we need to know about retirement results from the kinds of questions that get raised about it, and the kinds of people who pose them. Nate Rumsfeld, Alice Armani, and Donna Younger, three of the town's elders, each complained that statistical studies ask about the issues that researchers and politicians are interested in, not necessarily those that retirees themselves care about. What Nate pondered most was this question: Was the life I've lived the one I wanted to? And what can I afford to do with it now? Alice asked in her turn, Did I fulfill my potential? Can I still be the artist I once thought I was destined to be? For her friend Donna, faced with the end of a long academic career followed, in short order, by the death of her father, the heart of the matter was meaning itself: Was she still a scholar? Was she too old to be an orphan? Such were the questions that numbers alone could not answer.

These issues, and related questions about later life, first came to my own awareness during the research I did with elderly people and their families in four other cultural settings. In projects carried out between the late 1960s and the early 1990s, I had learned about the varieties of the aging experience in the Canadian subarctic, on Cat Island in the Bahamas, in a working-class neighborhood in London, England, and at Shelby's downtown nursing home, Elmwood Grove.[25] Among the Hare Indians, a hunting, fishing, and trapping people with whom I lived in the Canadian North during 1967, 1968, and 1971, individuals in their 70s, 80s, and 90s still traveled with their families by dogsled and, to the best of their ability, helped to hunt, fish, trap, build canoes, care for children, tan hides, sew clothing, cut firewood, and preserve the oral traditions of their people. On Cat Island, where I worked in the late 1970s, many young adults, as indicated, had left the island to seek work, and I found in their place a whole generation of elders who had taken on primary responsibilities as farmers, fishermen, herders, healers, spiritual leaders, and caregivers for their grandchildren. Living in the North London borough of Islington between 1987 and 1991, I discovered large numbers of families who—with the help of social workers and health care providers—were trying to maintain frail, often demented parents and spouses in their own homes, rather than place them in institutions. And at Elmwood Grove, in Shelby, where I had worked from 1982 to 1992 with the relatives, staff, and community volunteers caring for elders who *had* been placed in a nursing home, I witnessed, the full spectrum of love, guilt, commitment, burn-out, altruism, anger, and faith experienced by the many generations involved in the life of a geriatric facility.

These earlier projects revealed persistent, sometimes painful tensions between cultural values and personal experience in later life. All four communities exposed conflicts between autonomy and dependency, intimacy and privacy, public and private good, mortality and morality, and the emotional consequences of caring *about* versus caring *for* others—dilemmas which carried a heavy weight in the decisions that older people, their relatives, and their caregivers faced. As I approached and passed my 50th birthday and watched my friends, my neighbors, and the members of my parents' generation all age, I came to appreciate that retirement is a period that crystallizes many of these same issues. But when my students and I surveyed what was known about this time of transition, we found that retirees themselves had rarely been followed in a continuing, personal way—one that would reveal the daily diversity in how the elders of one community dealt with life after work. It was this gap in our cultural understanding of aging—and my belief that anthropology had something valuable to contribute—that prompted the study presented here.

The Setting and the Methods

I chose Shelby not as a "typical" American community, but because, being within an hour's drive, it was convenient to where I taught. Yet it also turned out to contain some of the essential variety of our society. It embraced a mix of rural and urban lifestyles; of farm families, businesspeople, and intellectuals; of light manufacturing and "high-tech" research facilities; and of conservative, mainstream, and liberal sentiments. It was home to professors and store owners, environmental activists and developers, members of communes and fundamentalist churches. Its resident population of 28,000 swelled to 35,000 when students returned to start the school year at nearby Seneca College. The combination of Shelby's location, economic mix, and educational features once led its local paper to characterize its quality as "rural cosmopolitan."

In the fall, a rich, pointillist palette of autumn colors covered the landscape wherever Taylor County's corn fields, orchards, dairy farms, and vineyards had spared woodlots, forests, and state parks. The clapboard homes in most of Shelby's neighborhoods climbed the hills that bordered the north end of Allegany Lake, a gift of the last glaciers. And the higher up the hills you looked, the higher your gaze went up the community's social ladder. Below, in "The Flats" that lay on the lake's floodplain, the town's business district stood on one side of Allegany's outlet, and an area of low-income housing and a strip mall on the other. Half a mile north, the college and the county hospital faced each other across an old barge canal, which now served boaters and tourists rather than trade from the west. Downtown, the war memorial, shops, the courthouse, the Greek revival town hall and library, movie theaters and churches, a synagogue, Elmwood Grove Nursing Home, the Crown Electronics factory, and three one-block-square parks filled in the patchwork of the community's layout.

The 26 older people of Shelby who collaborated with me were white and mostly middle-class but otherwise diverse, with a secretary, a banker, teachers, a farmer, and a mail carrier among them. And they shared with one another, as well as with me, an abiding interest in some central questions about their own retirements. Were they entering this new phase of life willingly and with great expectations? How did they feel about leaving jobs, careers, and co-workers? What would this change mean to their ties to friends and families? And what sense of security, purpose, and meaning were they building their new lives around?

Only astronauts work in a vacuum. Anthropologists, by contrast, live in an atmosphere filled with theories, and they prefer certain ways of approaching social reality. So candor compels a few words here about the concepts and methods that underlie what follows. The older women and men I have worked with have taught me that retirement is best viewed as *an ongoing process* rather than as *a single or time-limited event*. Though a person actually has a "last day at work," that hardly constitutes his or her retirement. Such an individual may have been thinking about and planning this change for months or years, just as the effects of retiring will continue to reshape that person's emotions, relationships, and activities for a long time to come. Retirees constantly experienced change. Alice rediscovered herself in painting, but found that she also had to make her peace with the politics of the local arts community; Nate realized that he needed to look for work again, not just for monetary but also for emotional reasons; and

Donna learned that it was okay to fall apart a bit and turn to friends in a moment of frailty. A life stage such as retirement, then, unfolds and alters with time.

Several concepts and theories have been especially helpful in my attempt to understand it.[26]

- The concept of *consolidation,* developed by Robert Atchley, directed my attention to the way some newly retired people built on interests and roles that they already have in order to construct a life, and thereby maintain a *continuity* of personality.
- I also came to appreciate, however, that there were retirees for whom vitality was based on the search for novelty and the unexpected. They traveled, sculpted, volunteered, or worked in new ways, discovering their own version of what art historians have called *altersstil,* a distinctive *old-age style* of creativity.
- These contrasting emphases on new and old enthusiasms illustrated the concept of *age heterogeneity,* which emphasizes that people become more differentiated and individualized, not less so, as they age. Elders, in other words, can be more unlike one another than adolescents are. That differences in skill, health, attitudes, and competencies can become more pronounced with time suggested that I could expect people to react to retirement in highly diverse ways.
- The theory of *age stratification* indicates that in the United States, as in African age-villages, people born and entering retirement at around the same time may experience themselves as members of a cohort, a group shaped by a distinct set of historical experiences. The Depression, the Second World War, and the American politics of race, gender, and war after mid-century proved indeed to be common points of reference for many retirees.
- Erik Erikson's argument that older individuals seek to achieve *ego integrity*—a sense of order, acceptance, and dignity in later life—sensitized me to the many sources of meaning that people drew on for a feeling of personal worth. Spirituality, parenthood, friendship, service, and art turned out to be of primary significance here.
- Retirees' search for a meaningful account of their lives, and their ways of speaking about themselves at different ages, reinforced Sharon Kaufman's notion that older women and men have an *ageless self,* a long-

standing image of who they are that is centered on their unique config-
uration of values and qualities.

* And in both their reflections and their actions, many retired people also
  evaluated themselves by stressing their personal conduct and their family and social commitments, thus revealing that they were deeply concerned with what philosophers call their *moral agency*. That is, they
  judged their lives, and those of their peers, in ethical as well as material
  terms.

Working with these ideas fostered a view of retirement as a process
rooted in personal experience, history, and community—what gerontologists call a *life-course* approach.[27] And recognizing the diversity and depth
of older people's lives influenced the methods with which I chose to study
them. Participants were recruited in various ways. First, letters and notices
about the project were sent to major employers and labor unions in the
Shelby area, asking for volunteers who were approaching retirement.
Then personnel directors and the town's Chamber of Commerce were informed about the study. A bit later an article about the research also appeared in the local newspaper.

Over a dozen people eventually contacted me and a colleague in the
psychology department who was planning to examine cognitive changes
in retirement. Those who offered to participate were then asked to suggest
other individuals who might be interested in collaborating with us. Where
possible, we tried to use these new contacts to branch out to other areas of
the local community and its labor force; men and women in farming, finance, education, law, civil service, medicine, human services, business,
and science were among those we were able to attract.

This method of "snowball" sampling eventually brought us over 50 individuals, all of whom defined themselves as "about to retire"—though
some, as it turned out, were uneasy with the very word "retirement." I selected half that group to work with in an intensive, ethnographic way. I
was able to choose an equal number of women and men representing a
range of work, family, educational, and socioeconomic backgrounds. The
decision to have a gender-balanced group aimed to offset the relative neglect of women in earlier retirement studies, despite their increasing role
in the labor force since the Second World War.[28]

Participants included teachers, doctors, a lawyer, a secretary, a postman, a designer, a media consultant, an accountant, a farmer, a hotelier, a social service worker, a biologist, a librarian, professors, administrators, a musician, and a man who was both a minister and a salesman. These were variously married, single, or divorced individuals, some of whom had children and grandchildren and others who had neither. Their states of health varied too, as did their financial situations, ranging from the fit to the forgetful, from the well-heeled to the worried. Their ages at the time of retirement ranged from 54 to 77, and about half had elderly parents or in-laws still alive. Despite their age spread, these men and women also had some shared historical experiences to lend a common shape to their lives. But though they had lived and labored through some of the same times, it turned out that their approaches to retirement were diverse; some were about to leave work willingly and on their own initiative, others were doing so grudgingly and involuntarily. Among their emotions were hope and anticipation, fear and trembling. Thus, though white and largely middle-class, these individuals faced issues similar to those of retired people from other backgrounds, including the challenges of making meaning out of their work, identities, and family ties, and forging a sense of passion, place, and well-being in later life. The Appendix shows some of the diversity in the employment and personal histories that these women and men brought with them.

Doing anthropology, whether in the jungles of Brazil, an Asian city, or the small towns of rural America, is a very labor-intensive enterprise, and this dictated the small size of the group I decided to follow. Spending a lot of personal time with people over a long period of time has long been the hallmark of good ethnography, and that requirement limited the number of men and women whom I could reasonably hope to develop rapport with, as well as visit, drink tea and hang out with, and keep track of as their lives evolved. The intimacy and intensity of this approach were also rooted in my decision to adopt the basic methods that anthropologists have successfully employed in other cultures and in various settings in our own society: participant-observation, informal and structured interviews, and life-story analysis. They had served me well in my earlier work with small populations in Canada, the Bahamas, Great Britain, and Shelby itself. At Elmwood Grove, in fact, I had come to appreciate that looking at even one institution where life and death are daily concerns can connect you to the values and networks of an entire community. Participant-observation for this study had several elements. I attended both the formal and the improvised retirement parties held for people and spent casual time with them in coffee shops, concert halls, shopping malls, the local farmers' market, and other settings where retirees tended to congregate. The very texture of life in a small community also led to many unplanned contacts at dinners, parties, stores, and such public events as ball games, movies, school board meetings, and local fund-raisers. Certain weekday mornings I could stroll over to the Clockworks, a downtown coffee shop, and count on finding 80-year-old Frank Ryan, a former health worker, chiding some of his cronies there about their diets and the overweight state senator they had voted for. I could also pop into the Shelby Bakery to pick up fresh bread on my way home, and not emerge for an hour because I had run into Johanna Alexander, retired from a bank at 64, who had invited me to have tea and talk about the meditation class she was taking. One day I went to an art gallery opening and discovered that Alice Armani, 68, the former head of a social agency, was one of the painters being featured in the new group show. In essence, whether it was over coffee or tea, art or politics, I was able to approximate to a degree the anthropologist's ideal of sharing and immersing himself in the life of the community he is trying to understand.

Only after the study was launched did I begin to appreciate how these 26 people were tied together into Shelby's social fabric. Alice was a good friend of Donna Younger, a retired historian, whom she had gotten to know through her church. Ed and Harriet Trayvor, a fund-raiser and medical administrator, lived in the same neighborhood as Johanna from the bank and Sandra Golecki, who had taught and performed music for over 40 years. Before their separate retirements, Martin Karler and Sophie Malounek had both worked at Crown Electronics, he as a designer, she as a secretary. And early in Petra van Osten's career as a pediatrician, she had treated the children of several people who would later retire just about when she did. These included postman Nate Rumsfeld, who would one day question the kind of life he had led; accountant Lester Ulanoff, whose wife had left him and their son and daughter in the children's early adolescence; and lab technician Zoe Leven, who would one day bemuse her own offspring by turning her retirement into the serious study of *tai chi*.

People reacted in several ways to the methods I was using. They praised, questioned, and made suggestions about research techniques, though regardless of their preferences they all stayed loyal to the project. Nate, a 59-year-old veteran of the post office, said it was good just to talk, because he felt that none of the retired men he had once worked with were being honest with him, or themselves, about how hard a time they were having. "But I can tell *you* what it's like, and hopefully you can tell others." Ursula Chalfin, a retired biologist, was more sanguine about direct communication. She suggested I "get some of the retirees together as a group" so that they can "learn directly from one another." When I took her advice, and then invited several of my students to join us at one of these sessions, we all heard just how anxious some of these young people were about the way their own parents were going to deal with retirement. They asked the retirees what advice they would give to people of college age, and I followed up by making that a standard question in future interviews.

Carl Withen, a retired lawyer who had once earned summer money in his own student days doing political surveys, was curious—a bit dubious, in fact—about the participant-observation approach I was employing. He wanted to know, for example, whether I could believe what people told me, and whether I was "seeing all there was to see." I asked him, in turn, how he had found administering questionnaires and tabulating the results. He thought for a moment, smiled, and then replied: "I guess it was what you'd call real 'hands-off' research. It answered a lot of questions. It just didn't tell me anything I really wanted to know."

As participant-observation, anthropology sometimes becomes a kind of serendipity: you go where life, and people, take you. But not entirely. Besides making a careful point of attending people's retirement rituals, my students and I conducted a planned sequence of interviews with all participants. The first ones, built around a structured set of questions, took place before formal retirement—about four months, on average, before people stopped full-time work. Two additional rounds of interviews were subsequently held: the second took place between six and 12 months after retirement, and the third round between 18 and 24 months after it began.

In addition, we continued to meet informally with participants, unburdened by a pre-set agenda of questions. Interviews, and casual conversations with retirees, their family members, and friends, also yielded a considerable body of life-story materials.

Since studying people's feelings about retirement is also to study their attitudes toward work, each of the brief biographies given here devotes ample space both to employment histories and to retirees' feelings about the various jobs they have held. The other topics we gathered information on included people's educational, marital, and medical backgrounds; their financial status; their families and living situations; their expectations of and reflections on retirement; their mode of planning for this stage of life; their perceptions of individuals who they felt constituted good or bad models of retirement for them; their views of how their new status was affecting their relationships and activities; their involvement in travel and volunteer and paid work; and their views of the meaning of life.

There were a number of unexpected twists and turns. Some individuals who agreed to help embraced the very notion of retirement, while others objected to it. Stefan Nokalsky, a former army officer and hotelier, insisted he had not retired so much as he had "gone on to the next stage of life." Teri Rogers, who had taught English in the local high school, loved the idea that she was leaving work but stressed that she would "let my life define my retirement rather than let my retirement define my life." Stefan and Teri were also among the people who were avid and thoughtful readers, and who cited the influence of some key books on their lives. As part of the research, then, besides looking at the scholarly literature on retirement, I followed in Stefan's footsteps by reading Marine hero Lewis B. Puller Jr.'s Pulitzer Prize-winning autobiography, *Fortunate Son;* took Teri's suggestion to absorb Thomas Berry's ecological plea in *The Dream of the Earth;* searched Willa Cather's *My Ántonia* to understand why it resonated so for Donna Younger; and went back to Saul Alinsky's *Rules for Radicals* to appreciate why, in what Ed Trayvor called one of his "earlier reincarnations," it had inspired him as a citizen.[29]

The research developed a rhythm of its own, and this book's organization echoes that. Since many of the study's ideas and insights arose out of informal talks with retirees, each of its sections is introduced by a conversation—the reconstruction of a real talk over a cup of coffee or tea. Each dialogue focuses on a particular issue or contradiction in retirement that these people faced. The first cup examines the tension between the formal and informal ways they found to celebrate their entry into this life stage. The second compares the rewards of careful planning versus spontaneity in their strategies for how to prepare for retirement. The third considers the kinds of fulfillment people discovered in fostering either their sense of place or their freedom from encumbrances as retirement began. The fourth cup contrasts the commitments of different individuals to following their passions or their sense of responsibility in maturity. In the fifth talk, attention shifts to the balance people tried to create between the calls of family and those of friendship. And the sixth cup explores the efforts of women and men to deal simultaneously with their emotional, material, and medical well-being.

The dialogues that open each section are followed by a set of life stories that show how a variety of other retired people from Shelby—those of a different gender, a different economic or marital status, or with a different work and family history—have dealt with that same dilemma. Every chapter concludes by highlighting the lessons that can be drawn from the experiences and reflections of the retirees who have spoken. By the book's end, all 26 men and woman have had a chance to give their accounts of past and present, and to indicate something of what they think the future may hold. A final section considers some of the main cultural themes that their retirements have raised, including concepts of freedom, time, space, gender, work, diversity, creativity, identity, fulfillment, fantasy, family, community, and meaning.

Motives and Meanings

Just as I had my own motives for pursuing this study, I discovered that the elders of Shelby had their own reasons for agreeing to participate in it. One lay in the disarming truth that, quite often, people are not so much repelled at "being studied" as they are pleased by it; the uncharacteristic attention of a researcher bestows a sense of worth on them. Some wanted to express gratitude for what life had so far *given* them, others to revenge themselves a bit for what others had *done to* them. But there was another, implicit reward. In a society where people are anxious about retirement—in both the positive and negative senses of "anxious"—for older people to be invited in as expert witnesses, to be asked to turn their personal experiences to some kind of moral profit, was not just flattering, it was reassuring. In Johanna's words, it turned "merely living" into "something educational—if not always exemplary." Without my initially realizing it, my request for people's help also spoke to a value that later emerged as a central theme in many of their lives—the impetus to be of use. Thus, what was at first affirming for a few later became redemptive for many.

Curiosity, flattery, reassurance, gratitude, revenge, edification, redemption—there were at least a dozen such needs and gratifications, a sufficiency of human substance, with which to create a project and invest it with purpose. It brought me, over the course of several years, to the conviction that the older women and men of Shelby have some valuable lessons to teach us. First, though 26 lives cannot be reduced to one profile or formula, their collective experience, their central insight, was the one expressed by Teri Rogers: *these are people who have defined retirement rather than letting retirement define them.* To be identified simply as "retired" was, variously, an insufficient or stigmatizing identity for most because it implied that they were necessarily either happy and secure, or jobless, pointless, and unproductive, or merely enjoying a well-earned rest. Instead, the elders of Shelby showed that people work hard at having a meaningful, purposeful retirement, just as they have struggled for comparable meanings at earlier stages of their lives.

Second, *to make their retirements meaningful, these people have used their sense of creativity and morality—much like the figures of Greek drama—to wrestle with the contradictions of their culture.* Specifically, they have taken on the American conflicts between personal needs and public commitments, passion and duty, prudence and spontaneity, responsibility and self-fulfillment, and decorum and desire. There was a related and classically American theme at work here, too, one voiced in the very phrasing of Teri's moral: the tension between culture and the individual, the struggle of men and women to put their personal stamp on a stereotyped and misunderstood stage of life. In effect, if "retirement" is a cultural construction, then retirees are continually deconstructing and reconstructing it.

A third lesson, I found, was that *the everyday lives of older people possessed the kind of poignancy we too often relegate to the realms of dramatic fiction or the philosopher's quest for answers to the "big" questions about life, death, and meaning.* Retirees often struggle with these same issues, but their reflections are commonly couched in the mulling over of seemingly mundane decisions about how to help aging parents, ailing spouses, or needy grandchildren; about whether to give long hours for the next two years of life to a community board; or about the "justice" of devoting one's time and resources to being a sculptor or painter or dancer or memoirist. In their dilemmas I saw what writer James Agee called "the cruel radiance of what is," which lies in the "normal predicaments of human divinity."[30] As one of my students expressed it after conducting three interviews that showed her the unexpected fate of people's desires, "In the end, everyone is interesting."

The way Shelby's elders spoke to us about duty, creativity, family, passion, and the other issues in their lives also revealed a fourth lesson, one about the poetry of everyday speech. People were not reaching for new rhetorical heights when we talked; they spoke out of the hope, or joy, or pain, or reflection of the moment—moments that took place in coffee shops and living rooms, in gardens and hospitals, not on daises or speakers' platforms. Yet the words they used often had the poetic qualities of metaphor, irony, and imagination—suggesting that *common people have less trouble capturing the poetry of everyday life than poets sometimes have in capturing the commonplace.*

Finally, the older men and women of this community reminded me that *as life expectancy rises and the age for leaving work falls, retirement can now constitute up to a quarter of one's life.* Understanding its cultural, personal, and community dimensions is thus of considerable importance for those experiencing or anticipating this passage. What follows is meant to reveal the human and moral diversity of ordinary Americans confronted with the last major stage of existence.

A FIRST CUP

AT THE FIREHOUSE

In later life we sometimes revisit the pain and passions of our childhood. Our sibling rivalries may finally be resolved, our artistic dreams revived. We can confront again the vulnerabilities of love and friendship, or rediscover such youthful virtues as idealism and candor. For Felix Davis, the recovery of the past was more concrete. It took the form of his favorite toy, the centerpiece of the boyhood, basement fantasies he had acted out over half a century ago. But now it was serious play with real fire engines.

They were behind us, framed in the two bays of Shelby's central firehouse. Felix and I sat against the station's outer wall on wooden folding chairs, early morning coffee mugs cradled in our hands. Eyes closed, Felix breathed in his cup's steam as if it held medicinal vapors. "These are the day's most intense moments," he said, nodding agreement with himself. "Silence. All the senses opening." His head shook side-to-side twice, as if completing a benediction.

At age 58, at 8:15 A.M., in the first September and third month of his retirement, this is where Felix took the measure of the world.

We were talking about the shape and taste of his new life. "Doing this had nothing to do with retirement." Felix hiked a thumb over his shoulder, exonerating the engines, the firefighters, the whole department. "I did it," he laughed, "for this terrible coffee. Believe it or not, it used to be worse. They had a vending machine when I started to volunteer here, ten years ago. The coffee was lukewarm, pale . . . piss. Then I organized these wonderful men—they're so active they leap out of bed at night to save people's homes; and they're so passive that they put up with dishwater for coffee—so I got them each to put up $5, and we bought this real coffeemaker. How did I sell that? I said, These are real engines. We're real firefighters. And these are real alarms we go to. So let's have real coffee."

"So, Felix, you do this for the coffee?"

"No, no. Of course not. When I retired, I decided I'd do it for the pay."

"But you're a volunteer, wise guy!"

"Oh, yeah. Right." A pause. "I guess it's the uniform."

"The uniform?" I asked. "What . . ."

"I mean the hat," he interrupted. He tapped the helmet on top of his head and laughed again, lifting it for a moment to run his fingers through short, blond-gray hair.

I had seen the helmet before, perched on Felix's desk at Seneca College, holding up a leaning tower of papers and files. His faculty office boiled over, as unkempt, as improvised, as his lectures on ecology, responsibility, parenting and politics, dying and love. When I visited him at his department a month before the end of his last semester, the fireman's hat, doubling as paperweight, was a strange but fitting punctuation to a career's accumulation of reading, agitation, talk, struggle, and moral outrage. It crowned but did not quite cap the fires of ideas which had kept his work life intense for 32 years.

In the front of the firehouse Felix settled the helmet back over his hair and reflected that "retirement was so hard I had to do it twice." He added, even more cryptically, "Even the second time I didn't know I was headed for the retirement that 'never was.' " He raised a finger as if launching a lecture, but before he could move to explain the "never was," I asked him to back up, to tell me about his first attempt to retire.

"I went to see Grayson, the provost," he began. "You know, I'd already been living with this idea of 'getting out early' for a few years. I loved teaching, but it was too much to do that and still do everything else." He waved his cup in an arc. "I wanted to write, to clean up this environment *and* the fire department in this town. My wife Teri and I, we'd been over it.

We figured with her job, and the pensions we'd be getting, that we could afford it if I just did some part-time work.

"Grayson—he was incredulous. 'Felix,' he says to me, 'you're only 54. Are you serious? At this point? You're at your peak,' he tells me, and goes, 'Why? Why?!'

"I tried to tell him but I couldn't do it well. I'd never worked out the reasons as clearly as I'd figured out the money. It was more in my guts, where it didn't need words. So, because I'm so intent on pleasing people, I started off by saying things that were agreeable with what he'd argued. About teaching. And why it mattered, to them and to me. On and on, you know the way I go sometimes. But at home that night, I realized I was back where I had been. Not just at home, but *in my life*. I hadn't retired or resigned. Or anything. I blamed Grayson. But really now I see: I talked myself out of it."

I had bought some donuts on my way to Shelby that morning, and when I went inside the firehouse to refill my mug, I brought out two of them and a fresh pot to share with Felix. But he declined both, protesting that he was trying to lose weight and learn how to live with his middle-aged prostate. "Ten, maybe fifteen pounds. I'm looking too much like Leo, my father, did when he was my age." He flicked a finger on his stomach and curled down the corners of his lips with disapproval. "Puffy. Soft around the middle. But with him it was beer, not dessert." Felix gazed off for a moment, and blew out a small pocket of breath. "Bastard didn't even make it to retirement. Didn't deserve to."

Felix described his father's life as "one long ride." His dad had gone to and from work, from one town and bar to the next. He was in construction, a carpenter, and "it wasn't that he loved work, or hated home so much; he just resented his life, and took it out on his wife and kids. Work was a better place to be when he couldn't be with friends at a tavern. I guess some people want to escape *from* work; he escaped *to* it."

Then his father got killed in a car crash. "Or, people speculated, he killed himself. They didn't investigate that sort of thing all that carefully in those years, but . . . drinking, driving, a long trip home for the weekend from a job near Rochester. Right off the road, on a straightaway, into a big old sugar maple near Warren's Hollow."

That was 1951. Felix was 17, and as soon as he graduated from high school he enlisted, ending up an MP in Korea. "Maybe," he joked, "maybe that's where I was seduced into loving uniforms, and helmets, and dressing up for work. Or it could have been my early years as an altar boy. Anyway"—more seriously—"by the time I was discharged, my mother and family, they saw the real change in me I owed to the service." By Felix's own confession, even speaking now as a latter-day pacifist, he had to allow a debt to the army for teaching him "a kind of secular discipline," one that helped him contain "long-suffering anger," the kind that "lapsed Catholics seem to enjoy so much."

Out of uniform, Felix went to college on the GI Bill, met Teri in his junior year, and married her the month after taking his degree in English. Only a few years beyond his own adolescence, Felix did a stint of substitute teaching in high school, and found himself "seduced again"—this time by the painful, familiar problems of the young adults in his classes. In their own words, "in their silences too," he found the echo of his own teenage traumas turning, day by day, into a source of fascination, a calling. He decided to teach, working where he felt he could help others as well as meet his own demons "one last time."

But in classic, mythic fashion, the demons kept changing shape. And Felix ended up with a long, shifting career during which he himself periodically resurfaced in some new form, as if he were always climbing, reborn, out of a burrow, reaching for some helpful, hoped-for daylight. After several years in the school system he started graduate work, eventually finished a Ph.D. in education, and moved on to teach at the college level. Even then he kept moving his venue and, finally, his field. From his first post at a state university he went to Seneca, a private institution, transforming himself from a trainer of teachers to a critic of society, and convincing the dean to move him over to sociology. Felix invented and taught strange, unorthodox courses there that had his students entranced, his colleagues bemused: Death as Life, Leisure and Liberty, Paths to Intimacy, The Nature of Responsibility.

He was notorious for the wide range of issues and the rage in the letters he wrote. He took on administrators, arms merchants, land developers, and local polluters. His opinions were a regular presence on the "Letters" page of the *Shelby Herald*. He organized protests, raised funds, and lobbied legislators, doing it all in such a relentlessly public way that his students—

and his three children—could not escape noticing the kind of citizenship he wanted them to emulate. And Felix sent extra copies of his many letters to a long list of friends and colleagues, giving his causes greater publicity and putting the prime recipients under more pressure. His special, personal touch was to add an apocryphal string of prominent figures to the bottom of each letter's mailing list. Professors, mayors, and senators learned that the document in their hands was also being sent to Ronald Reagan, Mother Teresa, David Rockefeller, Benjamin Spock, Pope John Paul, Toni Morrison, the Everly Brothers.

The kind of demonic energy that drove Felix throughout his career finally drove him out of it. The scarred face of justice; the fate of peace in an unruly, overarmed world; the desire to put out his own society's fires; and the health of the physical landscape itself—these were the moral concerns that propelled him. For decades he taught about them with great personal passion, and then—reluctantly, anxiously, apologetically—he began to think of leaving education because he wanted to give what he could "to *doing* instead of *teaching*." He once explained, "Look: I've been outraged. Now I want to be outrageous."

Felix admitted, over our nearly coffeeless cups, that "negatives" had also brought him to that point. By his mid-50s, for all his frantic energy, he had grown very tired: of campus politics; of grading papers; of the college's demeaning reviews for each year's raise; of the apathy of the graduating seniors he often had to face. But whatever the balance of forces that pushed and pulled him, he knew that if he retired it would mean giving up not only a career he loved but also, as a teacher, an identity and a role that he needed and feared to live without.[1]

For months I watched him play with his ambivalence over and over in his mind, touching it tenderly like a tongue toying with a sore tooth. At the firehouse he admitted that "after that disastrous talk with Grayson, I realized—Teri saw it right off—that the provost never could have persuaded me to stay on if I hadn't already half-persuaded myself."

It helped to fail. Felix would later recount to me his first, flawed attempt to retire as a cautionary tale. "I think, now, that I *needed* to live with the idea itself for a while longer. Teri once said to me that I couldn't bear to be parted from my students, from the stories of *their* lives, because those had become so much the story of *my* life. To retire I had to get past that, she said, to decide to become more complete myself. Also, I probably had to figure out ways to say goodbye—and Teri knows I'm terrible at letting go. If I hadn't been forced to take that time, to get really clear in my own mind, I don't think I'd have been capable of doing it.

"I'm not sure why it finally hit me last August. Probably something to do with a new school year starting. Also, I think with all three of our kids finally out of the house, it began to dawn on me: all the things I'd dreamed of were really possible. Then I got scared, as if someone had called my bluff. Probably, the last year or two of teaching, I'd been holding on partly because I was afraid of getting what I said I wanted—the chance to write. To organize. To be a player. I mulled and mulled it, but like my friend Peter says, 'Don't meditate. Agitate.' Still, could I do it? Could I take it?"

Teri had her own theory: that what in the end decided the issue were "Felix's own words," their echo, which came back "to haunt and goad and hold him to account." He was never a great practitioner of privacy or reverie, she told me, and Felix had made his retirement hopes so public to so many people that their inevitable questions about his plans became a regular refrain, "a reminder to him of the promises he had made to himself." In the end, she argued, he felt compelled to do what he had led others to expect he would. Confronted by friends with his own testimony, he finally found retirement not just a matter of dreams but one of integrity, credibility, and self-respect.

This time, when Felix went to see the provost in November, he was ready. Two years of talking to others had rehearsed and fortified him well. He had also seen his lawyer and his accountant, and brought with him a formal proposal. It detailed options about part-time teaching, long-term health coverage, and compensation for giving up tenure. The document went to the college's lawyers, and the process of negotiation began. It went on and on. And on. There were compromises. The time frame contracted. So did the dollars and benefits. The game grew tedious and wore Felix down, just as his lawyer said it was meant to. It was then that Felix found he had more time than patience left, and that what he was most impatient about was time itself. He bought the compromises. He felt he could afford to financially, and that he could not afford *not* to emotionally.

What he did not realize he had bought in the bargain was a particular form of language. Felix thought he was retiring, but in fact, in the terms of the Letter of Understanding signed the following March, he had agreed to a "voluntary separation." He explained, "When I realized this—I wasn't even sure why at the moment—I was very upset. I called my lawyer, but he was out of town. So I went to the provost's office, and tried to cool off while waiting outside. I saw the vice president, Donna Younger, in the hall, and I told her: they took away my 'retirement.' She was sympathetic, but she really didn't get it. 'Just change the word,' she suggested, but probably spoke out of turn. So when I went into the provost's office I almost lost it. Grayson was puzzled. Genuinely. I really shocked him. I said something like, 'Bill, slavery was "involuntary servitude." This "voluntary separation," it sounds like you've agreed to free me, or I've agreed to be freed. Was I your slave?! Or did I just "quit"?'

" 'Of course not,' he tells me. 'Don't get so upset. But there are legal and contractual meanings to "retired." Our Handbook and Pension Plan say that. And what you're doing, technically, skirts those particular obligations. You got some things, Felix. You gave up others. Look,' he went on, 'this is what you wanted. Don't get distracted by the language, the lawyers' ways of putting stuff. It adds up to the same thing.' "

Felix turned to me in his firehouse chair. "But I tell you, Joel, I knew what I had meant it to be, and I knew what it was called. So did Donna. Even if what they gave me was basically what I wanted, to *call* it something else *made* it something else. It made *me* someone else. I was not a quitter or a freed slave. But there I was. I discovered I'd sold my 'rights' to the word 'retirement.' "

That was just the first of two discoveries Felix made that spring. The second, derived from the first, was that with the "rights" went the rites. When the college's newspaper printed a list of retirees to be feted in May, he found that his name was absent. He inquired, he protested. It was *his* turn to be genuinely puzzled. The provost and head of personnel relented—a bit—but stood by the words of the Letter: separation, not retirement. Nevertheless, they agreed to include Felix among those to be "honored."

Whether he was a truly honored guest or an afterthought, it was important for Felix to be there, to have wrested that token of acknowledgment from those in authority. The formalities themselves were another story, less a discovery than a few hours of déjà vu and disappointment. Three other faculty members from other departments were retiring that year—two women whom Felix barely knew, and one man whom he had clashed with over issues of tenure and free speech. They all attended the reception hosted by the dean, president and provost. Held on a May afternoon in one of the college's more comfortable lounges, it featured wine, cheese, fruit, and remarks by each administrator—elements virtually identical to the retirement parties Felix had attended at other people's departures one, two, five, and nearly ten years ago. This year, the average age of those in attendance was somewhat older, the wine a bit younger.

In the only improvised aspect, personal remarks made by colleagues were addressed individually to each of the four honorees. When his turn came, Felix was toasted and roasted by Ron Santucci, his department chair, who spoke with affection and something short of total candor about Felix's idiosyncrasies, his passions, his memos, and "his inimitable forms of dress, address, and redress."

Felix was touched by Ron's regard, his choice of words and emphases, even his feigned sense of discretion. But those warm currents were soon lost in the larger sea of rhetoric and ritual during the hour and a quarter of the celebration. The event, in Felix's memory, was "mostly standard issue," those honored "more like members of a line-up than stars in a spotlight; kind of the 'usual suspects' for that year." The glow of good feeling was sincere, but it lasted, he felt, about as long as "the buzz produced by the wine." Along with the regulation gifts that he and the "real" retirees were given—a plaque, a chair with the college's seal, a clock—it was not much to take home after 30 years of service. One consolation for Felix was that missing even that much, he would have felt even worse.

The season had one other redeeming quality, and that surfaced as an act of invention. Felix had a wide network of friends, and he had not kept hidden from them his escalating anxiety about his upcoming departure. Sensing his need for recognition and reassurance, three of those closest to him—Peter Blaustein and Chris and Ginny Hansell—proposed a party in

Felix's honor at the Hansells' house. Once they had pushed him beyond the first blush of perfunctory protest—"these things are silly," I told them. "Why bother? Who cares? Who'd even come?"—Felix did not need a lot of convincing. What he needed, instead, was some serious coaching.

The problems with planning the party, once Felix himself got into it, were those of scale and personnel. How many—and who—should be invited? At a lunch that Chris and Ginny set up with Felix to decide this, he arrived at the Clockworks, a local coffee shop, with a roster of 106 people. He was embarrassed, but professed helplessness against the numbers. "I told them that when I'd sat down that weekend to make the list, I didn't know where to begin. But once I'd started, I didn't know where to stop."

Ginny later recalled her own dismay. "Felix," she had told him, "this is a shopping list, not a guest list. Your wife, your kids, your colleagues and friends—yes. But committee chairs, old deans, editors, your Volvo mechanic, the people in your car pool, the fire chief, the guy who arrested you at the sit-in last year?! Come on," she cried, "except for the Dalai Lama and the head of the state Assembly, I think you've got everyone. Am I right?" Felix roared. But after the patrons at nearby tables turned back to their meals, his own face turned sheepish. Weakly, he tried to answer Ginny. "They're all . . . ," he began, but his voice broke and trailed off.

Chris stepped in. "They *are* all part of your life in some way. Or have been. But you have to think of the party, and what you want *that* to feel like. It's not that we don't have room in our home. The real question is about your real life." Felix conceded, "Okay, it's too much, too many. Yeah. But I don't know how to do this. Everyone fits somewhere . . ."

"Sure," Chris interjected, "but let's figure out where *you* fit." So they began again, walking and talking Felix through his "Who's Who" as he explained, defended, but gradually deleted individual names and, sometimes, whole categories of people. Chris later remembered how the conversation turned into "a sort of sorting"—of the relationships that mattered, of those that had simply happened. Just being a colleague, for example, turned out *not* to be a criterion for inclusion. Those who remained were people with whom Felix laid claim to some measure of passion or engagement, including those with whom he had had what he called "the great arguments." Ginny worked hard, pushing Felix to break through his tendency to make professions of universal love, to include people he *wanted* to love or who he wished would love *him*. Periodically, she put her head down to where it hung just above the table, between the yellow pages of foolscap and Felix's face, and then she'd finger a name and turn her gaze up at him to plead: "Do you really *care* about this person? Does he really care about *you*?"

It was "the longest lunch I ever had," Chris told me. "Felix had a story about nearly everyone. And the moral of each explained why this or that person stayed on or got crossed off. Every decision had to be justified. Felix was having all these dialogues with people who weren't even there. Ginny finally had to leave, but I stayed on. I knew Felix needed to do it this way."

Three weeks after the college's official reception, the "short list" of guests for the "real" retirement party assembled at the Hansells'. Teri, Chris, Ginny, Peter Blaustein, Ron Santucci, a dozen of Felix's good friends and colleagues, and all of his children were able to come. People brought dishes of food, a lot of beer, sufficient gifts to cover a coffee table, and enough anecdotes to last till midnight.

The dinner was free-form, neither a sit-down nor stand-up affair. Unlike the restrained circle of people posed around the college's white-table-clothed wine-and-cheese spread, the women and men at the Hansells' house moved, mixed, ate with appetite, and joked loudly. None of them was retired, yet most took great—if vicarious—pleasure in Felix's decision, and his history, and what Peter called his "victory."

Around ten o'clock, as a knot of noisy people gathered around the coffee urn for dessert, Ginny took them on as a ready-made audience. "I remember . . . ," she began, and the other voices dropped. "I remember when Luftkoff was the dean, and he tried to lower the hours that some secretaries could work—all so the college wouldn't have to pay them benefits. So Felix organized faculty to send in drafts of their letters and tests and bibliographies to Luftkoff for him and his assistant to type. Felix had us invent stuff for them to do—I heard someone took a page out of the telephone directory, said he needed it typed up for a random sample—just for Luftkoff to get the point that *we* needed those secretaries, and *those women* needed enough hours to make a decent living."

The "story hour"—as Teri referred to it later—had begun. One person after another told a favorite tale about Felix—everyone seemed to have at least one. Peter described the time Felix and Teri "had given away—not loaned—$500 and an attic of furniture to a group of foreign students who had been burned out of their apartment." Ron talked about, and mimicked, the way Felix paraded at each year's graduation wearing his fireman's hat and cape. Then Chris read a memo he had found, dated October 1973, in which Felix had defended the college's first co-ed dorm against its critics by arguing that it would lower the school's fuel, water, and repair bills by generating more body heat, fewer individual showers, and less vandalism because of the increased "energy of love."

When Chris finished, the room's eyes and energy all moved to Felix. He had prepared nothing to say, he claimed, but Teri pointed out that this had never stopped him before. Felix nodded, confessing that fighting with the college to be acknowledged as "retired" was perhaps just another opportunity to contest authority. He actually liked the *idea* of being retired, but wasn't too keen on the word itself. He said, " 'Re' means doing something again, like re-treads, getting new 'old' tires. But we really need a word that talks about new energies, a new phase of life. It is 'new,' not 'again.' I'd prefer 'renewal' or something Teri suggested: 'realignment with life.'

"Look, language is important. Sometimes it *does* say it all. When Mark and Kate had their first child, and Teri and I became grandparents . . . oh my God, that's new! And Liam, their first, when he comes over now, he talks. We take him one day a week since we retired. We go for long walks. I show him nests. He's in the garden with Teri. You know what he calls us? I'm 'Grandbird.' She's 'Grandflower.' "

Felix told his friends that if he had decided to hang on and become a professor emeritus—an "extinguished" instead of "distinguished" professor—he could have kept an office, phone, secretary, even a copier. "But staying at academic places like Seneca is like 'Welcome to the Hotel California': you check in, but you can't check out."[2] He admitted wanting to tell some administrators off, and how it was hard to let go, to give up the admiration, the pay, and the title. The horns of what he dubbed his "tragic little dilemma" had sharp, estimable points: to educate or activate? to reap the cash rewards of work, or those of a leaner, meaner, more morally meaningful life? Could he write the book on "love and the environment" he'd been promising to do? He even worried that his department would not try hard enough to find someone to carry on the special courses he'd developed. "My therapist—she's so beautiful, who'd want to get past the transference?—she calls it my 'delusion of indispensability.' "

When Felix paused, it was easy to see how moist his eyes had gotten. And one could sense him looking, as he did when lecturing, for a final, redeeming note. He found it in a metaphor for time and motion. He told people how differently he and Teri were moving through the world now, just in retirement's first few weeks. "I call it 'drift time.' It's not being in a fixed frame of work or routine. You bicycle instead of drive through life, letting each day unfold, taking you wherever it does. You know," he said, raising his hands as if to steer, "you know in a high-speed car, at 65 or 70 miles per hour, you hardly see anything—just the blur of other cars, not the streams or the trees? On a bike, in 'drift time,' you don't hit or kill anything. You can stop, or watch, or let your look absorb what's there. You hear the stream."

When Felix wiped his eyes after the anecdotes and his own remarks, it was ambiguous: tears of laughter? nostalgia? regret? gratitude? "I was moved. I was amused," he recalled for me at the firehouse. "It was so many things. I don't think I could have named the words for some of them. And then, *then,* they started to give me the presents to open!"

People had brought a medley of gifts which, considering how unrehearsed they were, played remarkably well together. Some reached into Felix's past, others to the future, and they variously spoke of who he was or what he hoped to do. There was a birdwatcher's journal where sightings and counts could be recorded; a CD of protest songs from the 60s; a GI Joe doll for the ex-MP as counterpoint; and a gift certificate for a tree from Teri and Felix's favorite nursery. Individually, each present might have gone to a number of the people gathered there. Together, however, they added up to one group's collective portrait of just one person, in all his complexity and continuity.

The very last package Felix opened neatly lined up his past and present alongside one of his favorite sociological truths. The gift, from Peter, was a bright, magenta-colored T-shirt, its front showing the outline of a large bar graph, with thick double columns reaching up from navel to neckline. Felix turned away and cheered as he slipped it on, then turned back to the room so that everyone could read the words printed below the bottom line of bars: the legend proclaimed the wearer, like the chart, to be "Broken Down by Age and Sex."

CHAPTER I

THE UNBEARABLE LIGHTNESS OF RETIREMENT

RITUAL AND SUPPORT AT THE END OF WORK

Culture has often been thought of in terms of tradition, but modern culture is more often noted for its inventions. The novelties of our time include not just obvious and dramatic new technologies—gene-splicers, CAT scanners, word processors, and spaceships—but also new social forms. Feminism, single-parenthood, nursing homes, rap music, psychobabble, and deconstructionism are just a few of these innovations. But one of the most important developments has been in the life course itself, where our century has seen the invention of retirement as a new stage of existence with its own name, organizations, magazines, and economic and legal infrastructure, as well as ceremonies, symbols, and full-blown planned communities.

Traditionally, when anthropologists have studied tradition they have focused a lot on ritual, and many of the rituals they have addressed are rites of passage.[1] These ceremonies help individuals move from one stage of life to the next by transforming their identities, and by investing both the passage and the person with deep cultural meaning. Societies that fail to provide timely and appropriate retirement rites may lay themselves open—as the Mesakin herders demonstrate—to intergenerational tensions and discontent among their elders.

In the culture of modernity, the potential dilemmas have been exacerbated: rituals have been played down, and to act ritualistically is to risk being put down rather than socially elevated. Later life in particular is characterized by a scarcity of clear expectations and helpful ceremonies in industrial societies. And these deficiencies occur during a period of great discontinuity in people's lives—a time of altered work and family roles, when rites of passage could potentially be most helpful to older individuals and the social order. For most retiring employees, sociologist George Maddox once observed, "this significant transition appears to be unceremonious, perhaps intentionally so, as though retirement were an event which one does not wish to mark especially." Since traditional European culture had no place for retirement in the life cycle, it lacked rituals to dramatize people's transition into old age. Gerontologist Ronald Manheimer has noted that retirement is still "a rite of passage we haven't figured out how to celebrate." Felix Davis would probably say "amen" to that.[2]

One of the most attentive students of retirement, Robert Atchley, has argued that we do not know much about retirement ceremonies, or how commonly they occur, or what part they play in this important process. Atchley stresses that retirement ceremonies, unlike weddings and graduations, are not standardized in our culture. Some end-of-work rites are personal and informal events, others highly organized and elaborate; some honor one person, others feature a group of individuals; some are sponsored by employers, others by friends; some bestow meaningful gifts while others fail to; and though the atmosphere of such occasions is usually festive, the speeches and rhetoric focus on the past rather than on the transitions that lie ahead.[3] The ritual experiences that Felix had, both at his college and the Hansells' home, reveal some of the good, the bad, and the ambiguous in these ceremonies.

Given the lack of attention to these rites, the absence of standards for conducting them, and their uncertain significance, there are several important issues worth addressing. What happens, ceremonially, when people enter the new life stage of retirement? Who organizes these events, and how are they arranged and put together? And, most important, what are the sources of meaning and support that retirees find, or hope to find, in these ritual experiences?

Several lessons became clear to Felix and his peers, and then to me, during the ceremonial season that ensued. First, we found critical differences in the nature of the *formal* as compared to the *informal rituals* that were held for them. Second, in both forms of ceremonies we came to appreciate the kinds of *symbolism, fantasy, social support,* and *personal control* that mattered to retirees. Third, in the period following actual retirement we discovered how important *travel* was to some people as a ritual means of transformation and transition into their new status. And finally, in the language and rhetoric used at these times we uncovered the varied *metaphors* that individuals employed to conceptualize the nature of retirement.

Formal Rituals

Retirement marks the end of work but not of responsibilities, one of which is to mark retirement itself with ritual. Employers usually feel obligated to host farewell ceremonies, and prospective retirees feel compelled to attend them. The formal nature of these events tends to follow a fairly basic formula: advance announcements of the party's time and place; brief speeches by supervisors or senior personnel; the bestowal of a gift and, sometimes, a commemorative certificate or plaque; and the serving of food, accompanied by a toast. Although the course and content of such rites are fairly predictable, the expectations of workers and the best laid plans of mice, men, and management are not always congruent. Nor are the results necessarily fulfilling.

At the age of 61, Martin Karler had been anticipating his retirement for months; he knew that it would only take one day in April to finish off the work of 37 years. For over three decades he had been employed in the production department of Crown Electronics, a Shelby appliance manufacturer. Rising slowly in its ranks, he wound up his career as an industrial designer in charge of advertising and media. Martin was content with what he called his last promotion's "comfortable responsibility," and in the last five years he had especially enjoyed being a kind of mentor to younger workers just starting out in the division.

Martin saw himself as a very practical man. And other than attending his children's college graduations and weddings, and a 25th anniversary party they threw for him and his wife Inez, he was no great lover of ritual. But with the end of work looming, he privately hoped that a public celebration would make the passage to retirement easier for him. He wanted some validation for what he had accomplished, and an acknowledgment of the unknown world he was about to enter. But the ceremony held to mark his last day of work was vague, a disappointment, moving like a hand that did not know what sign to make before an altar.

Like others who had been walked and talked down the same path, Martin found the formal ritual at his workplace to be "nice" but pallid and predictable. His boss said a few words, a plaque and a present were given, glasses were raised in salute, and people quickly turned to the buffet. Like Felix, Martin had been witness to nearly identical ceremonies held for older co-workers, and what these other men and women had once seen was now what he himself got.

The climax to years of work, then, was anticlimactic. For Martin and his predecessors at Crown there were, of course, minor variations in the content of the speeches, the words on the cards, and the value of the check or gift each individual received. A few anecdotes were told, and the retirees' contributions recounted; but only the most general remarks were made about each person's family ties or future plans. The rhetoric and the proceedings followed a well-known formula, and in Martin's experience "even the laughter came on cue and sounded canned."

People retiring from some of Shelby's larger employers—Seneca College in several cases, a financial corporation in others—were faced with another dimension, the fact of numbers. For Johanna Alexander, an administrative assistant at Evergreen Savings and Loan, or for teachers such as Felix Davis, the work year fell into well-defined periods—semesters, tax seasons, business quarters—providing clear junctures in time when groups of employees, approaching retirement, were expected to leave and mark that event together. Felix's joint college party was one case in point, and Johanna's experience at age 64 another.

When Johanna's boss Walter Baylen, a vice president, was compelled to retire in a bank merger and reorganization, she was "encouraged" to move up the date of her own retirement by several months so that both their positions could be closed out at the end of the fiscal year. A few weeks before her last day, Johanna discovered, on the invitations sent to all administrative staff, that the bank's new directors had also merged her and Walter's departing celebrations. Though Walter had worked at the bank for only half as many years as Johanna—ten for him, almost 21 for her—his senior position earned him top billing on the notice and center stage at the dressy dinner held at the Stonemill Inn. Johanna was far from devastated at being overshadowed in either place—her methodical, meditative character ran more to kilims and quiet than speeches and limelight—but having a fairly formal relationship with Walter, she would have preferred either no ceremony at all or a room and ritual of her own.

In situations such as those faced by Johanna and Felix, retirees were made to share an already weakened spotlight with others whom they were either not close to or who—in some cases—they actively disliked. These experiences underscored how distinct the retirement rite could be from a seemingly similar ceremony such as a graduation, which usually marked a person's entry *into* the world of work. Though adolescence and the "young" end of old age may parallel one another as times of transition, powerlessness, and identity confusion, their rituals can differ in significant ways.[4] Unlike the finale of high school or college, there was no collective or "class" consciousness at the end of work to bind retirees together. Employees generally began and lived their work lives as individuals, not as a cohort; and yet at the end of their careers they were sometimes lumped together for ceremonial convenience.

Even some of the people who looked negatively upon the formal rites still felt compelled to attend them. In some instances they did not want to disappoint those desiring to acknowledge their departure. In other cases, like Felix's, the compulsion was their own. Whether hollow or not, the ceremony was still an important form of closure they preferred not to forgo. For postman Nate Rumsfeld, the story began in his own mail bag, where he found a letter informing him that his district's supervisors were opening a "window" of time during which senior employees could take an early retirement. Encouraged by younger co-workers anxious to move up, pressured by staff from above, and given "precious little guidance" by his union, Nate took the window at age 57—but he did so with great ambivalence and uncertainty. His situation bore a kind of kinship to that of a besieged Mesakin elder.

Several others at the post office also made the same decision to retire when Nate did, and no one thought of organizing even the most minimal of departure rites for them. Though Nate said he would not have especially enjoyed such an event—a claim his wife Charlotte dismissed as "sour grapes"—he nevertheless resented the absence of all celebration. Unlike Felix's situation, there were no ceremonies that Nate could lobby to be included in. It was one more insult in a hurried, unsatisfying, and alienating process.

Another reason "official" rites of retirement were so unfulfilling was that their organizers—the bosses, supervisors, and administrators—only knew retirees in a one-dimensional way, as employees or co-workers. Since this was the only part of a person's identity they could speak to, they could not address all the other dimensions of his or her life that would be affected by this transition, such as family ties, personal dreams, and life goals. Only people who knew a retiree in a more rounded, multifaceted way—such as Felix's close colleagues and friends—could relate to these other aspects of who they were. In contrast, the informal rites that intimates organized were far more meaningful; conceived by individuals who were better informed, they provided both closure on work and an opening to the future.

Informal Rites

The inventions that greeted Alice Armani at her career's end reveal the structure and significance of one such successful event. For Alice, retirement came at the end of 15 years of administrative work for Homebase—a small nonprofit human service agency—in a very demanding, low-paying, yet high-profile position. This organization had had only two previous directors—neither of whom had retired upon leaving—and so there was no institutional culture to frame a ceremonial tradition. When Alice decided to retire at 67, her decision was prompted by a combination of burn-out, a growing sense of her own age, and a feeling of diminished capacity and trust in her memory and attentiveness. She was both proud of what she had accomplished in her work and haunted by doubts of her own efficacy.

The retirement event created by Alice's staff, her board of directors, and the agency's volunteers included a dish-to-pass supper, the presence of Alice's adult children, a dance band featuring several of her colleagues, a song composed in her honor, and five speeches—brief but rich in detail—recounting episodes from Alice's career and highlighting the qualities of her character. There was also a "memory book" in which most of the six dozen guests wrote at some length about their feelings for her. Finally, there was a gift of a hand-carved easel, reflecting people's awareness of Alice's intention to focus on her passion for painting once retirement began.

The presentation of the gift, which Alice's grown children participated in, emphasized the kinds of watercolors Alice loved and some of the actual landscapes she dreamed of visiting. Those who spoke obviously knew Alice's heart as well as her art. What also made the evening so memorable to Alice was not just the personal attention and warmth but "the knowledge that my work had not been in vain, that I wasn't as incompetent as I feared I had become." The main reward, then, even more valuable than the easel, was the gift of reassurance about her worth. By the following week, on the back wall of Alice's studio, her artist's hands had added two key words to a sign her office staff had given her: it now read, "Alice Doesn't Work or Worry Here Any More."

The very steps by which such informal rites were planned unveiled another of their essential attributes, namely, the importance of process and selection. As Felix's experience revealed, preparing the guest list for a private celebration was itself a priceless opportunity for retirees to "work through" the people in their lives, to decide who constituted their real support system and circle of significant others. Along the way, possessions and old passions could also be reconsidered.

These features came out in the process of weeding and winnowing that biologist Ursula Chalfin went through. After 31 years of work at "The Station," a research facility run by the state's agriculture department, she had retired, quite contentedly, at the age of 63. Reflecting on her recent party and her role in planning it, Ursula compared the experience of making the guest list to what she had gone through cleaning out her office and lab. She had been helped in both the social and the physical tasks by Leanne Hoffer, her colleague and long-term companion, but there was some emotional work she had to do herself. Ursula discovered that these two processes of sorting had enabled her to figure out what and who was meaningful in her history. Just as she had combed through her library, deciding which books to keep, which to recycle, and which to give to people she cared about, Ursula had also had to separate out individuals who were "simply" co-workers and acquaintances from those who truly mattered.

"Plowing through all those papers and people, I saw that certain projects and staff were really from a distant past—the grants I'd never reapplied for, the technicians I used to have coffee with—and I said to Leanne, but more to myself, I guess: 'Okay, that was fun then, but it's over. These are not part of what I'm all about *now*.' " Deciding what to keep and who to invite, she felt, "put things together by putting some dreams and people away."

These informal or intimate rites revealed yet another important dimension of retirement, namely fantasy. In the safe, supportive company of friends, colleagues, and families, the more inventive and imaginative retirees articulated their vision of what they *would* have wanted their ideal departure to be like. Sparked by the presence of confidants and a bit of alcohol, they mused about who they would have told off, and in what words, or with what degree of drama and fanfare. Hearing them talk was like listening to people's fantasies of how they would have wanted to leave a bad relationship; their remarks had all the theatricality, flair, and well-considered words we come up with only in our dreams or on the morning after.

One retiree who acted out a rich example of this genre was Felix Davis himself. At the Hansells' party, after opening the last of his gifts—the graphic T-shirt—Felix spoke of a vision he had had, one in which he dreamed of holding his official retirement rite on the main quadrangle of the Seneca campus. In his fantasy he saw himself dressed in golfing clothes and awaiting a vintage Sopwith Camel, which would fly low over the college, land on the quad, and taxi up to where he stood, surrounded by dignitaries. Stepping onto a chair, Felix demonstrated how he saw himself mount a wing of the plane, hurl piles of bureaucratic forms and invective on the unprecedentedly silent college president, emit one huge fart, and roar off into the sunset.

To be able to describe such dreams, mouth the words, and—in at least a few cases—act them out before an appreciative group lent a cathartic quality to the opening act of retirement. Like court jesters, clowns, and other marginal figures who are licensed to express outrage and ridicule, retired elders such as Felix were able to use ritualized fantasy, humor, and their own privileged status as opportunities for social commentary and criticism. As anthropologist Victor Turner has emphasized in his studies of ritual, being marginalized does not necessarily disempower people. In fact, it is often from the margins that individuals can see, and voice, what those in the center of things may miss or choose to suppress.[5] For retirees, ceremony here was the chance for the repressed to find its voice, for intimates to become an audience, for kin and colleagues to stand witness to an adulthood's accumulation of love and hate.

Travel

In listening to people talk about retirement, and in following their rituals and fantasies during the early phases of their new lives, I came upon an unexpected and unceremonious way that many of them had for dealing with this transition: travel. Ursula Chalfin took Leanne on a long-dreamed-of trip to Siberia and Lake Baikal; Alice, divorced, treated herself to a two week Elderhostel program painting watercolors on the Maine coast—and found herself flirting there with the first serious, romantic relationship since the end of her marriage six years before; and Martin Karler traveled south for a month's second honeymoon with his wife Inez to visit old friends and a married son in the Carolinas.

For many women and men, however, such major trips in the immediate postretirement period were more than just special rewards they gave themselves. Whereas vacations were once a break between periods of work, travel now marked a separation between periods of life—what Alice called a "true punctuation." It also served significant emotional and symbolic functions on the home front. Travel itself, beyond its inherent pleasures of leisure and excitement, allowed new retirees to separate from work, hometown, the daily round of life, and the common flow of social ties. They found that when people persistently (and sometimes irritatingly) asked, "What are you going to do in your retirement?" they could simply answer, "I'm going to take a trip," and that this would often satisfy others and shut them up. Ursula actually suggested that "even if you're not going anywhere, tell them you are—and they'll leave you alone." But travel was more than merely the excuse for a quick, convenient retort. Recent retirees used the time away not only to relax, but to reflect on the past, put its immediacy behind them, and give thought to what they wanted from their future.

After Felix's wife Teri Rogers retired from teaching high school, for instance, she set out on a lengthy cross-country trip by train with her husband. The two of them visited many of the national parks that Teri had been dreaming about for most of her 57 years. The experience not only fulfilled a long-held ambition but built on her growing sensitivity to environmental issues, which Teri had developed while serving on her local civic association's executive board. On her journey, Teri had also read—"devoured," she said—a retirement gift from her children, Thomas Berry's book *The Dream of the Earth*; this account of a priest's spiritual encounter with the natural world moved her almost as much as her own passages through Mesa Verde, the Tetons, and Yosemite.[6] The messages of her trip and her reading grew even deeper the next fall, when a series of extraordinary October sunsets filled Teri with two sorts of wonder: one over the beauty unfolding before her, and the other over how many such autumn evenings she might have left in her life. Within five months of her return home, and after the interlude of "drift time" that she and Felix had bicycled through, Teri had decided to put her trip, her retirement, and her consciousness to work by joining Shelby's fledgling efforts to develop a land preservation trust. Her life review had taken a redemptive turn.

Teri's experience bears out the remarks of novelist and memoirist Lawrence Durrell, who has observed that "Journeys . . . flower spontaneously out of the demands of our natures—and the best of them not only lead us outwards in space, but inwards as well. Travel can be one of the most rewarding forms of introspection."[7] Like Teri, other veterans of retirement rites said that when they came back from their trip, their new identity as a retiree was "more real." They acknowledged that except for the absence of work, the things around them were still the same; yet *they* had somehow changed. It was, in effect, easier to go away and come back as a different person than it would have been, in Teri's words, "to simply change in place."

These experiences add a special dimension of meaning to the role of travel in the period after people exit from the work force. Gerontologists have noted that one path retired individuals follow is to pursue activities they had not been able to engage in before. Among men and women who start out adopting this euphoric "honeymoon" approach, extended travel is common. Even those with limited resources, such as postman Nate Rumsfeld, took a modest camping or fishing trip in order, as Nate phrased it, "to mark the end of one life and the start of the next." Older women and men of Shelby suggest, then, that for persons on such a path, the pursuit of this particular form of pleasure is also a transformative process.

Travel for them thus constituted a de facto rite of passage in the classic sense of that term: that is, the initial postretirement trip served to mediate between statuses, to create a transitional or liminal period between an individual's separation from an old identity and his or her subsequent reincorporation into society as a new person. In a modest but meaningful way, retirees' trips also echoed the journeys of self-discovery—the odysseys— which mark the mythic emergence of great cultural heroes throughout the world.[8] As Victor Turner has persuasively argued regarding people who are "betwixt and between" life's stages, it is in this liminal phase of ritual that personal identity is truly reconstituted. This quality of leaving one's old self behind reinforces the ceremonial emphasis on "separation" in retirement's broader meaning.[9] But whereas members of many cultures, from India's elder *sannyasins* to American Indian youths, successfully incorporate travel into such rites of passage as pilgrimages and vision quests, for retirees travel itself *is* the ritual, helping them pass from an old stage of life to a new one.

Ritual and Rhetoric

Modern times have presented Western peoples with many forms of novelty in lifestyle as well as technology. These innovations have prompted critical reflections on the idea that one's job is a central source of personal and social meaning. Just as the Industrial Revolution and the nineteenth century gave birth to the weekend and modern forms of leisure, they have also restructured the life course of current workers by creating the very concept of retirement.[10]

Studying how individuals cope with the transition into retirement is neither trivial nor esoteric. This passage is the gateway to a period of time that, as noted, could amount to a quarter of a person's life. The experiences of retirees such as Felix, Martin, Johanna, Nate, Alice, Ursula, and Teri indicate, however, that exiting from work can itself be hard work, and that the rituals held to mark people's entry into retirement take a number of different forms, just as they vary in their degrees of fulfillment. Two key points stand out from this diversity.

For most individuals, the formal and public recognition of retirement is commonly marred by the pale content of the official rites meant to dramatize it. These ceremonies tend to be formulaic, predictable, and clichéd; they are officiated over by individuals who commonly do not know the retirees in a rounded way; and they sometimes lump together a group of honorees who want to be acknowledged as individuals. In these circumstances ritual does become "mere ritual." Since most of the people I worked with in Shelby were in decent financial shape, what they were faced with as retirement began, then, was not the culture of poverty, but rather the poverty of culture.

The private and informal ceremonies created for retirees prove to be more fulfilling because of their style, their substance, their process, and their audience. They allow people to leave work on a good note, and give them a sense of control over this transition. The specific virtues of such occasions include the content and tone of their rhetoric; the informed and sympathetic presence of people who have really known the retirees, along with their histories and their dreams; the thoughtful process of selecting gifts and the reflective experience of formulating a guest list; and the opportunities such rites provide for retirees to engage in fantasy, physical separation, and freedom of expression. The latter features of these ceremonies open the doors for catharsis and personal transformation.

These rewarding attributes suggest that the ritual entry into retirement is heavy with meaning and full of potential. Unfortunately, the language of American culture and the rhetoric of formal ritual continue to convey the subtle and airy nature of this new phase of life, its aura of nothingness. People retire *from* work, which is an activity. They retire *to* bed or Florida, which are simply places. But there are still no prepositions or figures of speech to indicate what retirement is *for*. Older individuals do not retire to a purpose or function. What they *do* in the place they retire *to* is ill-defined and largely up to them.

Going through retirement strips people of a long-held identity and bestows nothing concrete to replace it. In contrast to our adolescent initiations, which often define individuals as "adult" who are really not yet capable of being economically productive or sexually reproductive, retirement rituals may communicate the uselessness of people who are actually still full of capability. This disjuncture between culture and biology, between functional and chronological age, can be deeply disconcerting for those caught in the gap between their sense of self and society's silence.[11]

Lacking a consensual model of retirement, most of Shelby's retirees tended to invent or seize on a metaphor for it that felt suitable to them. Retirement was a "vacation" to those who anticipated its freedom; it was a "sentence" to those who could not escape its confinement; it was like "adolescence" to those who saw it, with either fear or hope, as a kind of "starting all over again." Like being itself, whether people consciously followed the weighty philosophy of Sartre or floated along passively with Milan Kundera's characters, it was this undefined nature, this cultural lightness of retirement, which made it so personally heavy to bear.[12]

Anthropologists and historians have shown how people faced with the unexpected circumstances of modernity commonly create new forms of behavior to pattern their unprecedented lives. The historian Eric Hobsbawm, in fact, has pointed out how a good deal of what now passes for tradition—from Scottish kilts to royal coronations—is really of recent invention, created mainly in the years since the start of the Industrial Revolution. And in Barbara Myerhoff's now classic study of elderly East European Jews in California, she observed how an uprooted people created "definitional ceremonies," that is, their own rites of passage, when their newfound culture failed to provide them with meaningful ways to mark times of hope and renewal. The ancient Chinese recognized "ritual" itself as one of the most basic of "human arts"—which is an aesthetic sensitivity we might do well to cultivate.[13]

Shelby's elders have, in fact, shown that there are several positive ways in which the ritual handling of retirement can be made to work for people, just as their celebrations suggest that all of us—those who are retired, those who expect to retire, and those who may be called on to help others retire—could give more careful regard to the design of these critical events. It is not only God who dwells in the details; there are valuable and practical lessons lurking there as well. In that spirit, and based specifically on what retirees themselves have found in their own experiences, I would suggest that colleagues and kin pay more attention to the following six areas in planning people's ceremonies.

- *Informal rites.* The rites that people invent for their friends and family are a rich source of cultural creativity. They do, and say, and provide more than the standardized rituals that have grown up in the American workplace. Such private, intimate, and informal ceremonies need to be encouraged, learned from, and adapted to individual circumstances, and not overshadowed by the pro forma events that usually occur at people's places of employment. Whereas the latter celebrations, like Johanna's, homogenize participants and obliterate their singularity, invented rituals give control to retirees and their peers and allow the uniqueness of each person's life and its passages to be celebrated.
- *The gift.* The gift a retiree gets would ideally have some direct relationship to his or her history and hopes. All-purpose presents, such as money or gift certificates, are best avoided; retirement is a meaningful transition, and its meaning needs to be reflected and expressed in what is given. A gift connected to an activity that the retiree is looking forward to, such as Alice's easel, makes the ritual more personal, more future-oriented, and thus more fulfilling.
- *The guest list.* Though the gift for an informal event may be a surprise, the guests should not be. Rather, it is better to prepare the guest list with care, and give the retiree a primary role in drawing it up. As Ursula and Felix found, family and friends who work on this process with the individual being honored can help by encouraging that person to talk about the reasons for including or excluding people; this turns the process into an opportunity for individuals to sort through their social ties and their history of work.
- *Travel.* Travel turns out to be a potent and even transformative experience for certain retirees, and its functional equivalent to a rite of passage needs to be recognized and promoted. Those planning their own retirement, and those who help others make such plans, would do well to consider the efficacy of travel in this light and think of ways to enhance its potential. The most effective journeys occur within a reasonable time (approximately six months) of actual retirement, and involve—as Teri's experience shows—an itinerary that has special meaning for the retiree.
- *Rhetoric.* The silence that afflicted Nate and the fulfillment enjoyed by

Alice highlighted the power of language and rhetoric as part of ritual. Words matter. What retirement is called, what retirees are called, what is said *to* such people, and what they can say *for* themselves can make the difference between a rite of reassurance and what Martin once dismissed as "eulogies for the living." Good rituals do not require formal speeches, but they can easily incorporate moments for thoughtful language, well-chosen words, and meaningful self-expression.

• *Fantasy.* Finally, retirement is a transition that brings out both memories and dreams, and so it bears a strong link to the unconscious world of fantasy. The ritual celebration of this life passage offers a rich occasion to express and act out those fantasies, and people benefit greatly when they are given—or, as Felix showed, when they give themselves—a chance to enjoy this possibility. If the American dream is one that has been built around the world of work, perhaps it is time for people to dream new worlds, and avenge themselves on old ones, when this time of transition is at hand.

A SECOND CUP

LIFE IS WHAT HAPPENS

Older people commonly like to be thought of as wise, but some take perverse pleasure in questioning their own wisdom. Alan Freudenberg liked to tease himself and others with that kind of humor. Having spent much of his adult life teaching government and history at Shelby's high school, and years of evening hours on the planning board of Common Council, he advocated learning from the past, assessing the present, and managing the future. But when it came to preparing for his own retirement, he reflected on what he called "the fallacy of misplaced prudence," proclaiming—borrowing, perhaps unconsciously, from John Lennon's song "Beautiful Boy"—that "life is what happens while you're out making plans."[1]

If there was a clear plan or order to Alan's life, it was not apparent from the state of his desk. Tucked into a corner of the large work room in the town hall that served council members as an office space, it supported a forest of files, blueprints, reports, and maps. One stand of papers, poised near the edge, seemed to be braced by a bag of golf clubs resting against the side. We each held our coffee cups in our laps because there was no safe place to put them down. Alan had even propped atop one pile of folders a printed plaque he had taken from his old office on retiring from the high school. It read: "A Clean Desk Is the Sign of a Sick Mind."

Alan, however, saw real symptoms in other places. His community, for example, despite its robust appearance, its well-kept woodframe homes and barns, and its neat red-brick storefronts, also had "its share of aches and ills." He was most concerned about Shelby's need for affordable housing, good youth programs, and adequate parking to keep the downtown business district vital. Yet he badly wanted to find ways to provide these without hiking taxes—"because if we raise them, then rents go up, retailers close, and the whole process turns self-defeating." Moving close to his old classroom style, he hit the desk and argued that "the responsibility of good government is like that of the good physician: when you're looking at illness, your job is not just to care but to cure. But above all, to *do no harm*. It's too bad," he mused, "they don't make politicians and lawyers take the same Hippocratic oath as doctors."

For over three decades, government at one level or another had been a central concern of Alan's life. But during much of that time it had mattered to him only in an "academic" sense. He had moved his short, round figure through its paces in front of countless high school classes, holding forth on laws, vetoes, checks and balances, voting blocs and civil rights, lobbies and wars. On his good days Alan had a slight bounce to his walk, which became more pronounced when he got excited. And it was speaking about the great legislators and justices that pumped him up: Daniel Webster, Robert LaFollette, Louis Brandeis, and John Marshall were favorites. Alan's voice and step then picked up speed, and his head—with close-cropped hair that had long outlived its 1950s fashionableness—stood a bit higher against the backdrop of blackboards and time lines. Since his early classroom years, Alan had loved and taught "Civics." "I still do," he told me at the start of his last term, "but now I have to call it something else. If I walked around using words like that, or 'civility' or 'social contract,' people would look at me as if I were wearing a powdered wig. My crewcut is bad enough!"

Fifteen years before, Alan had been bouncing and raging in front of a room of first-semester seniors, their faces as resistant to old truths as their tastes were to yesterday's music. During a lesson on Roosevelt's New Deal, a favorite theme of his, Alan made a grateful reference to the lovely stone trails that Roosevelt's Civil Conservation Corps had built in the state parks near Shelby. Then suddenly—out of context, almost out of character—Alan was railing about the state's current plans to tear down a scenic old one-lane bridge near his home and replace it with a modern, two-lane, "totally unnecessary eyesore." No one, he fumed at the first row, no one in the local area wanted it, or had even been consulted. Is that how our government is supposed to work? Our tax dollars used?

Alan's burn about the bridge got no looks of recognition, little sympathy, and just one response from one student. Bryan, a bright, laconic basketball player raised his hand, shrugged his bony shoulders, and asked: "So what are you and your neighbors going to do about it?"

Shocked both by the question and the quarter it came from, Alan stopped pacing. He leaned back against his desk, surprised at how reflective he felt. Years later he told me how visceral that moment remained in his memory. He looked past me for a second, pushed some papers aside, and made a small space for our coffee. "I remember: my impulse was to get defensive. But I didn't have the strength for it. I took a deep breath— you know, sometimes the way you breathe tells you how you're feeling?— and I knew then: I was about to 'lose' this class. I wasn't having a good day. But it wasn't just at school." His head shook. "It was the home front." He cradled his cup.

"My wife Anne had started on me at breakfast. She'd been halfway through her nurse's training when Garth, our third, had been born. We hadn't planned to have three, but there he was, 17 already. And Anne said, that same morning I'd railed about the bridge, how she finally wanted to go back, finish her degree, get her credential—by the end of next year!" Alan replayed her arguments: "She'd raised three children, worked only part-time as an aide, and Garth was now in high school. So, she said, 'It's my turn.' That's how she put it," he shrugged, raising his shoulders as if helpless. "I was not ready for that. But of course she was right. And the truth is she only needed about two more semesters to get her license. Still, I hadn't known she was going to come on like that just then." In the kitchen Alan had calculated quickly: Anne's reclaimed life meant less golf for him, more cooking and home duty, more summer school to cover Anne's college tuition as well as Garth's.

Three hours later, at the head of his class, Alan was still tasting the family fare from breakfast that day. He heard his own mind, caught between the claims of his wife and the bridge, echoing Bryan's words: "So what are you going to do about it?" Not knowing what he would say, Alan launched himself off the edge of the desk and toward the first row of students. In that small and unpremeditated move, he set his future in motion too.

"Maybe we'll rebel or start a revolution!" he offered. But as soon as he said that, he knew it was too pat. Though he tried to challenge the class, they seemed determined that day to challenge him. "How would you *do* it?" Bryan responded from the back of the room, giving the right word just the right amount of needling emphasis.

"How would *you* do it?" Alan countered, hiding his uncertainty behind a question, trying to sound Socratic. To his surprise, that philosophic trick of the teacher's trade worked this time. Asking students for rebellious ideas, he recalled, "was like asking them what's wrong with their parents." Sitting across from me, he amused himself with the far-off echo of their words: " 'Blockade the bridge.' 'Mine it.' 'Sue them.' I shot back, 'Sue who?'

"Now they were hot. 'Anyone,' they said. 'Everyone.' 'The highway commissioner.' 'The legislature.' They were into it. 'The governor.' 'Maybe the builders are breaking a law.' 'Maybe they're giving bribes.' 'Maybe . . . ' 'Maybe . . . ' From the chorus of offers Alan knew he had found fertile ground for angry minds. And by the bell he realized that one of them was his. The morning's class had taught him something about himself, which was what he had always secretly loved about teaching. It was the kind of moment he sometimes missed now, even when he was, in all other ways, glad to be retired from the classroom. But on that day back in 1977, he had gone home on fire. By ten o'clock he had called four families from nearby streets and organized an informal neighborhood meeting for that weekend. The first roadblock to the bridge was about to take shape.

In the end, Alan found, it took years to insure "that 'progress' was defeated," but the process, besides dismantling the bridge project, was also a kind of political coming-of-age for him. From chairing West Shelby's "ABC," the Anti-Bridge Coalition, Alan was drafted to serve on the town's transportation and highway commission. In the give-and-take of programs and budgets, he began to mature as a politician, learning to negotiate with some of his counterparts in state government—even John Sant'angelo, the strong-willed chief engineer with the Department of Transportation, the very man he had once "headed off at the bridge." A few years later Alan "graduated" to the local planning board and, finally, election to Common Council. By the time he taught his last classes, Alan had developed a teacher's pride in his in-house expertise, his notoriety as an official of government who taught students about its workings from the inside. When Bryan's successors in the back row now confronted him with their "show me" tones of voice about "the whole point" of politics, Alan could cite his own modest victories—with playgrounds and tax reforms—alongside the more dramatic ones of his New Deal heroes.

Alan's retirement was, and was not, planned. He knew when it was scheduled for, and looked forward to its promise. But in the months leading up to the freedom of a life without daily work, he did not really know what he wanted to do with it. "My father, from the 'old school,' the labor-union Jewish radical from New York, he never retired. He keeled over at his sewing machine on Rivington Street. So did I deserve retirement? All I'd figured out was that I'd finally be able to buy and read the Sunday *New York Times*. Otherwise, I was floating toward it. Not aimlessly, you understand. I just wasn't sure which of the things I enjoyed most was going to be primary for me: Reading? Studying Spanish? Perfecting . . . ha! . . . my golf?"

Reluctantly, Alan agreed to let Anne and his colleagues throw a farewell party for him. "They were going to feel culturally deprived if I didn't relent. But the real ritual for me, if you can believe it, turned out to be going to sign up for Social Security. It was like a Bar Mitzvah: I had been called to the Torah, to get my reward. It was only filling out some forms, and not much of a setting, but I felt that I had officially entered the ranks. The first payment, when it came, was like a diploma, a certificate, a letter of acceptance. All those years teaching about government and entitlements, and the check was finally in the mail!"[2]

But there had been other papers and dreams to contend with before June. As he began to empty out his school office and clean up the files in his study at home, he realized that what was often in his hands were his fantasies and hopes: his notes for a book he had once thought of writing on great American lawmakers; an autobiographical sketch for a graduate program he had almost applied for; the college journal he had kept while a summer intern in the state assembly, which he had once dreamed of serving in.

A year later, in his home, he showed me part of that paper trail. "Why did I keep adding those folders to a pile of things I wasn't ready to throw out yet? Why be so compulsive? Because tossing them away would have meant admitting I won't live long enough to do a fraction of what I've thought up for my life. I'd have to admit I'm going to die. Joel—I just wanted to figure out how to retire! But doing that, trying to clean things out, I swear I sometimes found death hiding in my desk. I'd try to comfort myself: dying is so democratic, I'd say, everyone gets to do it. Cold comfort. The act of throwing away confirms death. Keeping things is trying to keep death away."

In trying to figure out *how* to prepare for retirement, Alan even bought a self-help book on "streamlining your life." It helped, he joked, by "telling you what you already know," which "is pretty much what consultants do." The one area it did assist with was finances. For the first time in his adult life he sat down and made a budget. "Can you believe it? I was 61, married 35 years, with three kids, and I'd never done that. I was watchdog for the budgets on two of Shelby's departments, but I'd never made one of my own! Well, when I finished, at least the news was good. I found I could not only afford to live, but that it paid to retire."

Alan picked up a folder, then put it down without looking at it. His lips pursed for a second. "There was this moment of truth at the kitchen table—with my pads, and the calculator, and the pension printouts—when Anne and I had to sort out how much more help we should give our kids. I used to be so liberal on that score, and now I was feeling they're too old for us to keep that up. But Anne, she wanted to do it more gradually for the two who still get a kind of allowance from us." He leaned in, confessionally. "The third one never took a penny, paid all his own bills—and became a Republican! Anyway, we made some compromises, and even so, I saw that if I'd kept working for another three years, I wouldn't have made much more than my pension and Social Security would be giving me. I tried to show this to the older guys at school, so that they'd see they were practically working for nothing. But they just couldn't hear it. I think my retiring early was actually threatening to them. What would they *do* with themselves? I thought. But they turned it around on me. They said: 'What are *you* going to do with yourself?' "

"A good question," he confessed. For though Alan knew *why* he was retiring—boredom, restlessness, the certainty that three and a half decades in the classroom had been enough—he was less clear about what he wanted to retire *to*. He held up his hands when he tried to explain it to me, palms facing each other as if forming a frame. "Those final months I kept seeing Dan Pastner, the guy who used to chair my department. He'd retired, but they let him keep a small office there at the school—it was really an old storage room—and he'd come in almost every day, go through mail, try to look busy, rearrange the bulletin boards, drink coffee, shmooze, shuffle around. 'A ghost,' I thought, 'this guy's a ghost.' "

If Pastner was the haunted figure in retirement's landscape, Alan had several other people in mind who helped clarify his choices. The first was his wife. "One thing that made doing this easier to consider, even without goals, was the limits. Anne is seven years younger than me, and finally she was enjoying her career. By then she'd been made Director of Nursing at Elmwood Grove the nursing home downtown, so we were committed to staying. She'd waited too long to give up that job. So the issue for me was: what do *I* want to do here? Other than staying on the council and finally reading the *Times* each Sunday, I wasn't sure. I figured I'd wait and see."

Alan also had other questions from that time. "What is life about? Am I going to keep teaching until I get old and decrepit and fall over? At a certain point I said I don't want that. I have more choices than that. What I finally thought I could face was something I'd always lived with, a kind of different ghost from the family closet, this immigrant ethic from my labor-movement parents: the idea that your own growth comes from struggle, from working in the community, to make things better. Part of this is giving, but you also help yourself." He slipped me a look, passing it on like a plea. "I guess some part of me needed to accept that I needed to do that, to make a difference. Making plans is good, but being realistic is better, especially about yourself. So if that's what I needed to do, the question was, how to do it?"

The answer for Alan finally came in the form of someone else's retirement. Three months after cleaning out his desk at the high school, he learned that Gene Marcus, the chair of Common Council, had decided to step down because of illness. A number of Alan's colleagues at the town hall urged him to accept a nomination for the post. "Really," he insisted, holding out his palms again, face up this time, as if to claim sincerity, "really, I hadn't thought of it beforehand, because the position wasn't even there. Who would have guessed that Gene's health would have taken such a turn, or that he'd actually decide to resign? It just happened. Life's like that sometimes. Just like you can't take the blame for everything, you can't take credit for all of it either—even when it goes well—though that's exactly when you're tempted to do it!"

Alan picked up his cup and moved a few more of the files on his desk, making a small gesture toward order. "Did I plan to do this, to head up the council? Is this what I thought my retirement was going to look like? Hey, did Ben Franklin 'plan' to make a revolution? No, not in the early phases. He did other things: he negotiated, he experimented, he organized, he fornicated ('early to bed!' my ass), he wrote essays and made money. But lots of those things were steps that only later turned into a revolution. It all seemed to be inevitable or intentional—eventually. In hindsight it looked like a plan—the kind of hindsight that keeps history teachers employed! I'm not saying that making your retirement is like making a revolution— my students would have loved that! But it seems to evolve. You plan, and then life happens."

CHAPTER 2

ZEN MASTERS AND MASTER PLANNERS

HOW PEOPLE PREPARE FOR LATER LIFE

At an age when elders are thought to to have all the answers, retirees such as Alan may be awash in uncertainty. Do plans pan out? Do teachers know what they are talking about, or do the real lessons lie in the questions that their students ask?

All of life's passages challenge conventional wisdom and values, but the special poignancy of retirement is that it is often being entered by people who reached this very point *because* they have lived by society's rules, and have done so with a modicum of success. Though they are giving up work, most at least have the luxury of choosing to do so. If they can afford to think about retiring, they probably have at least some of the means to afford living it. And if life so far has not been all they hoped, they have nevertheless survived long enough to consider what they might want to get out of the rest of it. As Alice learned from her ritual's gift of assurance, just making it *to* retirement can be a measure of one's efficacy in the world.

Even so, there are still major questions for those who get there. Carl Withen, a retired Shelby lawyer, once joked to me and his friends over poker that the key questions change every decade or two of life. "You wonder at 10: Is there life after death? At 20: Is there work after college? At 40: Is there sex after marriage? At 60: Is there life after work?"

Carl's observation had its serious side, that our obsessions and preoccupations—if not our paid occupations—alter with age. Alan Freudenberg's story suggests that in their maturity people are concerned, even perplexed, about *how* they should prepare for retirement, and whether, in fact, they *can* plan for its passions and contingencies. In the variety of ways that men and women make the passage into this life stage—Alice's art, Nate's anger, Felix's fires, Teri's land trust, and Alan's work on the council—there were elements of both forethought and the fortuitous. Some, like Alan, also detect the hand of fate and the weight of family. But a fundamental difference in how individuals deal with retirement is the extent to which they plan, or believe in planning, for this great transition.

Shelby's elders tended to fall into two groups on this issue of preparation, with each following a distinct approach to the planning process. *One set of retirees emphasized a kind of Zen attitude of unscheduled openness and unformulated expectations about what the future might bring. The second group stressed a carefully thought-out agenda of activities, resources, and priorities around which to organize retired life.* The advocates of each approach, dubbed by Alan the "Zen masters" and the "Master planners," had numerous, sometimes contradictory reasons to explain their posture on this issue. But their explanations often shared a strong reactive element: what they were hoping to do and how they were hoping to do it were often explained by retirees as a reaction against what their own work life had been like, or what it had done to their hopes, or what they themselves had learned from watching how other elders had dealt with retirement.

Some, for example, spoke of their reaction against the demanding, highly structured nature of their jobs by voicing a desire to be spontaneous and free to respond to whatever inspirations came their way. But others emphasized a wish to finally follow pursuits that a responsible work life had placed beyond their reach. And among both groups, the individuals whom they cited to explain their own course of action were usually the negative examples—the role models of retirement such as parents and mentors, who had made poor choices or stressed the wrong emphases in preparing for later life.

The life stories that follow—those of a health administrator, a fundraiser, and a musician—show the influence of these models, and they exemplify the the sharply opposed outlooks of those who took the Zen and the planning approaches. In their own words and experiences, Harriet Trayvor, Ed Trayvor, and Sandra Golecki, along with Alan, also reflect the levels of fulfillment that people found during the opening years of retirement. They provide personal if not definitive answers to Carl Withen's question about whether there is life after work.

Master Planners: The Pleasures of Structure

The first time I spoke with Harriet and Ed Trayvor was in the deep-cushioned comfort of their living room. It was April, and the outside of their home was an advertisement for orderliness. The lawn was laid like a table; the trees pruned; even the gravel at their property's edge, thrown up by late winter snowplows, had been raked back into the street. If the outsides of houses are better guides to who and what is inside than the covers of books, then the Trayvors' home was an exemplar of that truth. Ed's retirement would start right on time, in eight weeks, just as he had ordered it last May. And as soon as I entered the kitchen, he showed me Harriet's last day of work neatly marked on their calendar for the following fall.

The Trayvors both talked easily, but they too needed their props. As Harriet poured tea, Ed started several answers to my questions about what he expected to be doing next, but he dropped each in mid-sentence and then said, "Wait. I'll show you." He left the room, with its rich blues and soft lights, and returned in a minute with a yellow legal pad, placing it proudly in my lap. Harriet laughed when she saw what he was about to offer in evidence.

The pad featured four pages of neat handwritten notes listing in detail all the things Ed hoped to accomplish, and avoid, when he left work in two months. One page had a column headed "What *Not* to Do." It included abstinence from "boring meetings," "boring people," and the "dry professional literature" Ed had needed to keep up with in careers as a personnel manager and fund-raiser. The positive side of the ledger was a very personal mix of the private and the public. Among the directives Ed had written to himself were: "Devote more energy to the YMCA." "Get involved in community health." "Spend more time with the grandchildren." And "Refit the sailboat." He had added a red-inked note about their 26-footer: "Take it out for whole weekends on the lake." Making the list, he said, had been the best thing about the whole last year of work.

He tapped the pad with a pen. "You need to have a *plan*," he emphasized, "otherwise life gets away from you. What did I do? I counted the months backwards from 65, to when my Medicare and COBRA could start, and that fixed the date so that I wouldn't lose money, or coverage, or time." Harriet nodded as she offered us the sugar bowl. "If you don't plan it out," she observed, "you wake up and hours, days, a whole week is gone, and you don't know what happened. It's the way weekends disappear for working people. Laundry. Errands. Shopping. Bills. Repairs. And then suddenly it's Sunday night. I think that's what 'lost weekend' really means." She shrugged at her guess. "Anyway, we've waited too long to do too many things to let that happen to us in *our* retirement."

The Trayvors' proclamations were not couched in the form of complaints. For his part, Ed acknowledged that he had had a good and privileged life so far: financial security, a long marriage, good health, professional success, and public regard. Together, he and Harriet could account for one large home, two Master's degrees, three grown daughters, and five grandchildren. They had each grown up in New England prior to the Second World War—Ed in Maine, Harriet in Connecticut—then met in Boston during college and, after Ed's army service, gotten married in New York just as they were starting graduate school. "Our families thought we should have waited till we had real jobs," Ed recalled. "They were hard rock 'Pilgrim's Rock' stock: your 'work now, play later, if ever', people." Still, all their parents came down from Portland and Hartford for the wedding, and again, two years later, to see Harriet get her degree in public affairs and Ed take his in business.

Family loyalty kept the Trayvors in the Northeast in the years ahead, but Ed eventually made a risky but rewarding move; from corporate management in Philadelphia he went to philanthropic fund-raising for the Harris Foundation, one of upstate New York's largest private charities. He confessed, "It finally gave the extrovert in me a chance to be the matchmaker between money and dreams." And though he and Harriet had launched their professional lives and family during what Ed called the "Eisenhower-and-Father-Knows-Best" reign of the 1950s, Harriet remained very "goal-oriented," very much her own person. By the time their third daughter was out of diapers, Harriet had begun a separate, respected career as a medical administrator, ending up associate director of Taylor County Hospital.

"I started a bit later than I had planned," she told me. "We thought we'd only have two children. But in retrospect I couldn't regret getting the girls started on their lives before I started on my own. Don't tell Columbia, but in terms of administrative skills, raising three kids was probably more helpful than getting a Master's."

There is a common observation that long-married couples eventually come to look alike. This was one "truth" that did not fit the Trayvors. When I stood on their deck the following October, just a week before Harriet's last official day at work, Ed's 6'1" frame, his jogger's leanness, straight sandy hair and ruddy cheeks, were not likely to be confused with Harriet's 5'4" figure, her salt-and-pepper curls and clean complexion. But the Trayvors had shared enough of one another's lives—almost 39 years by the autumn Harriet retired—to share an outlook. They were both, in Ed's words, "grateful people." He capitalized the reasons: Favored Backgrounds, Opportunities, Good Kids, Health. "Maybe," Harriet theorized, "we look at things the same way because of what we've shared. Or maybe we're still together because we've had a tendency to look at some things the same way all along."

Whichever was true, it helped frame the way both Trayvors thought of retirement. They had each deferred a number of gratifications during what Harriet called "decades of hard work and conscious parenting." "Honestly," she explained, "we like to think of ourselves as fun-loving people—and I *do* think we are—but our daughter Tracy has teased us for years that we should get bumper stickers that say 'Puritanism Rules.' She says then it could be with us at all the meetings and hearings and debates we dutifully go to."

Harriet shrugged a concession. "Okay. We still want to do things for the community—but we also want to get on the boat and away from it. And we're not clones. Other than the lake, Ed and I move in different directions. He still consults part-time for the foundation, and promised people at the Y he'd help them with a new building, whereas I've begun working with the League of Women Voters. It's not only that our lists aren't identical," she added, raising her tone to signal the next detail as a telling one. "It's also that we have different means of keeping track of what's on them, and the ways do say something about who we are."

When I wondered what that meant, Harriet's right hand moved to my elbow. She coaxed me through the door that led into their study, and in quick succession, turned on the lights, her surge suppressor, and her laptop. "Poor Ed's still in the pen-and-paper stage," she said with mock sympathy, watching a menu come into focus. "Maybe it's because he was always traveling to see people and raise money, or give it away, but he never settled down to a desk and hardware. For me, being stuck in a hospital office at least had the virtue of forcing me to get my mind and my work wired. Look at this." She moved the mouse and clicked a few times, and in seconds the screen unscrolled Harriet's list for *her* new life. Reminiscent of Ed's, it had its "Dos" and "Don'ts."

The former came first, and included: • Walk 3 to 4 miles *every* day. • Write Jenny, Kyle, Loren and the twins [her grandchildren] when we can't see them. • Speak with Gladys about the League budget. • Clean out the basement. • Clean up this hard drive! • Replace the dishes on the boat. • Buy simple software for doing our taxes. And then there were the admonitions to herself, among which were: • Don't go to the hospital . . . for *anything*! • Don't take another credit card. • Don't listen to people telling me I have to listen to modern music. • Don't buy books I won't read in the next three months. And finally: • Don't make more lists . . . just work through this one!

From careers built around boards of directors, both Trayvors were used to giving annual reports. So a year after Harriet "checked out" of the hospital, they were ready when we met in their study to take stock of the first phase of retired life. Each of them adopted a pleased tone, just a touch competitive, in recounting their progress. Ed pulled out the pad again, noting his recent work with the Y's building committee, his relief at how different its members were from the indecisive people he used to see at business meetings. He implied some credit, probably well deserved, for the speed with which this volunteer group had secured money for a new wing and pool. "And when I'm helping them," he observed, "I don't get nervous the way I did at work, thinking the world would end if I slipped up or was a bit late. What are they going to do now? Fire me?" Then he tapped his chest, but in a gesture literally about his body, not buildings. "Five miles, just what I swore I'd jog." He fingered the pad where it said,

"Run five times a week." "Okay, I go three, maybe four days. But it's steady. I know I'm committed."

He turned to the next page and beamed. "Yes, yes," he said, showing me the line that said "week-ends on the lake." "This summer we did almost every one. Right through September. We even took our grandchildren—twice!" He switched to his captain's voice: "Drop anchor. Reef the sails. Eat simply. Bless the absence of a telephone."

He stopped just long enough to take a deep breath. "My father never would have done it—never, in fact, did it—this way. Looking after his health, giving something to the community, playing grandpa: those were not part of his plan." Ed admitted thinking a lot about his parents the past year, unable to refrain from comparing his own retirement with theirs. His mother had "never worked seriously, so retiring—from her little jobs with the arts council or the Thrift Shop—was no big deal for her. Then she developed cancer and didn't live very long. But my father's real retirement was when he remarried a few years later. He went with his new wife to this upscale 'Sun City' kind of place in California to be near *her* children. Now, I never could do that: move away from my own children, and grandchildren, *and* leave a place where I had put down roots. But I admit, he was quite happy with his choice. There were so many widows there and he liked being in demand as a man—fixing things, chauffeuring, knowing about stocks. Not my kind of retirement at all, but it suited him."

Listening to Ed on his father cued Harriet. "I don't know if there was a generation gap between him and us, but there was certainly a gender gap. I want to be around my children, not just to help them but because I genuinely enjoy their company. And just because I'm a woman with three daughters doesn't make me their role model. Take my own mother. She was a school teacher who 'hung in there' at work till the end because she couldn't bring herself to retire. She had no other interests, just her home and family, and she wasn't happy those final years because your home and family don't always need you when you need them to need you. But my father, he retired as a railroad engineer, then worked part-time for the city of Hartford, and was delighted to still be at it on his own terms. And he wasn't like his wife—he enjoyed his grandchildren in the same way as his job. So he was okay. He did it well."

Harriet touched her chest. "Me, I'm not much like either of my parents, especially my mother. I care about my children and their kids, but I don't smother them. In fact, the problem for us is that when our grandchildren come here, they're so undisciplined and unscheduled—their parents set so few limits—that *we* are the ones who create rules for them. What a reversal! Now it's the parents who're indulgent, too afraid to 'stifle the kids,' and we grandparents lay down the law. What else is different from our parents? Ed and I are active in the community. There's lots of room for family, but other things too. That's good to model, and I think our daughters see it—yes, we're retired and we love them, but we still have our own lives. And we planned them. To be full. That's why we're fulfilled."

Her comments brought to mind a parental judgment for Ed as well. "My father once said something to me—it was kind of grudging, so typical of him—but he did mean it as a compliment. When I was in college he'd always been unhappy that I was studying liberal arts. He thought that was so pointless, 'so unmanly.' But years later, after my mother died and before he remarried, he was kind of floundering—and he could see that Harriet and I were busy, not just with our family, but in the town, church, Rotary, the art museum. And he gave my life, and the lists he'd seen on my desk, he gave them their due. He said something like the value of a good education is not so much to make you interesting to others, but to make you 'interesting to yourself.' I think, maybe, he finally understood something about me."

As their reflection on their families suggest, the early stages of retirement were filled for the Trayvors with both models and attitude. Besides the lessons of parents, they each cited as inspiration one of Shelby's "stars," their neighbor Rowena Darman. A retired physician, an international expert on infant nutrition, Darman was still lecturing and writing on children in developing countries. Recently, at the age of 80, she had decided to study for the ministry, and now commuted to Rochester two hours, twice a week, to attend divinity school.

The Trayvors had their individual favorites as well. For Harriet it was Maggie Kuhn, the founder of the Gray Panthers, who continued to agitate in her mid-80s "and show people how to 'think old.' "[1] To Ed the exemplar was someone from an earlier period of his own life, Saul Alinsky, the author of *Rules for Radicals*, whom Ed had worked with on community organizing back in Philadelphia in the 1960s. "He was the best coalition builder

I've ever known."[2] Neither Trayvor claimed to be a Darman, a Kuhn, or an Alinsky, but they knew who they would have been like if they could have been someone else.

Beyond personalities, it was still meaningful for Ed and Harriet to stake out some hopes of their own. "What kind of legacy do I want to leave?" Ed asked himself. "My immortality, I guess, is my children, and the trees I planted, and what I built in the community: real buildings and programs." Harriet cut in for equal time. "You ought to feel you've accomplished something in life. I did that having three nice daughters—though I'd like to be able to say I produced, not just *re*produced. Be like my college friends, who wrote books and became dancers."

"Oh come on, Harriet," Ed said. "Give yourself credit. You helped create that hospital from nothing but other people's pious wishes and words." His distrust of rhetoric had one other source. "I'm totally skeptical of folks who boast they'll make radical changes in their retirement. I think most of us tend to stick to the patterns we've always had. It's the rare person who goes from being, say, a corporate executive to a portrait painter."

"I object to it," Harriet said, "when I hear people say: 'When you retire, you'll get to do all the things you always wanted to.' If they were so important, you would have made time for them before. For me it's more of a chance to do more of the things I've been doing all along."

Ed continued, "That's why everyone needs to get on the ball about their health. Lose that, and probably nothing you've planned for retirement will happen the way you want. I was fat and dumb at 28. I'm smarter and thinner now. I get furious with people who joke that they get their exercise going to the funerals of their friends who jog. Those wise guys take better care of their cars and computers than their own bodies."

What does it take to change people? I asked. Ed had a joke for an answer. "There's this older man, Mr. Jones, late 70s, and he can't do as much as he used to. So he's getting depressed and he keeps telling his wife: 'I think I'm going to die.' He says this so often she finally takes him to see a doctor. The doctor gives him a complete exam, and then asks him to step outside so he can speak to the wife. Mrs. Jones comes in and the doctor says, 'For his age, he's actually in remarkable shape. In fact, there's nothing wrong with him that some home cooking and regular sex can't cure.' So outside Mr. Jones turns to his wife and asks: 'What did the doctor say?' And she answers:

'You're going to die.' " She had heard it before, but Harriet still laughed, and she tried one of her own. "When you're young and newly married, the three greatest words are 'I love you.' When you're retired, they're 'Let's eat out.' "

"We don't have all the answers," Harriet put in, "and I don't think the way we're doing it would have worked for my mother or Ed's father. But what has happened here," she went on, nudging me over to her laptop, pointing to the screen as it brought forth text, "is a good start." She paused, running a finger down her list: "Yes, I did help the League, and now I'm on their board. And that's *fun*, because we get to put candidates on the spot and in the spotlight—which is a lot better than being in the hot seat and having my old board sticking it to me. And I do walk more now." Another pause, moving down a few more lines. "Well, I bought the tax software, but still haven't learned it. Yes, I write to my grandchildren, and I cleaned up this hard drive."

Ed peeked over her shoulder. "Ah, but we still didn't empty out the basement." Harriet corrected: "No. *You* still didn't clean out the basement." "But that's on *your* list," said Ed. "Yes, for *you* to do."

"Hey," he shrugged in mock defeat, "whose life, I mean whose list, is it anyway?" And he turned to me, offering the wry smile that long-married men like to trade. Harriet rolled her eyes. "Okay," Ed confessed, "there are still lots of things I haven't gotten to, but it's a beginning. We're under way." To that, at least, Harriet could agree. What pleased them both was not that their plans or lists had been completed, but, as she put it, that "the plan *to* plan was working well."

Zen Masters: Planning Not to Plan

Most people feel retirement is wonderful in principle, but they disagree on how to practice it. In sharp contrast to Ed and Harriet are those who see a prospect devoid of tables and commandments, of "dos and don'ts," of "musts and shoulds." Instead, they conjure an image of their future that is clear but list-less. Close to finishing a long phase of adulthood characterized by work, schedules, family commitments, or other responsibilities, these individuals do not want retirement to be filled in before it has barely begun with scripts, agendas, or padfuls of priorities crowded with other people's figures and dutiful details. Instead, they have decided to plan not to plan.

One of those who embraced this approach was pianist Sandra Golecki, a retired 68-year-old music educator, who spoke of "the excitement of emptiness." Settled into a Bach chorale and her favorite easy chair one morning, she reached to a shelf behind her and pulled down a large artist's sketchbook. I thought I was about to be shown another roster of tasks. But Sandra turned back the cover and proudly displayed a completely unmarked surface. She explained: "I know some who'd be terrified by such a space, like a blocked writer staring at a blank page. But for me, this is what retirement has meant." She put down her coffee to fan her fingers over the vacant paper, staring at its whiteness. "An unexpected invitation. Something like the childhood dream of walking through a hidden door and stepping into—what? Some strange, magic land."

From her peers and colleagues, though, Sandra did not have a lot of support for stepping into retirement in that spirit of wonderment. They were puzzled, some to the point of disbelief, that in leaving work she was also effectively leaving music. "I told them I would play, but only for myself. And I've stuck to that promise, and enjoyed it. It's nice to be alone with the music rather than preparing it for someone else to hear."

Music was not all she had come to appreciate in a new way. In the 12 months since retiring, Sandra had also realized how being a musician and teacher had shaped her experience of time. "In a profession like mine, your thoughts are always on the future: the next student, the next concert. You never seem to have time for 'this moment.' But just because your day is untidy doesn't mean it can't be an offering or a promise. What I've learned is that the present is possible—I can 'be' in it. That's new. By habit I'm a very grounded person, and all those years of discipline die hard. I have to keep relearning that lesson. Even after a year, I still have to remind myself that this is where I am; I should enjoy today *today!* It's not a rehearsal."

There were other facets of her work that Sandra could not easily discuss until time and distance had separated her from former colleagues. "There is this terrible irony about certain musicians," she once began, recalling people's reactions to her decision to leave performing and teaching. "They can be brilliant but narrow," she explained. "For a while after I left, some friends and I occasionally met for lunch." Retuning her voice, Sandra did both her and their halves of a sample conversation. *"When are you playing, or conducting, next?* I'm not. *Oh, you're not?* Really. *Well, what piece [of music] are you working on?* Nothing particular. *Really? Nothing?!"*

She stopped a few seconds for effect, and turned to me. "You see? Silence. They had nothing else to say. It wasn't that music was all they knew, but it was all they knew *how* to talk about. It's as if suddenly we'd all agreed to play one of John Cage's 'silent' compositions—the kind where the orchestra does nothing, and you wait for 'found sounds' to happen.[3] Yet none of them liked that kind of music. Anyway, it seems funny now, but it was sad then. They were nice enough, really, but not much range."

Sandra shook her head and gave an embarrassed smile. "Oh they weren't all like that. But when I tried to tell some of them about what I *was* doing, they just weren't that interested. They didn't ask questions. Of course I could ask *them* about what they were doing or playing or performing—being the solicitous woman, you know, 'interviewing' the men—and they'd be relieved and go on at great length. Like it was a performance itself! I guess some musicians just want to be heard, but they don't know how to listen."

Educated as a "conservatory brat" with formal, intense training that began at six, Sandra had marched to that meter for over five decades. Now that she had decided to stop playing in public, conducting, teaching, consulting, and judging, it was not because she disliked music. She was just tired of building her life around it. And the nature of the work it brought her had soured in recent years. Teaching had become predictable, the bureaucracy at the conservatory increasingly petty, and too many of her colleagues too wrapped up in committees, gossip, and their small triumphs and defeats—"bagatelles magnified into a magnum opus."

There were also caveats from history. Sandra had seen older musicians whom she had admired, including her own mentor, grow stale and bitter by staying on too long in careers they no longer had the passion or talent for. "By the time he stopped, the man I'd studied with, Pierre Vallint, was way past his prime—as a pianist, even as a teacher—yet he couldn't see anything past what he was doing. I'd heard that he'd started flying off the handle at his students, resenting their talent instead of being inspired by it. He finally had to retire because of poor health. The illness wasn't life-threatening, but he was so tied to his career that when he left the conservatory and the phone stopped ringing, he became despondent. Dead within a year." Sandra stared into her cup. "It made me think of Leonard Bernstein, who died inside when he could no longer perform or be seen."[4]

Her eyes came up to mine again. "It's not that every musician is like that." She glowed a bit. "Now Fritz Reiner—director of the Chicago Symphony—he had a heart attack at 72, and six months later he was back on the podium conducting Mozart from a tall chair. When he died at 74, it was from pneumonia he got rehearsing the Met for a performance of *Die Götterdämmerung!* Now *that* is how musicians *dream* of going. Not me, understand, but I admire him; he went on doing concerts and recordings right to the end, and I respect that he did it his way.[5]

"My husband too," she went on. "Joseph, he's a composer, semiretired, ten years older than me, but he still teaches and lives part-time in Rochester. Comes home for long weekends. He has his studio, sees two students a day, and still gets commissions. He's been doing a lot of arranging. These have been some of the happiest years for him—happy *and* healthy. His passions have added years to his life.

"But we're all different," Sandra continued in a lower register. "We lead different lives. My temperament is mercurial, and I have to go with it. The unhappiest ones are those who try to lead someone *else's* life, or someone else's version of *their* life. For me, when I was approaching retirement, I distinctly remember saying to myself, Yes, music is superb. But there has to be more to life than this. More to *my* life at least."[6] Her eyebrows raised in remembrance. "One morning it dawned on me that even though I'd begun as a conservatory brat, I never really thought of myself as having a 'career.' Strange. But my sense of who I was, it was not so bound up with what I did. Maybe that's why I was never invested in my children becoming musicians. Men are more self-identified that way, which must be why retiring from a career is so much harder for my colleagues to think about. They can't let go of themselves."

In walking away from music, Sandra felt she had other parts of her self in place, and some still to develop. The fact that she had never had a comprehensive education turned out to be a blessing in disguise. She said she was now having "the joy of learning the things that others know, especially history, but doing it at an age when I think it means more." Her two children, grown and gone, were now raising children of their own. With a decent pension, a commuter marriage, relatively good health, and only mild arthritis, Sandra thought of herself largely as a free agent. In her one concession to planning, she and Joseph had already made out living wills and sent copies to their children—who disappointed her by not acknowledging the documents when they came. "They're too threatened, I guess."

Ends and beginnings troubled Sandra less, and her simple curiosity about the unknowns that retirement would bring—a Zenlike frame of mind—was, in her words, "death's gift" to her. Three years earlier, her 84-year-old mother, stricken with liver cancer, had moved into Sandra's home to be nursed and to die. For close to four months, the attention, company, and caregiving required had been a round-the-clock responsibility. Though the local hospice staff had helped her in the final weeks, Sandra felt that unexpectedly she had been given something precious. "To be able to do that for someone who's loved you, to be able to have the kind of time together that normal life never allows—you have to stop the music, be able to step out of your life to find that."

Perhaps it was a musician's sensitivity, but the tell-tale moment at the end for Sandra, heard through the half-open door of the guest room where her mother lay, was the sound of the undertaker zipping up the black body bag. "What does it mean when they 'zip up the bag' on you? What did your life mean? All that really matters, I've come to feel, is your connection to your own gifts, and to people—right down to the unknown nature of your talents and your influence on others, whether it's your children, friends, or students. Whatever the talent. And whoever the people are. But you have to be able to set aside the plans, stop fixing up the future, for those things to happen."

The thoroughly unmusical and unacademic nature of that death's legacy, of what Sandra's life after work brought, surprised even her; instead of pedagogy and performance, she got hooked on polo and politics. Both developments emerged within the first few months of retirement. On a fall evening when Joseph was away, a neighbor invited Sandra to an indoor polo match. She was aroused by the chill in the air, the unfamiliar sounds of shouts, hoofbeats, and pounding mallets, the smells of horses and the churned-up turf, and she became fascinated with the sport's grace and ritual. "During the warm-up," she recalled with amusement, "they played the Bach E-major violin partita over the PA system. I knew—this is where I belong!" What also spoke to her senses was the nature of the crowd: their workaday clothes, the presence of children and elders, the passionate talk about the kinds of skills and discipline Sandra had never thought of. She went back a few times, got to know some of the people in the stands and those behind the scenes, and soon found herself engaged in a dimension of life—and a social circle—she had never dreamed of stepping foot in.

Sandra's political "comeback" occurred differently: it had to be recalled and unpacked. It materialized out of her own attic, a few weeks after her last day at work, as she was putting away the books, records, and scores she had brought home from her studio. Rearranging the other boxes already stored under some eaves, she discovered two large cartons stuffed with posters, news clippings, and buttons; they were from presidential campaigns she had participated in during the 1950s and 1960s.

Sitting across from me, Sandra put her cup and saucer down on the sidetable with a clack, and eased back into her cushions. "When I saw Stevenson, Eisenhower, the Kennedys and Nixon, Johnson and Goldwater all staring back at me, I suddenly remembered a promise I'd made to myself back then. It was from a time when politics mattered almost as much to me as music—the Cold War, the Bomb, civil rights, Vietnam—because I was young, and my kids were young then, and I felt that what I did or didn't do would somehow affect all our lives. The present was so worrisome because of the past, the genocides. History plagued me. The promise was that if I ever had time, I would really try to understand our own—*my* own—political past."

She slapped the arms of the chair. "I had once been as passionate about that as the piano. And I'd almost forgotten that whole part of who I was! How embarrassing to lose it—and how wonderful to recover it." By the end of that first winter, Sandra had clearly come out of the attic. She had joined the Current Affairs Book Club and worked on the campaign of a neighbor, Stefan Nokalsky, who was running for the school board. She had also begun helping the Shelby Museum organize its collection of old election materials.

With mixed tones of pleasure and revenge, she told me that "the best part about this kind of work in retirement is that I don't have a feeling of compulsion—that I have to do everything right away, or perfectly, or else my world will crash. There was this constant tension at the conservatory, and I used to squeeze all the other things in my life around that sense of obligation. Now, I'm as conscientious as before, but the feeling is 180° different. I feel in control. No one is going to haul me on the carpet. It's work without the feeling of work. It's play."

By the two-year mark of Sandra's retirement, music had ceded the stage to activism. She had attended a regional conference for curators of political history, read a lot more, and begun, without embarrassment, to watch the History Channel each week. "Maybe by the next presidential campaign I'll be out there again." she mused. "If you listen and you're open to life," she reflected, "zzzzzip: these are the kinds of things that happen."

Mastering the Art of Retirement

The point of these exemplary tales is not so much the merit or purpose of polo or politics, of community service or sailing, or of whether people's pursuits are new or resurrected ones, or deferred or newly discovered. Rather, it is the realization that the "method in the madness" for some individuals lies in not planning, in traveling into retirement without a road map or chart, whereas for others the satisfaction lies in knowing that the route and the itinerary are clearly laid out, that there are known and worthwhile goals to be pursued.

Whether or not to prepare for retirement is far less of an issue, far less of a choice, in many other cultures. For the Inuit, the Bahamians, and the Abkhasians, there is no retirement to plan or not plan for. Among the Korongo and Mesakin of Africa, and the people of traditional Ireland and China, culture has laid out the main contours of retirement in regard to succession, land, herds, places to live, and social support. The one kind of long-range plan possible in those societies is to accumulate sufficient property and heirs in adulthood to make one's later life secure. And it is in India, a predominantly Hindu country that gave birth to Buddhism, where elders come closest to a Zen approach: *sannyasins* there do have an ultimate spiritual goal, but they follow a path to reach it that cannot be controlled, planned, or predicted.

In Shelby, the only planning issue that all retirees agreed on was to save and invest enough money during one's working years to have financial security when they were over. People otherwise followed distinct roads and offered a variety of explanations for their choice of routes. Perhaps because they had grown up in an age of psychology—from Dr. Freud to Dr. Spock to Dr. Brothers—retirees had a strong sense of their characters, and readily described themselves in such terms as 'goal-oriented' (Harriet), 'grounded' (Sandra), 'compulsive' (Alan), and 'extrovert' (Ed). Those terms, in turn, became a ready-made vocabulary with which to explain certain aspects of their work, life history, and retirement: why, for example, they chose certain careers, or shied away from others; why they did or did not accomplish particular things; why they approached retirement in a specific way.

Other factors such as class, gender, and ethnicity were also invoked by retirees to increase their understanding of their own lives. Alan cited his Jewish working-class roots to clarify his rediscovered sense of activism; Ed and Harriet their solid New England backgrounds as the source of diligence and deferred gratification; and Sandra the effect that being female had on her degree of professional identity. In sum, as people sought to explain their sense of integrity, their moral values, and the consolidation or novelty of their roles in life—as politician, artist, builder, child, parent, producer, or reproducer—they were quite willing to call upon culture, character, and history to make sense of their own retirements.

The distinct strategies represented by Alan, Ed, Harriet, and Sandra are, admittedly, those of people who have given retirement a good deal of thought. They made very conscious decisions about how to handle it. Their approaches also proved threatening to certain of their colleagues— in Alan's case because of the timing, in Sandra's because of what she was planning *not* to do. These four individuals mixed memory and desire according to distinct formulas, followed different time frames with their spouses, and drew on a variety of other people as exemplars of good and bad ways to manage this process. Their experiences point to important lessons in three connected areas of retirement.

- *Timing and time.* The outcomes of retirement can be good whether partners are close in age or not, and whether they retire at the same time or
  years apart. Ed and Harriet Trayvor, like Felix Davis and Teri Rogers,
  were about the same age as one another and retired successfully within
  months of their partner. In contrast, Sandra Golecki, and Alan Freudenberg were ten years younger and seven years older, respectively, than
  their spouses. Whereas for Sandra the difference in ages and retirement
  times was liberating, for Alan it created constraints—but ones that nevertheless helped him to narrow down his choices.

  People had to deal with the "gift" of time that retirement represented
  and figure out what *kind* of time they wanted to live in. Felix and Teri
  enjoyed the interlude of "bicycle" or "drift" time as an opportunity to
  play with a different way of being in the world. Ed and Harriet struggled to balance private and public time as part of their allegiance to distinct agendas of dos and don'ts. Alan searched for a way to make the
  ethics of his past a viable part of his commitments for the future. And
  Sandra fought not to let concerns for the future control her life, but instead make room for the present and not treat play as a rehearsal or a
  leisurely prelude to more labor.[7]
- *Role models.* In preparing for retirement, and in making decisions about
  when and how to do it, people often had the examples of other elders in
  mind. Retirees looked to people they had personally known, or known
  of, as positive or negative role models because there were no generally
  accepted cultural heroes or heroines they could turn to in this regard.
  Even Benjamin Franklin, that American prophet of prudence, once admitted that he found planning the hardest of his own precepts to practice.[8] So we find Shelby's elders reflecting on such diverse individuals
  as Harriet's mother, who "hung in there" unhappily as a homemaker
  and teacher; Felix's father, who may have killed himself before retirement could; Alan's former chair Dan Pastner, who now haunted the
  halls at the high school; and Sandra's mentor Vallint, who withered and
  died once he left the studio and concert hall. These people provided lessons on how *not* to handle later life.

  On the affirmative side, Sandra could cite her husband Joseph, just as
  she, Ed, and Harriet were able to point to others who had clearly enjoyed later life—Ed's and Harriet's fathers and Fritz Reiner among

them—though each had done it in ways that none of the retirees was choosing to emulate. Even the admirable exemplars such as Rowena Darman, Maggie Kuhn, and Saul Alinsky were not thought of as realistic guides. In both the positive and the negative role models, then, it was the negative lessons that stood out.[9]

In contrast to the attention people gave to individual models, their participation in formal preretirement programs was minimal—a pattern noted before among other working Americans. Alan spoke with people at Social Security and Nate with union representatives; and staff at personnel offices were consulted by Johanna at the bank, Ursula at "The Station," Teri at her school, and Harriet at the hospital—but this was mostly to fill out forms. Some people talked with financial advisors, just as Felix sought the help of his lawyer and accountant. But none of these retirees' employers offered much that was attractive in the way of organized preparation. Planning sessions found about as much favor as official parties—they were sometimes necessary, but rarely sufficient.

• *Process.* There were two distinct approaches that people used in preparing for and entering retirement. One was a well-planned process that emphasized carefully laid out purposes, reasons, and agendas, and the other a philosophy that stressed a Zenlike mind-frame of openness, uncertainty, and expectation. The positive experiences of Alan, Ed, Harriet, and Sandra in the first period of retirement suggest that these alternative approaches worked equally well, given the distinct kinds of values, work histories, role models, and family circumstances that each brought to this new stage of life. All roads may or may not lead to Rome, but there are clearly several that lead into retirement. The experiences of these women and men indicate that each route will get you there, but that you have to know how you want to travel, and whether you want to take a sketchbook, a laptop, or a legal pad for company.

A THIRD CUP

HOW DO YOU CATALOG THIS?

Each generation makes meaning out of the landscape on which it lives. Over the years Tom and Rita Ellman had superimposed an intimate geography on the physical map of Shelby. To the south there was the library, where Rita had worked for 24 years, and north lay the Women's Center, whose choir she had sung in for almost as long. In the western part of town stood Feldman's, the department store where Tom had been a salesman for nearly two decades. Retired now, he was more likely to be found on the east side, either at Lakeview Baptist Church or the nearby county hospital that Harriet Trayvor helped run, both of which Tom currently served as part-time pastor. House and hospital, library and church, workplace and choir space, these landmarks turned a town into a hometown for the Ellmans.

Time was also part of their sense of place, and it helped fix Shelby as the only setting they had really considered for their retirement. Primary among the community's fixtures was the home the Ellmans lived in, which had been passed down in Rita's family, the Claremonts, for four generations. Its main section had been built on Iroquois Ridge in 1857, when it had had most of the hill to itself, with a clear view down to the village and the lake beyond. Much of that prospect had since been interrupted by newer buildings, tall-growing maples, power lines, and the smokestacks of one of Shelby's few factories. But the home seemed to have a kind of pride in itself, and even its altered views, its chipped paint, and the northward sag of the front porch floor could not diminish that.

Rita adored the house, and Tom adored her. And both forms of adoration were evident in the way they staged their tea ceremony. In the small living room behind their porch, a dark mahogany sideboard with a tea service stood against a long wall. The wood had been brought to a high polish by decades of Claremont women's hands. Tom and I sat across from it, sunk into armchairs near the fireplace. Rita picked up the teapot, another Claremont heirloom, its surface covered with a garden of high-glazed Chinese flowers.

Rita served with delicacy and precision, placing the pot back in its original position. "Everything in its place, and a place for everything," she had once said to me at the library—making gentle fun of herself in repeating this one-liner her colleagues tweaked her with as retirement approached. When she finally had to empty out her office, the task was notably easy; she had actually been cleaning that room all along, discarding old files, shredding outdated memos, and filing necessary papers in their proper drawers. The only perplexity, tucked behind the geraniums, was a small carton of photographs, most taken by Rita herself, of staff parties, public exhibits, the mountain of snow that had closed the town down in the great storm of '78. Her last week at work, Rita put a few pictures of special people in her purse, labeled and dated the rest, and gave the box to the library's archivist. Now at her home over a year later, with Tom and me, and the tea service and Rita herself all fixed in our places, it was easy to sense again how pleasurable order was to her. It had the quality of a duty, freely taken on and well fulfilled.

Duty, in all its domestic, Christian, and community incarnations, was as much a part of the landscape the Ellmans lived in as any building or hillside or vista. Rita had retired in June 1992 at age 62, earlier than she had planned to, in order to care for Pearl, her widowed mother, who was moving through the stages of Alzheimer's. Tom was still working as an appliance salesman then, and had recently also taken on a part-time pastoral position. When Dale Trinka, the minister of Lakeview Baptist, had been struck down in his pulpit by a stroke, the elders had asked if Tom would step in during Dale's recuperation.

Trained in the ministry as a young man, Tom had not had his own congregation for many years. Back in 1964, when the small rural church he had been serving was closed because of its inadequate size, Tom, then 33, "didn't lose faith" but allowed that he "did lose heart." After two more years as a "circuit preacher" for farm towns in the western part of the state, he decided to return to Shelby, his birthplace as well as Rita's, to be close to kin and childhood friends, and to take "a regular job" and "join the world of sinners." The way Tom now told it, "I had to give up my calling to make a living."

Decades later, with Dale's illness, Tom returned to the pulpit from the pews. He was happy because "that chance called to mind a great uncle of mine, who'd retired from the ministry but found a way to keep caring for his people by making 'sick calls.' To tell the truth," he said, "in those months, serving Feldman's and the church, I was more than a little amused— 'pushing' both washing machines and God."

That summer, however, had more earnestness than humor to it. During Pearl's decline and Tom's renewed ministry, the Ellmans got to see one another only in the late evening, after Rita got home from Elmwood Grove, her mother's nursing home, and Tom from his pastoral calls.

But within eight months, the order of things, and the nature of duty, both changed in unplanned ways. In November, five months after Rita's retirement from the library, her mother died after a rapid, surprising decline. Pearl's appetite had suddenly diminished in mid-September, and she soon moved from agitation to quietude. The slide seemed to begin almost two years to the day after Pearl's husband had died of congestive heart failure—a loss, according to Rita, that "destroyed all the plans they had made for their retirement. It made my mother a bitter, an uncharacteristically bitter person. After such a long life of hard work, I saw they'd waited too long to enjoy the last part of it." Within weeks after that "anniversary," Pearl seemed to have descended into a condition of unreachable peace. Six days before Thanksgiving she took her final breath.

Her daughter Rita could only make a speculative kind of sense out of it. "I had seen a few people die, and a fair number of them during the dying. Helping Tom make calls, you know, it comes with the territory. And I thought mother's spirits had picked up a bit after I stopped work and was with her every day. I told myself, 'She's getting used to Daddy's death.' But then she just got quiet. Anne Freudenberg, her nurse, said she just seemed to 'go away' a lot of the time. By the end, when she died, I don't know whether I was a presence or merely a witness for her."

Life's sudden and unplanned freedom was almost as shocking for Rita as her mother's passing. She had been working, in one way or another, since her junior year in high school. Her family had been poor, "not dirt poor, but real struggling farmers," and so Rita had been a waitress and then a doctor's receptionist during her summers. After marrying Tom, she had continued as a bookkeeper and secretary for a local dentist, stopped for the births and infancies of her children, and then began work again, this time as a part-time clerk at the library. Starting at the check-out desk, Rita proved her worth, moving up step by step till she was head of circulation and special programs. Her mother's death made her reflect—somewhat uncharitably, she feared—that she could have worked for another year and a half had she not stopped to be a caregiver for what turned out to be such a short period.

In the months since Pearl's funeral, Rita had been helping Tom with his ministry, had made a start on some house repairs, and had been giving her daughter Rose a hand with her youngest grandchild, Marianne. Tom said it was good that Rita was "having a break, a time to relax and"—he smiled—"put things back in place." But Rita felt in limbo. She said that, off and on, she was guilty: " 'Tom's working two jobs,' I'd say to myself, 'and I'm not working any.' How do you square that with yourself?"

And then Tom took her guilt away. Ninety-two days after Pearl passed on, he had a heart attack. Quickly, some roles altered and others reversed. Rita, who had gone from dutiful daughter to helpful grandmother, now became caregiving spouse. When Tom came home, Rose would come over with Marianne a few times a week in order to sit with her father, or take him to the doctor, so that Rita could get out a bit. When she could, Rita swam to take the strain off her sciatica, and to take off some of the weight that resulted from her stay-at-home life. Neighbors and congregants whom Tom had ministered to now came to call on him. Thinking back almost a year, to the very first time we three had sat over tea, Tom could not help but compare his new situation to that of Dale Trinka from Lakeview Baptist.

"After they realized how serious Dale's stroke was, he and [his wife] Hannah decided to stay in Florida. He could tell by then he wouldn't be able to come back to the church. Now I hear Dale's doing all right, though to my mind the hardest thing would be trying to get better while living in a new place. I guess the weather down there's a real help in his situation, but everyone needs something different. For me . . ." He shrugged and stopped, and Rita chimed in for both of them, "For healing, not to have the rest of your family, your neighbors and friends around, now that's hard to imagine. For friendship and comfort. This house *itself* is comfort."

Rita lifted the teapot for one last offering. "Illness, God, life itself—they test you." Then she dipped into her memory to explain "comfort" in a different way, drawing up images from books she had once browsed in her office. "I always liked what I saw in photos of other countries—Japan and India and China, if I'm right—where people keep pictures or statues of the gods who guard and protect the house. They're on either side of the doorway, or in the kitchen, so that when you enter, you must think, Okay, we're all right. Now those aren't my faiths, but I like the idea. How different that makes a home feel." She didn't need to mention the crucifix over the mantle to finish her thought.

For the moment, Rita said, she was leading "an unexpected life. I'm retired, but not really 'living my retirement' yet. Without work, it's nice not to have to worry so much about the time, getting to the library, fitting in all the other things you need to do. I thought it would be pretty open, but it fills up—with other jobs and other worries. I think it makes the ease of being home that much more important to me. I'm enjoying organizing the house."

"It's her 'new world order,' " Tom put in, but Rita was quick.

"Now you hush up! I realized just the other week that, finally, I'm 'at home' being at home, fixing small things, putting stuff away. I even got back to choir rehearsal. I think I can be content just doing things like that until Tom *really* retires and catches up with me."

The cup in Rita's hand went down with a clink on the saucer, her way of punctuating a point. "The truth, of course, is that we'd decided to stay on here in Shelby well before any of this happened with my mother, or Dale, or Tom. Oh sure, I'd hoped—I *still* hope—for us to do a big trip to the South, to see my brother in Texas and our oldest daughter in Louisiana. But here is where we've got our church, our friends, most of our family— our life, I guess you could say."

Despite her gratitude, Rita's face bore the faint signs of resignation, the things she had spoken to me about at other times: the modest budget they were living on, the narrowing of life's daily orbit, the places she had traveled to in her reading but could not see in the flesh because of Tom's illness. These were there for him too, phrased to me more privately in his regret that he was "the cause of her disappointment," that money—and now his health—were frustrating his desire to show his wife as much of the world as she wished.

Rita herself, in Tom's company, was more circumspect, and gave gratitude its day in a time of surprise, disappointment, and relief. "Still," she began, "still, it's just as true that when I retired, I didn't imagine all this: my mother's death, Dale's stroke, Tom's attack, Rose and all the others helping. But finally we're moving back, in slow stages—to working with the church, and visiting the hospital, and being more active in our lives. Now," she chuckled, "if there's a place for everything—and every librarian knows there is!—what do you do with this new life we've been given in this old house? Cardiac arrest, house arrest, Tom rescues the church, people rescue us. How do you catalog this?"

AT WORK, AT HOME, AT LARGE

THE SENSE OF PERSON AND PLACE

Figures of speech often tell us where we stand in our relationships. They marry the social with the spatial. In the heat of argument or insult, we are sorely tempted to put the other person "in his (or her) place." Our antagonist, we commonly feel, has "stepped out of line." If that person persists in raising points that are "off the map," we say they just don't understand "where we are coming from."

In retirement, which is a major *time* of change, people also need to know where in *space* they belong—where they are "coming from," where they are "going to," where they will now "fit in." Just as their rituals help them to negotiate when and how to retire, and their stance on planning helps frame what retirement might involve, they also have to wrestle with questions of where their retirement will be lived out, and what possesssions, places and people they will surround themselves with.[1]

As Rita's and Tom's experiences suggest, even before people formally left work they were facing a number of important decisions in which their sense of self turned out to be intimately bound up with their sense of place. This became evident when they had to clear out their offices, reorient their daily lives to their homes, decide whether to move their residence to a new house or apartment, and choose between staying in their current community or moving away. A few proclaimed their attitude in the way they decorated or appointed their space, as in the prominence given to Harriet's computer, Rita's teapot, or the sign in Alice Armani's studio disclaiming both work and worry. But for most people, the solutions were less obvious. The three stories that follow show how a biologist, a secretary, and a media consultant dealt with these issues. Along with that of the Ellmans, the histories of Ursula Chalfin, Sophie Malounek, and Bruce Palanos reveal the different paths that emerged in this phase of retirement. In their variety, they also point to several lessons about "person and place." First, that *sorting through one's material world can be a critical part of self-examination, and of moving on to the next stage of life.* Second, that *home, land, community, and possessions carry different weights and meanings for people.* And third, that *in retirement, as Americans consider where to live and what to live with, they are forced to struggle with fundamental, often contradictory themes in their own culture, particularly the tensions between freedom and rootedness, adventure and security, and family responsibility and personal fulfillment.*

At Work: Leaving the Lab

While many women of Ursula Chalfin's generation kept house, she scrutinized the musculature of rats. A biologist for New York's agriculture department, her lab was a home away from home, her rodents' anatomy a lifelong passion, an enduring and wonderous mystery. In "The Station," the facility where she had worked, Ursula had studied the lives of pests and the effects of pesticides, the health of plants and the fate of the creatures who ate them, the chemistry of life and the anatomy of death. Where the poet William Blake saw "a world in a grain of sand," Ursula detected evolution's handiwork carved into the tendons, nerves, and articulations of small bodies.[2]

When Ursula's own time began to inch toward 63 years, she decided she was fulfilled and spent, and after 37 years of microscopes and scalpels she was ready to move on to some other form of life. It was not that her profession now repelled her. Rather, as with Sandra Golecki's musings on music, Ursula felt that there were other things to do, but that she would "never discover what they were if I kept on doing what I'd already *been* doing." She had decided, in fact, to move to Georgia to care for her widowed mother Estelle, 86, who had already fought several rounds with melanoma. "When I was a child, I'd watched my mother care for *her* mother in our house, where my grandma Minna lived in the same room with me. I still have this quilt she and I sewed together there when I was ten. Anyway, when my mother suggested coming down to share her seaside cottage and 'the good life,' it was not an outright request for help—it never is with mothers, at least not mine—but as her only childless child I was the logical choice."

Making the move to Georgia had to be made to fit in other ways. Ursula and her companion Leanne were on different timetables, with Leanne not scheduled to retire from the medical branch of the state's prison system for another year and a half. And whereas Ursula had grown up in the South and loved the warmth, Leanne still had her roots, an old house, and the bulk of her relatives in the timber country of northern Minnesota. So, as these two had done before in their long-term relationship, they juggled calendars, weighed the weather, and argued the calls and claims of their respective families. At the end of a two-year conversation the two women agreed, each with reservations, on a new partnership for retirement, one as committed as ever, just more dispersed and differently choreographed. Ursula would move to the Georgia coast and come north in the summer to stay with Leanne. The first year's warm-weather reunion would be in Shelby and the next, after Leanne's retirement, in Menominee. Leanne, in turn, would travel South each December to escape the worst of the winter.

Moving out of the lab, her current house, and Shelby itself, then, was a course that had a multitude of determinants for Ursula. On her first visit north, we took a walk along Allegany Lake and took stock of what the leavings had meant. "Believe me, I don't miss what I threw out, or the weather. From what I heard of last winter, I'm happy I'm out of it. The town? Well, you know we never made friends here like we did when we were in college. People were friendly, but didn't know how to let us into their lives—even the women. Maybe because we're an odd couple and because we're scientists too. So moving away wasn't as hard as you'd imagine. I've rather liked the freedom of starting over—getting to know the parks and storekeepers, and just walking new streets. I've even done a bit of volunteering at the library. It isn't much, what with looking after mother. Her melanoma came back and metastisized, and she's had two surgeries this winter and spring. There was a lot to deal with and adjust to.

It's illness and intimacy," Ursula summed up, not needing to elaborate. But she did add that it taught her a good deal she needed to know about the intricacies of Medicare, insurance, Social Security, and "dealing with the system."

Fifteen months after Ursula's arrival, and six months after the cancer's resurgence, Estelle died peacefully, eased by the attentions of her daughter, a hospice nurse, and morphine. Near the end, Ursula reported, Estelle abandoned her habit of implying what she wanted and became very directive instead. She told Ursula where to find the clothes to bury her in, who to contact for the funeral service, and what to do with her knicknacks, seashells, and jewelry. Visiting her mother's church to make the final arrangements, Ursula discovered that the organist already knew what music Estelle wanted to have played. The sheet music, she told Ursula, could be found inside Estelle's piano bench. Shaking her head as she recounted all this to me on one of her last visits to Shelby—the one where she helped Leanne clean out *their* house—Ursula observed of her mother, "She may have led an unplanned life, but she sure had a well-planned death."

Ursula decided she liked enough of the life in Georgia to stay on. It took her several months to settle Estelle's estate, plow through piles of old papers, and distribute the belongings that she did not want. The house itself suited her; the one investment she made was to put on a small addition—expanding a mudroom into a study—so that she and Leanne would each have some space of their own when they were both living there.

The renovation came with only one surprise, and "it was not, surprisingly, the usual problems with the contractor." When a worker moved a bookcase to break out a wall, he found a small, built-in storage space behind it, and inside, three cartons covered with dust. Two contained old curtains and table mats, but the third held drawings, books, and sketch pads from Ursula's and her brothers' childhoods. Among these was a diary that Ursula had kept between the ages of 12 and 15. Reading it a half century later, she told me how she had found its pages "full of struggle"— to control her moods, to make sense of her friends and parents, to find enough discipline to keep the diary itself. She saw how her language had changed. She could "read herself" in the process: becoming less naive, mildly hopeful, then backsliding, more reflective again, but all in all growing up. On the last page was a cryptic note about a girl who had rejected

Ursula's friendship: "I will never, ever like her, or *be* like her." After that the entries stopped.

Reading the diary brought Ursula to conclude that "the way people change, or don't change, is fascinating. The holding on, the letting go. Fierce, quick to judge—I used to be my harshest critic." The memories resonated with what she had felt when she retired and left "The Station." "It was great, but now it's over. Other people will do things differently there, for better or worse, and you've got to accept that. So even when there's a part of you that feels you still belong at the job, that they should do it your way because of all those years you gave it, you have to let it go. In that, at least, I've matured. Which is why I regret none of it—and I miss none of it."

Retirement, when it came, had meant a succession, a ceding of Ursula's work space, a winnowing—and anatomizing—of its contents. The equipment, of course, had stayed. But as Ursula went through the drawings and photographs she had made, the articles she had contributed to, and the models she had built—mostly cross-sections of cornfields and orchards, showing soil layers, root systems, water tables, and rodent tunnels—she chose a few of each to keep. They were her own handiwork, landmarks of a scientific trek measured out over nearly four decades.

As for the books, much to her surprise Ursula found herself taking home some of the heaviest of the lot, the ones that gave the "big picture" of what her field had become in her lifetime—that is, the context of what she herself had done. The highly technical books and the specialized journals, though not worth keeping, were well worth giving to significant others. Ursula spent weeks conferring with favored colleagues over which publications they wanted, and the pleasure she felt in walking into their offices and passing on the volumes was personal and visceral—with Danny, for instance, a young trainee she had helped over the rough spots, and with Cathy, who shared Ursula's feeling that microscopes had a kind of grace and poetry to them.

Sorting the possessions and paraphernalia of her work place, then, was not just an act of emptying out. She was bestowing, not merely divesting, and learning that paring down was not necessarily about loss; it could embrace the moment of giving. As with the Georgia house she would one day clean out and the diary she would discover and re-read, it was also a process of clarifying. Where Felix had sorted out people by giving invitations, Ursula did so by giving away books. It is the type of process people commonly go through at many stages of life, be it with childhood toys, teenage music, adult tools and jewels, or a grandmother's hand-sewn quilt. Each decision about what to keep, what to discard, and what to offer to whom is a statement about how we see ourselves and others at a given point in time. As anthropologists have discovered in the offering of gifts and feasts among indigenous peoples, we connect through what we give away.[3] Ursula's short strolls through the rooms of "The Station" and her visit to an interrupted adolescence had shown her not only where she had been but what she had done, whom she had learned to value, and who she herself had become.

At Home: Planting the Garden

Starting in late May, Sophie Malounek took tea in her garden rather than the kitchen. It was not only the lush carpets of her flowers, the tapestried backdrop of mulberries, and the faintly perfumed anthology of herbs that drew her. She said she came there to listen to the silence, to taste nature's handiwork as well as to admire her own.

She had first told me about her plans for that rare and special pleasure two years earlier in the unquiet space of her cubicle at Crown Electronics. The company made a range of small appliances—the ones that Martin Karler had helped to build and market when he had worked there, some that Tom Ellman had sold while on the payroll at Feldman's. Sophie's job was in procurement, helping Cal Wenger, a division manager, acquire the paints, plastics, metals, and wiring for toasters, blenders, sanders, and drills. Sophie had a comfortable but windowless area on the main building's third floor. She had worked there for nine years as a secretary, moving up from Crown's assembly shed after half a decade in shipping and inventory.

A farmer's daughter from birth, Sophie had grown up growing things, but had reluctantly moved away from her roots in middle age. Married right after high school, she and her husband Urpo had eventually bought land from his parents and started to farm. Both their families were Finnish, as were a score of others in the area, but since "Urpo" was too exotic for Americans to deal with, her husband's name had become "Herb" back in childhood. He and Sophie had been brought up 15 miles north of Shelby in the village of Horace, whose croplands would one day be displaced by vineyards running in low rows down the hillsides. Now, sitting in her garden, tasting her mint tea and her retirement, Sophie spoke of her early married life with touches of humor. "We lived quietly those years, especially Herb, not like some of the people we'd gone to school with—we raised corn and children, not hell. I'll tell you, though," she added as an aside, "if I had to raise kids nowadays, *that* would be hell. Corn's easier."

By her mid-forties, a number of other things had been settled for Sophie. Crop prices had fallen, four of her five offspring were out of the house, and a back injury had made active farming increasingly difficult for Herb. Though she noted, with pride, that "we left a better farm than the one we found," the Malouneks decided to lease out most of their land to a neighbor, fix up an old carriage house on their property to rent out for income, and take new jobs. Herb joined the maintenance department at Seneca College, and Sophie, starting out as a packer, made her way up at Crown to clerk and, finally, department assistant.

Whatever the deficiencies in her work environment, Sophie nevertheless felt that they had treated her "pretty well at Crown, and my boss, Mr. Wenger, was very decent to me." He let her take off when her son Andy's wife gave birth, and when Sophie herself "had to go to the doctor and get all these tests." She had been struggling with a weight problem, high blood pressure, and low energy when her internist, Dr. Krigstein, finally traced it all to diabetes. "I think I knew it before the doctor. Mr. Wenger's wife Millie had it and I'd heard a lot about her symptoms from him. Hers were so bad she had to retire, and she wished she'd left her job earlier so she could have enjoyed herself more. You know, she lost a leg to it."

Sophie's case was not as bad as Millie's, and changes in diet and medication eventually brought the diabetes under control. But she had done her homework, too—researching the disease, talking to Millie, and joining a support group—enough to know that there was "no steady state with this. Too much insulin, it's shock. Too little, coma. You have to be careful of your eyes, your kidneys. It'll keep on changing, and I'll always have to be on top of it. Be my own doctor." Her eyes looked away at a horizon of hemlocks. "I'll have to get rid of my daughter too, put her in her place—

Marsha, the youngest, who insists on going to Krigstein with me. Criticizing me to my face in front of him for 'doctoring myself.' I finally told her to shut up; my older sister had treated my mother like that, and I couldn't stand it, then or now. Marsha says, 'we're concerned,' and I say, 'rightly so.' But I'm not over the hill yet, and haven't lost my mind. And I'm not lying down or giving up. I *know* this disease."

The diabetes did not become a formal disability or make Sophie eligible for SSI, but her age did put an early retirement within reach.[4] "I decided I'd retire as *early* as I could so that I could enjoy life *while* I could." She aimed to make the "magic marker" of 62, qualify for Social Security and Medicare, and "still be covered by Herb's health insurance." The government people "told me I'd have to be retired for 15 years before I'd see the cost of not waiting till 65. Well, I'm not waiting." Along with the income from their land, the carriage house, and her pension, Sophie calculated that she could retire from Crown, "especially since Herb had no intention of not working—*ever*—which was fine with me if that's what he wanted."

It was not that all of Herb's likes, dislikes, and inclinations dovetailed with those of his wife. When their son Andy got injured on his job as a roofer, Sophie took on all the work and worry of helping him with doctors, insurance, depression, and unemployment. "I know Herb loves him and was upset, but it wasn't the kind of thing he could handle well or talk about." Sophie also referred to her husband as a "pack rat" who held onto old tools, bank books, and catalogs, which she then struggled to discard in order to make her life and her house simpler. When she looked hard enough, she found discomfiting parallels between her own marriage and those of her parents and her grandparents. "Men tend to take to the kind of inactivity that killed my grandfather after he retired and sold his farm. Grandmother knew he'd made a mistake. So? What did that change? Herb could be that way; he works, bowls, mows the lawn, and that's it. So I guess he's better with a job. At least it gets us both medical benefits."

History played other parts in moving Sophie to retire when and where she did. Her father had developed myasthenia gravis in Sophie's childhood and was crippled by the time she was seven. She could still picture her mother's constant care for his unwilling body. Necessity thus made Sophie skillful from the start—with tools, canning and freezing, making butter and her own clothes. "I know what fresh food tastes like. I love the outdoors. The weather here? I'm more worried about inactivity than the cold. My background served me well. My mother insisted all her daughters have a trade before they got married so they wouldn't end up like her—with a crippled husband and no skills. That's why I learned bookkeeping, not just farming."

That Sophie's and Herb's histories had the same rural and ethnic roots foretold little, then, about their characters or their relationship. He loved work and had little interest in socializing and travel. Those traits laid a substantial furrow between him and his wife, who was partial to people and winter vacations. "And he won't go for a walk to see the fall leaves or waterfalls," she added. So, rather than worry about a reluctant spouse, Sophie had arranged to begin retirement by golfing and lunching each week with her women friends, and by substituting now and then—"what they call a 'casual appointment' "—when someone at Crown was sick or away for a few days. "The nicest part is that I only have to go in if I feel like it." And she had made reservations for a trip to Florida with her sister and sister-in-law in January—"the dark time of year when I get restless."

Sophie had one other idea, and this was a scheme her husband was more amenable to. It was that they should move into the carriage house when she retired and rent out their home instead. With just the two of them now, she reasoned, they needed less space but more income, and as long as she could use the two small fields they had held onto in back of the main house, Sophie felt she'd be content. "Sure I like this house," she told me later, "but the truth is I'm more a land-lover than a homeowner." So 14 months after hatching that plan, Sophie stepped out of her cubicle at Crown for the last time, moved into the smaller house, and began to plant her gardens.

On the day we drank the mint tea she urged me to put down my mug and take a tour of "the new world" she had created in two and a half years. "Retirement's like 'a month of Sundays,' " she claimed, "and this is what I've done with them so far." The flower beds had gone in the first summer, beginning directly behind the carriage house. The next spring she had staked out a number of other plots which now extended across a gently sloping meadow that backed up to her kitchen window—a vegetable garden for summer salads and fall canning, a melon patch, and a third area, near the woodlot, where Sophie experimented with wildflowers and herbs supposed to be good for blood pressure and diabetes. She pointed out yarrow, fenugreek, Jerusalem artichoke, and huckleberry.

"Those years at work were quite a change for me," she reflected later, gazing out at the vegetable patch from our seat on a stone bench—a retirement gift from her children and grandchildren. "Even now, I don't really miss the farming, but I did miss the growing. I wanted to get back to it. Every one of these plots is a little world where I can work something out, watch it happen—kind of a divine plan unfolding. It's as if I *live* in all of these places now, each separate but tied together, like the squares on a patchwork quilt."

At Large: Going on the Road

If Sophie was disposed to find God in the garden, Bruce Palanos's enthusiasm was for machines, and they took him far away from home. As a media consultant, a shaper of images, he had spent his adult life in advertising, moving with success from radio and print to TV and CD-ROMs. After retiring from the Ad Lib Agency, he bought a commodious, state-of-the-art RV.

Although Bruce wanted to keep a home base in Shelby, where he and his wife Nikka had raised their family, his main dream for the first phase of retirement was to travel the country, joining what he called "the new tribe of gray-haired nomads." Nikka, who had worked for years as a buyer at Feldman's, was interested but not yet sold on the idea. While she voiced quiet concerns about leaving her "things" and her friends and being far from their children, Bruce pushed on, approaching his objective as he would have an advertising campaign. He did background research on "the mobile life"; he conducted an "audience survey" by speaking with scores of experienced RVers; he studied the packaging and people's perception of this new way of life; and he picked concrete goals and the appropriate vehicle to achieve them. Though Bruce learned a lot from others in the process, he emphasized that he and Nikka wanted to do this in their own way, at their own pace, and with their own itinerary.

Though the proverbial born salesman, Bruce had to console Nikka as much as convince her in order to win her okay. They would keep a place of their own in Shelby, he agreed; she could put her favorite furniture and belongings in storage; and they would find a way to stay in touch with their son and daughters when the time came to leave. But first they would experiment. A full year and a half before either retired, they sold their family home and took an apartment. By that time they had bought a used Airstream trailer and taken it on several trial trips or "shakedown cruises." They learned two lessons from these. First, in Nikka's words, was that though they "loved the life," they did not want to emulate "full-timers," those who stayed on the road for years and years with "no place to call home." Second, in Bruce's spin, was that "we realized we also needed more 'inner space' in order to enjoy all that 'outer space.' " So they traded up to a large new Winnebago in anticipation of what he termed their "continental drift."

When Bruce did retire, his colleagues at Ad Lib presented him with a cake cut in the shape of a trailer and decorated with a drawing of a credit card. Along with it came a contract to consult with the agency each summer on some special accounts he had developed. The cake and the promise of work both pleased Bruce, but in truth it was his new RV that excited him most. He was sold on it, and he once guided me through it as if he were selling it to me. He pointed out "the full bedroom, couches, eat-in kitchen, loads of storage, and rustproof, faultless fittings." Outside, he patted down the walls as if they were the flanks of a favorite horse.

Even with all that conviction, it turned out that there were some leases on the Palanoses old life they were not yet ready to break. In the month before they set out, prompted by Nikka's reluctance to pull out every local root, she and Bruce arranged for their unmarried son Neal to give up his own apartment in Shelby and rent theirs instead. This not only preserved some domestic tranquillity for Nikka but also addressed her last bit of family angst. With her and Bruce's parents deceased and their two daughters married, Neal was the one remaining familial uncertainty. With his 'on again, off again' career as an actor and writer, Neal, even at 30, still felt obliged to both of them. His lease was thus a relief all around.

The Palanoses took good care of themselves in other ways. When they set out on their journey—what Bruce called their "honeymoon"—they took a lifetime membership in "the cadillac" of RV clubs. This was "The Explorers," a national organization that maintained resorts—"small paradises," Bruce called them—all over the country, places that were clean and secure, that took reservations, that you could count on for comfort and help, even spare parts. He and Nikka had also equipped their mobile home with every convenience they could think of, including a service that forwarded mail and phone messages and a computer system that gave them e-mail capability. And Bruce's response to his children's concern about their parents "living somewhere out there in cyberspace" was a play on words that reversed roles and history. "I used to work for a TV station in New York City that broadcast a public service message at 9 o'clock every night. 'Parents,' " he intoned, 'do you know where your children are?' Hell, it's time for the torch and the worries to pass to a new generation. Now there should be broadcasters on PBS asking: 'Children: do you know where your *parents* are?' "

Their first two nomadic years took Bruce and Nikka across a landscape that turned out to be as rich in people as it was in places. They made "scores of wonderful friends" whom they stayed in touch with by phone, e-mail, and "snail mail," and whom they later reconnected with at prearranged dates and locations around the country. Even with the long summer stops in Shelby, the experience matched Bruce's notion of retirement as "an odyssey." He said he loved the idea of waking up in the morning to a fresh environment with new neighbors who were "real characters—active, engaged, and engaging."

At the start of year three the Palanoses "downsized" once again. They gave up their "safety net," the apartment, which meant a tremendous labor of sifting and negotiating. A lot went into storage, but each spouse gave up valued things, including some of Nikka's furniture and all of Bruce's *Playboy* collection. Nikka also had to fight her maternal guilt that she was "throwing her son out on the street," whereas Bruce said he was glad to be free of the "$500-a-month albatross of a rent check." In place of their apartment, they leased a fully serviced campsite at Jackson's, a

Shelby trailer park, which they have been returning to every year now as part of their evolving annual migration.

For the Palanoses' friends, who questioned the quality of a life without lots of clothes and miles of plumbing, Nikka tried to explain that "we don't want to be possessed by our possessions." Bruce elaborated: "The RV rule is, travel light. You bring something in, you take something out." Also, he went on, "this American obsession with large bathrooms is incredible. For the people who doubt our decision, it's as if nothing else in life mattered but toilets. You'd guess they're thinking of India or Haiti or Africa when they imagine our lives. Don't they know what those countries can really be like? A nomad friend of mine said it best: we've finally reached the decline and flush of Western civilization."

Bruce's preferred account of their new life mixed humor and judgment with purpose. When I visited him and Nikka at Jackson's during their third August of nomadic life, they outlined their next winter's trip; this time it was centered on the South, specifically Alabama, Mississippi, and Florida, where they would rendezvous with West Coast friends to help build low-cost housing for Habitat for Humanity. In a number of ways, in fact, their lives had come to share several qualities with those of other "RV-ing seniors," people whom anthropologists Dorothy and David Counts have studied and travelled with across North America. Like the Palanoses, the Countses have described women and men who seek to balance their freedom and self-reliance with community, mutual assistance, and voluntarism. These friends and fellow travelers of the Countses also speak of not being "possessed by possessions" and, in some cases, devote part of their time to building homes for the homeless.[5] Bruce appreciated these commonalities but, not surprisingly, also dreamed of a distinctive role for himself.

"I'm going to use this video library I've made—300 ads from the 1940s through the '90s—and do seminars at RV resorts, looking at the history of our generation through advertising: the New Deal, War Bonds, Levittown, television, miniskirts, Geritol, Viagra. Hey, we love this life," he proclaimed, "but we also feel we need to extend ourselves, pay back in some ways for the gifts we've enjoyed. And it's the strangeness of things, the surprise of it all—that's what retirement should be about. It's not doing the same stuff in the same place."

There was, in addition, what Bruce called a "mortality reality" in all this. He said it "feeds on the thoughts of people we know—colleagues, neighbors—who retired late and died early. That's why I do this competitive planning, asking myself, Are the Joneses or Smiths doing it better than we are? Because, I want to make sure I have at least as good a retirement as the others. I don't want to be pointed to, an example of how *not* to do it. Is there *one* best way to do it? No, I know that. Still, you wonder, Did I screw up? Did I get it right?" His voice had taken a more serious tone. "Look, I know I may seem like a well-heeled, eight-wheeled hippie living out his footloose fantasies. But basically I just want to meet people who share my history, kindred spirits, if you will, who've looked at the kinds of images and read the kinds of messages I helped to create. Like Kerouac, I find them 'on the road.' My community is mobile, not fixed in place. Sure, you *look* for community, but you don't just *find* it. You have to *create* it. Like other things people want in retirement, it takes work."[6]

All Over the Map

In retirement, people were all over the map. As Rita and Tom, Ursula and Leanne, Sophie and Herb, and Bruce and Nikka demonstrated in their words and deeds, one of the ways women and men negotiated this life transition was through the decisions they made about the possessions, the places, and the company they chose—or chose not—to keep. It happened for them at work, at home, and at large.

In many other cultures, people are far less mobile, or faced with far fewer choices, when retirement comes along. Abkhasians, Bahamians, Inuit, Korongo, Mesakin, Chinese and Irish elders basically either stay at home or live with younger relatives. The latter choice is one that few Americans would opt for, whereas the Chinese and Inuit move in with a married son, and Irish elders cede their main household to their male heir. On Cat Island, it is the grandchildren who do the moving, coming back to live with their grandparents in the stability of the latter's homes and communities. The *sannyasins* of India are, again, the exception: they leave and take to the road, but they do so for very different reasons from those that motivated Bruce, Nikka, and their fellow nomads. Where North American RVers are moved by the spirit of adventure, *sannyasins* set forth on an adventure of the spirit.

In Shelby, few of the decisions made regarding place, space, and belongings were free of difficulty. Rita and Tom had to deal with disappointment born of illness, Sophie and Herb with marital incompatibilities in comfort and desire. Faced with family responsibilities, Ursula needed to reshape a long-term relationship, and Bruce had to accommodate Nikka's needs in order to make his own dreams come true.

People explained or grounded their decisions by referring to a number of considerations. They were seeking adventure or preserving security. They were helping relatives or pursuing their own ambitions. In the process, they were either building on old ties or seeking new ones. And they were taking their health into account, or they were taking to heart the lessons of role models—a great-uncle, a parent, a grandparent, or a colleague, including those who had "retired late and died early." Though few men or women do actually die soon after retiring, the cases that people were aware of occupied a large place in their consciousness, and provided the moral to their cautionary tales about the timing of retirement.

There was also the weight of the material world. In sorting through and deciding what to do with possessions, Ursula, Sophie, and Bruce had chosen freedom from encumbrance, opting either to "live small" or "travel light." Alan Freudenberg, in contrast, was reluctant to discard things that connected him to his dreams or his own mortality, just as the Ellmans kept the place that embodied their history. Ursula was one of several retirees who found the terrible weather of their first winter away from Shelby to be a confirmation of their wisdom to leave it, either permanently or seasonally. But there were others, such as Sophie, who were largely indifferent to the climate, and long-term residents like Rita and Tom who barely mentioned it, speaking instead of family, friends, and the fulfilling roles they themselves played in the community, to explain their reasons for staying.

There was a kind of unexpected symmetry in the fact that Sophie and Ursula both talked about quilts—a literal one for Ursula, a metaphoric patchwork of gardens for Sophie—to bring out what the things and spaces around them meant. Their accounts also show that making sense of place for these people was a process, not a simple one-time decision. As Ursula learned, the sifting through and disbursing of possessions took time and thought, and it occurred in several places, not just one. Over a three-year period, Bruce and Nikka downsized from house to apartment to campsite, while simultaneously going upscale from a small RV to a large one. Sophie reduced her domestic life from main house to carriage house while upping her income, but was slowly expanding her gardens to cover more of the acreage she had kept back from her tenants. These changes bear out other studies, which have shown that older people often go through several stages and relocations as they try to find the kinds of communities and homes that suit their evolving lifestyle and sense of self.[7]

In the process of creating their new lives, these people also had to contend with major cultural contradictions as they negotiated their sense of person and place. In particular, they had to confront their feelings about home and freedom, and comfort and fulfillment.

- *Attachment to place.* There were people who were deeply attached to their homes, their belongings, their land, and their community, and who lived with a very strong sense that who they are is grounded in these possessions and locations. Most Americans, as noted, prefer to "age in place."
- *Liberation through detachment.* There were others who could more easily downsize the tools of their trade, their personal belongings, and their living space, finding in the process of sorting and divestment not just a prudent reduction in what they could physically or financially manage, but also a kind of self-exploration and liberation.
- *Personal freedom versus family responsibility.* There were people who left familiar surroundings in order to be with and help out family, and others who did not mind leaving close relatives so as to travel or seek out other forms of community and self-fulfillment.
- *Adventure versus security.* Finally, the tensions between the familiar and the exotic, between the personal and the familial, encapsulated a related

dilemma for older individuals, which is their desire to have both adventure and security at a time in life when each of these contrary values receives great emphasis. The cultural images of the cowboy and the settler, two enduring icons of American life, capture these choices between freedom and responsibility, movement and rootedness. They suggest, as does the contrast of Zen master and master planner, that retirees might well heed the ancient Greek advice to "know thyself" as they decide where to make their lives.

The very range of options that our society now presents for elders—NORCs, assisted living facilties, congregate housing, RV parks, retirement and continuing-care communities—indicate that one size, one flavor, and one type of residence does not fit everyone. Without too much distortion, one could find in the words of various authors and composers suitable refrains for all of the individuals featured here. Songwriters John Payne and Henry Bishop's "There's No Place Like Home" would work well for the Ellmans. Ursula would probably subscribe to Thoreau's observation that a person "is rich in proportion to the number of things he can afford to let alone." Candide's dictum, compliments of Voltaire, that "we must cultivate our garden," might sound quite sage advice to Sophie. And Kerouac's restless odyssey "on the road," as Bruce himself saw, could stand as a serviceable metaphor for his and Nikka's current life.[8]

But even without such outside assistance, these older people show that retirement is played out and explored not only in one's life*time,* but also in one's life*space.* Be it in the lab, in the garden, or on the highway, retired people are variously re-discovering or re-inventing themselves—a process which is sometimes an opportunity, at other times a burden, in a culture that has yet to determine what later life itself is all about, or where it should be lived.

A FOURTH CUP

BEHIND THE MIRROR

In the popular imagination, passion is thought of as uncontrolled, devilish, and ephemeral. From the perspective of age, however, it is neither so daemonic nor so fleeting. "Perhaps some people's passion is like that," said Alice Armani, who once suggested to me, over her homemade bread and tea, that "Maybe it's true of lust. But it doesn't apply to art. Art endures. The artist's passion for art endures. It doesn't die with a sigh, or the wrong sort of glance, or a whiff of bad breath in the morning."

Alice knew. At least about the art. Probably about sex and other passions too, despite her disclaimer that she had led "an ordinary and often compromised life." Within eight months of her retirement, Alice was in a new long-distance relationship with Jeff Burlen, a retired businessman, widower, and watercolorist from Arizona. But even before they had met at an Elderhostel art course in Maine, Alice had already embraced something else. Divorced, a mother and grandmother, the former director of Homebase, a nonprofit social agency, Alice had retired three years shy of 70 to redeem a pledge to herself that she had once mortgaged to marriage, children, and necesssity—the promise to exercise her gifts as a painter.

In the weeks after her last day at work, Alice took the easel that family and colleagues had given her and created a studio around it in a spare room of her home. Each time she stepped through that doorway now, it was like "meeting some younger version of myself." With oil, water, brushes, paper, and canvas, the youthful and mature Alices tried to realize one another. The older one had the means—the time, the tools, and the space—that her adolescent self had known only in dreams. But the new Alice worried whether she had the talent. She had moments of cold, sweaty terror. It was such a risk, she told me, "to take on the work you've talked to yourself about for so long. To risk the judgment of others, and the unkindness of strangers. Maybe there's just no sense in it."

Common sense aside, Alice was a student of the other senses. Her interests showed, for instance, in her insights on the death of lust, its language of sigh, glance, and breath. Even the materials at hand and before us in her breakfast nook—the bread spread with her own preserves, the handmade teapot and cups thrown by her friend Doreen—these brought the aesthetic into each day's details. Now, two years into retirement, Alice's pleasure in her own tastes and others' talents felt as keen and as privileged as they had at the start.

It had not always been that way. Her community work at Homebase had been with the homeless and the marginal. She had run an agency providing emergency shelter and aid to runaways, the evicted, displaced homemakers, and battered women. She had begun as a part-time book-keeper, later volunteered to design posters and brochures, and went on to handling crisis calls when no one else was available to answer the phone. Overhearing her, Homebase's psychologist realized that Alice had "innately good counseling skills" and encouraged her to take the formal training program for regular staff. Alice ended up as the head of community education and outreach, and four years later she became director.

In the midst of her rise, Alice's 30-year marriage collapsed, and when Vincent, her alcoholic husband moved out, he left her with few resources. Though her son Chris and daughter Nell were not issues of immediate concern—they were both in their twenties by then and gone from the house—Alice had to assemble a support system, an economic base, and a life of her own. These were precisely the challenges faced by the women she herself was trying to teach how to network and reach out, how to develop skills and go after what they were entitled to, how to learn to respect themselves. She found herself taking her own advice.

In this work Alice found little room for the art she had trained for as a young student. In college, in her home state of Michigan, she had studied painting and design. But after graduation, marriage, and the quick start of a family, she had followed in the wake of Vincent's scientific career to St. Louis, Nashville, and then Washington, D.C. She had worked as an elementary school teacher, a technical writer, a budget manager, and a bookkeeper. "Those last jobs taught me to paint by the numbers," she joked.

Vincent's next move to Shelby was to join the research team at Gro-Plan, a new biotechnology firm, and Alice found herself starting all over again—for the fourth time. But she was not alone in this in a community with many other prefeminist, dutiful mothers and wives who had put their own passions aside for their children's lives and husbands' careers. Over the next few years Alice held part-time jobs as a bookkeeper and grant writer, and even made room to take a Master's in design at Seneca College. But these were, in retrospect, "bits and pieces, a collage—not a career." When, a decade later, Alice did find herself literally more alone, separated from spouse and support, short of confidence and funds, she had all but abandoned any dream of a life based on art.

In the next eight years, however, Alice did succeed, in Catherine Bateson's phrase, at "composing a life" for herself.[1] As she rose to levels of greater responsibility at Homebase, the agency's board gave her a lot of encouragement, particularly the single women on it such as Donna Younger, a Seneca College vice president who had also had to struggle for a life of her own. Alice wove together a network of friends and achieved some measure of solvency. And, as an amateur, she began to travel in Shelby's circle of painters, sculptors, and potters. "In the world of work, other people were ultimately in charge of things," she recalled. "But once I retired and started to paint seriously, it was between me and God. Since I committed to this, 15 layers of gunk have fallen away."

When Alice's divorce was finally settled, she could count on alimony from Vincent and the prospect of part of his pension. In the interim, she had managed to hold on to her home by getting her son Chris to repay a loan she had made him by doing the gutters and some house repairs. "I wonder if older men worry about money and maintenance the way we single women do. I doubt it. I'm not overly sentimental," she told me, waving a hand to take in the nearby rooms, "but this house is all that's left of what was once our family. I'll hold on to it if I can.[2]

"Motherhood," she reflected, "was the most wonderful experience in my life. We were happy here. But I've had to find a different meaning since all this collapsed. I've become more religious—not just Unitarian, or even Christian. I live by art, and the faith that there's some order behind all this. And friendship. I have two women, and two pupils, who come here every week to paint with me. And the company is wonderful, because art is so solitary. You have to find people who can tolerate sitting in stillness for hours. We withdraw into silences, our private world. At my age, it's often friends who constitute the true family—the spiritual family, not the biological one. It's not that I dismiss what my kids mean to me, but after all those years of raising a teenage son and daughter, the hope and heartache, you finally hit a point where you can take them in your arms, look in their eyes, and tell them those three magic words: 'Get a life!' "

At the age of 67, done with Vincent and done with work, Alice faced retirement with other people and troubles in mind. For one, she was preoccupied with her successor. Having expanded Homebase's presence in the community, having put her own stamp on its public image, Alice was concerned about how well the next director would carry those accomplishments forward. In choosing her replacement, the agency's board had solicited Alice's input, but in the end it had not followed her advice. She felt that Della Laurisohn, the new head, had the right background but the wrong character for the job, and feared that her style and politics would polarize people.

In Alice's first months as a retiree, that anxiety cropped up in many of her conversations with old friends and former colleagues. People connected to Homebase would phone her and ask for advice, as if she were still on staff. But after "blowing" several such calls by speaking her mind, Alice reined in her tongue. In the long run her doubts proved correct, but it took long enough for her prophecy to be borne out that by the time Della resigned, 20 months later, Alice's life had moved on to other concerns. And she surprised herself by not caring that much—or even troubling to say "I told you so." By then, she explained, "I was off the agency's board and was thoroughly engrossed in my painting. Also, I'd met Jeff and I had just joined the art gallery. It is strange, *so* strange, that the programs and issues I used to live and breathe not that long ago now felt as if they were from another life."

During this transition into retirement there was a different sort of pre-occupation. Alice's loss of attentiveness to details had worried her during the last 12 months on the job, and she was afraid that her trouble with focusing and remembering was a harbinger of a more general decline. Once she was away from the stress of the agency her concentration did seem to improve, but she kept thinking about the lives of other elders she had known. As we had bread and tea together, Alice described four older women and men who stood out most clearly in her troubled memory and imagination.

First there was her father, who had "dealt with retirement so poorly that he had died within two years. Of course you can't blame a brain tumor on that," she allowed, "but he had no real interests or hobbies, and the fact that he liked people and travel just wasn't enough. He had worked at shipping iron ore on the Great Lakes, which wasn't something he could do after retiring. He had nothing to keep his engines going. I saw that as a bad experience, a lesson. He'd come to this country as an immigrant from Norway, and he loved work and gave his all to it. But that was also all he knew."

Alice's mother Paula was a story with a different turn. "She just turned 95 and still lives alone in her home in Michigan, which is rather amazing. But she's rather around the bend mentally. Dotty, I guess you'd say, though in her own way remarkably competent and spry. There's a woman who comes in most days to help her, and my brother lives nearby, so he keeps an eye on things. We're so different, my mother and I. She was this truly incredible athlete, playing golf and tennis till a few years ago. Me? I feel virtuous if I take a long walk. I share none of her interests, but admire her singlemindedness, her persistence. I'd like to think I'm her daughter in that way. I just hope my brain doesn't give out before my body does."

On the other hand, there were a great uncle and a close friend who had handled old age and retirement with great spirit and success. She cited Burt Rossler, her grandmother's brother, who "they still hired, at 79, to paint public murals in Albany. He did it for Roosevelt's Works Progress Administration—great landscapes of the Hudson Valley, in the 1930s. He finished his last commission at 83!" And then there was Doreen Ginnish, Alice's neighbor, the potter who had made the cups and teapot we were using, who "went into her retirement like a cyclone. She remarried, got rid of her old house, and began to sell her work—all within the first 12 months after she closed her business. She put us all to shame. I seem to know people who've done it too badly or too well."

Alice had a sense of competition in retirement that was distinct from Bruce's; hers went deeper into the past and well beyond the bounds of Shelby. At a time in later life when darkness gathers for many, Alice sought the light. "Rembrandt and Dürer, they're the most challenging, the most daunting for me. They could look behind the mirror, beyond appearance. What they did with light, with *chiaroscuro*, is, to me, unsurpassed. With them, it's not the play *of* light, it's playing *with* light. And with Rembrandt, like Picasso, the older he got, the looser his approach was. He became less constrained by tight forms and lines. It's what's called 'old-age style.' I've found myself wondering: Have artists like that lost control, so that the work becomes formless, or are they experimenting, searching for a new freedom—qualities an uninformed eye would not see, or could mistake for laziness? I think the latter. What I've long wanted to do is see if I could see the way they did."[3]

She hesitated, then corrected herself—an honest habit that sometimes bred its own brand of irritation for Alice. "No, no," she said, hitting the table with a small fist, rattling our cups. "No. Not *'see the way'* they did. Not duplicate that, as if I ever could! No: I'm looking for the light to make my *own* relationship with it. To try and maybe fail, but to give myself to it, to see if I can make the light speak and move in the way that I want it to."

In talking to me, Alice also sometimes seemed to be explaining herself *to* herself. "What am I doing? Do I know? One thing retirement has shown me is that I'm not the kind of person I thought I was. I'd always seen myself as someone who lived in and loved chaos, and avoided planning. But now I look back and see how much I'd thought things out. That secretly I'd been planning for years to build retirement around my art. That all along I'd been economizing to get my life to fit into a smaller budget. That I'd gotten Chris to fix up the house. That after the separation, I overcame my terror of stocks and hired a financial planner. God, four years back I even started building up 'frequent flyer' miles so that I could travel when I stopped working!"

She shook her head, acknowledged the great gap between her insights and self-image, and then plunged on. "I don't know a single divorced woman whose life has improved in retirement. Being alone is the biggest problem. And art is done in such solitude. That's why I enjoy painting at the Senior Center—and I'm one of the youngest! All of us there are in various states of deterioration. But what we do is positive, and these are people who are looking at their lives pretty hard. Taking stock. I find meaning there I didn't expect to. It's like when I had a cataract removed last winter. I was scared out of my mind, and went through hell to ask my friends for help: Donna Younger drove me, Doreen cooked. But I hated it. And then I found out that nearly all the people at the center have had operations on their eyes, or hands, or hips—surgery of some sort. So they've come a long way and are still going—painting, talking, trying to make sense. When I go there I feel free. Free?" She shrugged. "I only worry about loneliness, and my health, and about money. That's all!"

She sat back, sobered by her own reflections. "Retirement is like a progressive illness—*and* a spiritual expansion. There's a loss of efficacy, but the moral side grows. This is what allows you to give up control over a lot of this other stuff. Now I'm making choices on the basis of values, which I didn't do so much in my youth. I have the freedom to decide how to live and what to live for, and I'll sink or swim on the basis of my decisions. Back when I was in the middle of my life, it was really easy to live in response to necessity—I've got these kids, so I've got to make a home, make money, be there. You have to do what you have to do. Someone else is calling the shots. Now I'm managing my own life. And retirement meant relinquishing a job I loved for work that has become spiritual. The switch is from a life driven by necessity to one driven by desire. Retirement is the gift of time, but its real burden is the rediscovery of choice, the responsibility for making up your own life."[4]

She caught her breath, took a sip, leaned back. "I want, at least, to get behind my own mirror, the limits in how I see things. I want to have something where my creativity will feed me. I've got to have a feedback loop. If it's not a work environment, I have to have art say to me, 'Oh yeah, I love you.' " That was why, she allowed, it had meant so much to her to sell some paintings a year before, and to have two people approach her to pay for art lessons. That was also the reason she had finally applied for membership in the Winepress Gallery, risking rejection and, once accepted there, assuming the pressure to produce at least one show a year. The other members were not quite the supportive community Alice had hoped for, but she found that was less important to her than "the provocations they provide me with. Their criticisms keep me on my toes. I just have to resist painting for them and the reviewers! I've learned, as an artist, that I need them more than I like them."

She reframed her life one more time. "Now you see why, when I met Jeff at the Elderhostel in Maine last summer, it was so exciting. Not just *that* kind of passion, which I guess is pretty good at my age, but the fact that we share *the painting* too. My art says, 'I challenge you to do this right.' Spiritually, you draw on whatever depths you have. And you surprise yourself with the lies you tell yourself when you get old. 'I'm not doing this to survive,' I say to myself, 'it's for the pleasure and joy, so who gives a damn.' But I'm experiencing everything a younger artist would. I go into a slump, and don't know how to get out of it. Two years ago, when I retired, I thought I'd finally gotten to a point in life where I'd be happy not to be judged anymore—you know, by parents, or husband, or boss. But then I joined the Winepress, and now I go through a kind of semiannual agony—so I guess I need it. This new work has as many anxieties as the old, the same fears as 40 years ago. Is it worth it?

"Look," she stressed, "this is no Snow White thing, looking in the mirror and hoping you see some pretty version of yourself. At 70? Ha! I want to see behind the mirror. I want to find out if I have what I thought I did when I was 20. It's so terribly hard to explain and do, and so exciting," she cried. "I love every moment of it, and on the good days can even take the ones that fail miserably. The damned truth is that when my marriage ended and I started to get ahold of myself, I knew I'd live, somehow, but I never thought I'd live like this. That anyone would want me, or that I'd want anything this much."

CHAPTER 4

LOOKING FOR THE LIGHT

THE SEARCH FOR PASSION AND PURPOSE
IN MATURITY

Philosophy embarrasses people. That, at least, was the opinion of Carl Withen, a retired lawyer who had grown up on Long Island but now considered himself "a refugee from existentialism." Philosophy's questions, he said, are too big; their importance too obvious. Men and women are chagrined not because they don't have the answers but because "they don't have the time, or the courage, to ask them." For some people, retirement changes that. They do not necessarily become philosophers but, confronted with the inroads and opportunities of age—with their withdrawal from work, careers, and clear-cut roles; with a sudden surfeit of time; and with a new, ill-defined life stage—they may now ask questions that could once have been easily ignored. They may be less interested in *how* things work than in *why* things are the way they are. And if they are not quite ready to ask, "What is the meaning of life?" they may still find themselves wondering, "What is the meaning of my life?"

This issue of meaning was the serious intent behind Carl's half-humorous, half-serious questions: Is there life after work? Speaking to me in his old law office, his place of refuge from his wife, Sartre, Camus, and those other "French imports," he allowed himself to muse: "What *is* the point of it all? What is the point of it *now*?" He tried on an answer or two. "I'm retired, or semiretired, but I'm going to Chile to negotiate a deal this winter. Is that it, or is it the pro bono work I do for our church, its refugee committee. Will *that* do it for me?"

When others from Shelby spoke about their retirements, like Carl they often brought their sense of passion into the discussion. Alice's journey behind the mirror was an especially hopeful case in point. The land trust for Teri, history and polo for Sandra, the Council for Alan, firefighting for Felix, Sophie's gardens, Bruce's travels, Tom and Rita's ministries, Ursula's caregiving, the Y and boating for Ed, the League for Harriet—these were the places where enthusiasm took root.

Some individuals, however, were far less sanguine about their prospects. Nate Rumsfeld "got talked into" retiring early from the post office, and four months later found himself desperately looking for work to fill his time and his checking account. Ginny Hansell, who had hosted Felix's farewell celebration, eventually surprised hersef with a different dilemma. A year after retiring as a social work instructor, and six months into a part-time job for a labor union consulting on family problems, she found herself wondering out loud at a dinner party: "To work again with working people was something I'd looked forward to. So why don't I feel the passion for this that I once felt for teaching?" That same week, at his town hall desk, Alan Freudenberg spoke to me of the reverse: for years, it had not felt as good for him to *teach* about government as it now felt to *be* in it.

Carl's questions, Alice's painting, Ginny's job, Nate's search, Alan's politics, and the various causes, hobbies and sports that absorbed people brought out the often unexpected but ardent ways that retirees pursued purpose in life. The stories that follow illustrate several of the paths they followed in their search for fulfillment. They feature:

- Martin Karler, a retired designer, who literally discovered sculpture by accident;
- Nonny Schein, a former gym teacher, who gave her life over to dance and a new partner;
- Stefan Nokalsky, who, when he checked out of the hotel industry, set out to carve a place for himself on Shelby's school board;
- Carl Withen, who sidestepped the law for his love of business, Spanish, and Latin culture;
- Glen McReedy, who concluded a unique career in medicine by starting his autobiography; and
- Zoe Leven, who turned from work as a lab technician to see what *tai chi* could teach her about the bonds between mind and body.

As disparate as these experiences proved to be, there were commonalities, too. The histories of these people brought out the importance for them of satisfying six purposes: (1) *finding a way to deal with their loss or recovery of passion;* (2) *fulfilling a need to reconcile their sense of duty to the community with their desire to serve the needs of the self;* (3) *facing the uncertainty of whether they themselves, or a successor, could carry on with the accomplishments and priorities they had valued at work;* (4) *answering a wish to make sense out of the past and their own life stories;* (5) *addressing their anxiety about how successfully they were handling their lives in comparison with their peers;* and (6) *acknowledging their hope that they would not repeat the mistakes of others.*

The Art of Retirement

As sources of inspiration, the Muses may be female, but they visit retirees of both genders and varied tastes. Whereas Alice used canvas and color to give light a voice, Martin Karler cut wood, shaped stone, and forged iron to bring out the full dimensions of what he called "the poetry of matter." A graphic designer by trade, he became a sculptor in retirement not by design, but by a combination of accident and magic. He had spent 23 years working for Crown Electronics, first crafting the appliances they sold, then drawing the posters, packages, and displays used to sell them. The switch in position saved "some pieces of my soul," he said. "Marketing was creative in a way manufacturing wasn't. I got to learn new things, and then teach the younger people who came up as we expanded. I really felt I grew. It was only my last boss, Freuler, who made work into an ordeal. I don't know how many times I told Inez, my wife, that he was a manager with 'no people skills.' Who—or what—did he think he was 'managing'?"

But then Martin discovered computer graphics—a kind of "extra hand for the mind," he called it. "A project that used to take me the better part of a week I could now do in a morning." But it wasn't just the speed that impressed him. Martin also had a love for illusion, playfulness, and turning things inside out—qualities that the newest software excelled at. And he had been primed for those skills decades ago. As a self-taught, amateur magician, Martin had his greatest moments in front of his own children, performing at birthday parties and "turning something into nothing, and nothing into something."

The sculpting that Martin discovered a few months after retiring represented a variation on that theme, which was to "make something into something else." But the process started out as a car wreck, and took shape in the back of the auto repair shop. On her way to work one morning, Inez had incurred major damage to her car when a young buck "had tried to mate with our Toyota at 50 miles per hour." The jobs of dealing with the insurance company, the claims adjuster, and Lazslo, down at the garage, fell to Martin.

Stopping by to pick up an estimate two days after the accident, Martin came upon Lazslo in back of the body shop, crafting a large set of ornamental gates for Heaven's Rest, a nearby cemetery. The heat seeping from the forge, the sounds of sparks, the smell of solder, the willowy scrollwork of the metal—all seemed like alchemy to Martin. Iron became art, a hammer beat new life into dead gray bars. He offered Lazslo a hand, got a welding lesson in return, and found himself inside a process that was too much for the magician in him to resist. After an apprenticeship of sorts with Lazslo, he turned the storage room of his own garage into a work space. By the second year of retirement Martin had begun transforming stone and wood as well as steel.

Martin's sculpture was as varied as his raw material. Car parts, tree trunks, the refuse from quarries—the raw and the cooked of creation—became geometries, portraits, political statements, whimsies. It was a way to play with the world's substance and "get inside its skin," and also a means of turning his devotion to entertainment into something creative and durable. Martin's art became a part of him—a novel experience for a man whose main form of self-expression at Crown had been to develop the wrappings, casings, come-ons, and disposable displays promoting other people's work. He had been successful at his job there, but it did not add up to a legacy Martin wanted to pass on. Unlike Alice, Martin had felt little investment in who succeeded him or in the handling of his old accounts. Now, however, he gave his sculptures as gifts, he donated some to charities and fund-raisers, he sold a few, and he placed the rest around the small island where he and Inez had their home.

One of Martin's closest friends, John Sant'angelo, a retired engineer, challenged him that he was messing up the land for no purpose, letting art conquer nature. But Martin felt he was working with the world, returning the earth's substance to it in new form. Sculpture allowed him both to be and to let go, to leave his mark and walk away from it. "This could sound corny, like a 4-H speech, but I told John that when I started at Crown, I was making things with my hands, then later with my head, and now, finally, I'm creating from the heart. It's not just that I've gone from two to three dimensions. I have the freedom to 'work' in a way that work never allowed me to. Instead of packages, I've been turning myself inside out."

A different Muse moved Nonny Schein. Where Martin had been inspired by Lazslo and magic to make art, Nonny saw art in movement itself. She was a dancer. "Not the classics or tutus," she warned. "Not fine art. *Folk* art. And I didn't have to wait till retirement."

Nonny had already discovered folk dancing as a result of her career. At college in Scranton, she had studied physical education, then worked for a while as a fitness instructor, and ended up teaching gym for 32 years in Shelby's elementary schools. Early on, both she and her pupils had become bored with the standard regime of sports and exercise. At a workshop Nonny attended on the use of new games in education, she met an Irish-American teacher who had begun to introduce Celtic dances to her students. Nonny, whose own roots were Slavic, became intrigued with the basic idea, and began to attend folk classes on her own. Within a year she was using dance to develop rhythm, balance, and coordination in her students, and was soon working East European and African materials into her lesson plans.

Over the next two decades this repertoire evolved into the centerpiece of Nonny's teaching, and as her work life approached its end, she hoped these innovations would outlast her tenure. But she knew, as retirement drew near, that there was no guarantee of that. Union rules and district policy gave her little leverage over who would take her place, or what that person would emphasize in class. Nor was she even convinced that her supervisor believed her methods had been effective. He had, in fact, encouraged her to retire so that the system could retain younger teachers while it downsized. And he had hinted that if Nonny chose to stay on, she might eventually be moved away from the elementary grades she loved to the more troublesome middle school. It was ironic, given the veiled threats and naked uncertainties, that Nonny felt so secure about her legacy in the district at large, where other instructors had adapted parts of her approach in their classes.

By the time she retired, Nonny's enthusiasm for East European culture had expanded. In addition to her broad knowledge of dance styles, she had become expert about traditional Slavic costumes, collected many ethnic dolls in historic dress, and begun to teach herself Croatian. She said that she celebrated her retirement not so much at the party the other teachers gave her, but by getting her teeth cleaned and booking a trip to Yugoslavia. When I visited her after her return, I found the living room of her apartment a small, homespun museum lined with dollhouses, tapestries, and festival posters.

Thanks, in part, to Nonny's passion for dance, her life became expansive in other ways too. She had been divorced from her second husband for over a decade when, just a year before retirement, she had met Ernie, her partner now, at a "theme" weekend on ballroom dancing at a Catskill hotel. Recounting those first three days of their relationship, Nonny said the music was almost as memorable as meeting Ernie. "Ballroom, the music itself, was such a big part of the world when we were growing up. How can you not want to hold onto that in some way? You hear it, and a whole part of your life comes back. Don't you think each generation has at least that much in common—the songs that everyone sang and listened to? What they fell in love to? We made the music—and the music made us."[1]

Her connections with Ernie and dance were two of several midlife surprises for Nonny. As a young adult she had expected to marry and not work, but after two marriages and three children, she needed a "self-supporting career." Back at the ages of 20 and 30, retirement had never been in her plans because she had not intended "to have a job to retire from." Nor had she anticipated being back in the singles scene—twice more—after her first march down the aisle. "I met some strange men when I was dating again," she reported. "There was one I knew who was a very good cook. He was more interested in getting into the kitchen than into bed with me!"

Ernie's interests were more diverse. He did not have Nonny's roots, but he did share her feelings for music, which drew the two of them together on and off the dance floor. When he retired ten months after she did, he moved to Shelby to be near her, taking an apartment in the same complex where she lived. Divorced also, Ernie had been in corporate law, and he soon began volunteering in a local Office of Aging program that gave free legal assistance to older people. His health consciousness and exercise regimen also set a good example for Nonny, who confessed that "retirement, like a summer vacation with no alarm clocks, had made me far too lazy." She and Ernie were "all but married, except for the license." They both had good pensions with health coverage, and he helped her handle the IRS, who slapped Nonny with a huge bill after year one of retirement because she did not realize she now had to pay a quarterly estimated tax on her income. She and Ernie ate or slept in one another's place as the spirit moved. Having separate places had the added dividend, for him, "that we don't catch one another's colds."

Nonny added a generational angle on their arrangement. "My so-called 'liberal' son and daughters, all of whom are 30–somethings with kids of their own, like the 'separate but equal' piece of our lives. But for two of them, religion rules their lives; they freak out when Ernie and I come to visit, and insist we sleep in different rooms so we won't set a bad example for the grandchildren! But when we stay with my 93-year-old mother in Scranton, she couldn't care less who's in bed with whom. Oh, she does complain that now I'm retired, I should come see her more. I'm still being treated like a child. Some weeks when we go there I feel like I had more free time when I was working. But at least when we do visit, she doesn't give a damn where I sleep. My children are so uptight! Where did I go wrong?"

By the opening of the third year of Nonny's retirement, time had proven the wisdom of both her decision to stop teaching—"I hear the district's a mess"—and the relationship that her offspring had disapproved of. Age, however, had taken something of a toll on her body. She had torn some cartilage in her left knee—"it was a slip on the ice, not the dance floor"—and she was essentially off her feet for two months. "The inactivity made me a worse wreck than the knee. I get agitated when I can't be active. I can be such a grouch." To spare Ernie her nerves, she sent him off to their folk class to dance with some of the single women who made up her circle of friends. "They all love retirement—everyone I know does—but they don't all have partners. So I always share Ernie this way." Still cautious with the knee by the summer, Nonny spent August with Ernie at his cabin in Maine. They were learning French-Canadian folk styles, and entertaining assorted combinations of their grandchildren. To everyone's relief, the middle generation made itself scarce during those vacations. Nonny felt that "our children are so happy to get rid of their kids for a few weeks now that they're willing to overlook our life of 'sin.' I can't wait until some of these young ones are old enough for me to take them to Greece. Despite what my children think, my world is *not* built around the flesh and the devil. Maybe I've never had that much talent or ambition, but I've accomplished something in this life: having these wonderful grandchildren, and passing my love of dance on to other people. I just hope my knees and my nerves hold out till the end. It's like one of my folk teachers said: You're only dead when you can't hear the music and be moved by it."

Life in the Service Lane

After careers in the military and business worlds, a life on the road among war zones, Marine posts, and luxury hotels, Stefan Nokalsky was now staying put, close to home, "to build better schools from the inside." That was his best slogan when running for Shelby's board. In a time of tight budgets and low enrollments, he used "build" metaphorically. But he used it seriously and managerially too. Trained as an engineer, he had served as a captain in combat and then as a corporate vice president. He knew how to make things and how to make organizations work. He felt he could make them work in the school district too.

A scarce four months after retiring as a hotel executive, Stefan had agreed to temporarily fill a vacant slot on the publicly elected, all-volunteer board. Carol, his second wife, was dubious at first, but with all the children from their first marriages out in the world, she conceded that "Stefan's life is his now." When he assumed his post, and again, a year later, when he decided to run for a full term, Stefan's reasoning encompassed an apologia for his earlier careers and his moral history. In his study one day, he told me, "I've always worked within the system. I guess I've always worked *for* it, whether it was in the Corps or the hotel chains. Which is not to say that the system can't stand improvement. I know it can, and I learned you can combat both inefficiency *and* injustice there, with openness and opportunity."

He swept his fingers down his vest, settling back into his armchair. "People may think I'm conservative because of my careers—and in style I am! But I took on racism in the service, and then bias against women in the hotels. I helped make changes, though I find it's always an uphill struggle. Good intentions are never enough; you have to foster organizations and leadership committed to those goals. In the past I used to say I wanted to grow 'professionally.' Now I'm not sure I can. I did want to leave work before my competence became incompetence. When they put in a new vice president above me at Camelot Resorts, I sensed he didn't like my style. His predecessor had mentored me, and now it was different—I could read the handwriting on the wall. So I got anxious, and retired first, but not the way I'd hoped. See, I'm a Depression baby, a product of 'you are your job.' I try to fight that idea, but it's how I am. It's so American. Europeans don't begin conversations by asking, 'What do you do?' But here, what you do *is* who you are. It explains you." For the last 15 years, Stefan noted, he had had very high-profile employers. "So when you travel or meet people, you're immediately identified that way. A Camelot executive, say. That's okay. It has cachet. Otherwise, it's 'Who are you?' Your answer: 'Stefan Nokalsky.' They think, 'What's a "Stefan Nokalsky" '?"

In weighing the words and values that mattered to him, Stefan said, "The fact is, I don't even like the word 'retirement.' I'm not stopping. I'm changing—pace, direction. I just want to enjoy whatever I'm doing. My parents taught me that the hard way." There was his 90-year-old mother, happy now in senior housing in Westchester. After raising six children and watching her husband's business and self-image slide, she had gotten a bachelor's degree in her 50s and begun a career as an accountant. His father was "a big, extroverted, charismatic man; earned big money; never saved. Mr. Generosity. Then his factory failed. The last 12 years of his life, till he died at 70, were miserable. He lost most of his assets, never got his business restarted, thought himself a loser and a failure. Even fishing, which he loved, was no joy to him anymore. He was heartbroken. My mother's the exception; I don't see too many people over 85 having much fun. Let that be a caution."

Stefan linked work with character. He said his father's experience had shown him that "satisfaction has to come from within and not without. Success is in the mind, not someone else or your job telling you you've made it. It's like the way I jog. I like to go alone. Not be tied to others' schedules or pace. Carol calls me 'The Lone Runner.' And I just can't stop to 'smell the roses,' go to matinees, the Farmers' Market, take morning walks. I have this guilt problem, the need to set goals and do useful things. I don't know any better than to want to do an excellent job. That's what I felt even as a teenage kid washing dishes at the old Albany Hotel. Back then I learned not to dream dreams that are so far ahead of you that you undo yourself. But work on yourself. So much of me—too much?—is the Protestant ethic or *Poor Richard's Almanac*: self-development, purposeful hobbies. Learn a new word each day, do more push-ups, collect coins because some day they'll be worth a lot." He threw open his hands in a gesture of helplessness. "I had a son in college who took courses just because they interested him." And sounding like Ed Trayvor's father, he admitted: "I never took a damn course unless it led somewhere."

He pushed his fingers through a sheaf of hair falling across his forehead, and the confession turned heroic, tragic, exemplary. "Sometimes it's the doers who undo themselves by talking too much. I just read this book, *Fortunate Son,* by the son of Chesty Puller, the most decorated Marine in history. The author's father, this legendary general, got it right when he was calling the shots in Korea, but then got in trouble every time he shot his mouth off back in the States. After years of fierce loyalty to the Corps, Puller kind of died inside when the Marines kicked him upstairs to get him out of the way."

The point for Stefan, emphasized during a walk we took, was that "you have to understand what an organization is trying to do, and what it takes to do it. You have to have people who can inspire and get things done within the constraints of money and human resources, not just by talking. But if they won't respect you and give you room to act, it's time to get out.

Take action, or take a walk. Puller's tragedy was not just that the Marines betrayed him but that he got his own son Lewis to enlist, and then the son got half his body blown away in Vietnam. After that the Marines basically left the son to cope on his own with what was left of his life. That's what Puller was looking into the face of in his retirement. He died of a stroke, but it was a broken heart that killed him."[2]

There was a curious convergence in Stefan's invocation of Marine history, heartbreak, and the father-son connection to explain his own commitment to the battles of Shelby education. The move from command post and corporate office to school board was, in one sense, a return to his own years as a parent. He and Carol had each helped to raise three children in their respective first marriages, and through most of Stefan's active time as a father the local schools, with their faults and strengths, had just been part of the landscape. It was only with the troubled experiences of his younger son Kenneth—bright, unmotivated, creative, and undisciplined—that Stefan began to notice, as a part-time single parent, just how flawed the system was. Despite a cadre of good teachers, the district's lack of accountability and policy became all too clear to him as he tried to get Kenneth help.

"He was failing courses, cutting classes, getting into scrapes, probably messing around with drugs. Still, he wrote wonderful poetry, amazingly mature for his years. But they weren't tapping into his talents. There was no concerted way for them to respond, no one who'd take responsibility. He was your classic bright kid about to fall through the cracks—and I mean really fall. It was frustrating, though I realize, compared to others, I was quite capable and articulate in the way I could advocate for him. After all, I was 'an organization man.' But if someone like me couldn't get the system to work well for my kid, imagine how hard it must be for others, the ones who don't have going for them the kind of background that I did."

It took counseling and some tough love to pull Kenneth out of the hole he had been sucked into. Most of the help had come from "outside the school," Stefan reflected, though the basic problems had manifested themselves "on its inside." And though the story was now over a decade old, the pain and struggle were not forgotten by others whom Stefan knew, mainly because such crises were not unique to the Nokalskys. These veterans of parenting continued to trade their war stories with one another. When their collective memory of that period in their lives resurfaced during a crisis on Shelby's school board, their conversations and recollections gave Stefan's retirement a new direction.

In the town's circles of power, Stefan orbited with people who had interest and influence in the schools, and who knew of both his work and his family history. There were some well-to-do neighbors, a former mayor— Sheila Stone—, friends such as Sandra Golecki from the Congregational church, and Ray Horvick, a golfing buddy from business. Ray in particular knew how disappointed Stefan was in the paltry amount of part-time work and consulting his old hotel chain had thrown his way. When Stefan had left Camelot Resorts, his former bosses gave him the editorship of an in-house newsletter, a few speeches to write, and two assignments as a troubleshooter. This "small change" left him wondering whether he had been worth as much as he once had thought. And it hardly filled the framework that Stefan had established for his life.

He had set himself up with a daily discipline so that he would not "slip into sloth": jogging around 8 A.M., breakfasting by 9, and sitting down to his desk by 10. Early in his 'nonretirement' he had had surgery on one of his hands, but that had only been a temporary setback. And since he now lived partly off his investments, Stefan considered managing these to be the equivalent of a job. He had also organized an electronic office for himself at home—computer, modem, fax—ready to take on the world at a digital distance. But the world had not called in very much.

Ray knew that Stefan blamed the token work that came from Camelot on his successor there, a man whose promotion Stefan had not supported, and whom he considered to be a company hack. "I'd hoped for someone who would carry on with what I'd done," he had told Ray, "and who'd keep me on as an active consultant. But he was one of those portable MBA types, the kind who don't care what they're selling, or know much about hospitality—or loyalty."

The unhappy succession was part of what left Stefan ripe for other assignments. Sensing this, Ray, Sheila and the others—with Carol's belated blessing—encouraged Stefan to let them put his name forward for the school board. One of its members, Lena Williams, had resigned in midterm after a bitter fight over the performance and promotion rates of minority students. Stefan's friends knew what *he* had to offer and to over-come as a candidate. Sheila Stone once remarked to me: "The thing about Stefan is not just that he has a 'can do' frame of mind; he feels he 'should do.' And since he's never been in this part of public life before, he's got a squeaky clean record." That he would be a white male replacing a black woman only made it more critical for Stefan to feel that he "*had* to do it well." He took office in June.

His first eight months on the board were absorbing, disturbing, and se-ductive. He ended up dealing with some of the same teachers and admin-istrators he had spoken to, or heard about, when advocating for his son over 14 years before. But now he could relate to them from a position of authority, and of passion stripped of the purely personal. This time around it felt good to have a mission and some of the means to affect the outcomes. When the nomination period for the next board's election opened, Stefan put up a perfunctory struggle over whether to seek a regu-lar seat: the time commitment was great, the issues complex, and several of the personalities to be dealt with were so self-absorbed or offensive. But his decision whether to run was never much in doubt, at least among Carol, Ray, Sheila, and others who were close to him.

The campaign itself was a novel form of education, Stefan's first stand for a public office—a purportedly nonpartisan, nonpolitical post that was contested in an intensely political way. Candidates were not pitted against one another directly; rather, the top four vote-getters would each serve a term. Still, the nominees had to position themselves well enough to attract sufficient support in what was often a low-turnout election. Once Stefan decided to run, his military and corporate discipline and his fitness as a runner served him well. He ran long and he ran hard. There was a gruel-ing round of public hearings, debates, interviews, position papers, visits to all the district's schools, and attendance at workshops on race and science education. The more Stefan did, the more it energized him.

His victory was a sweet and genuine surprise, but it proved to be more of a beginning than an end to anything—the beginning of what Stefan called his "public sector career." The challenges were a world apart from corporate struggles or training people in military strategies. Now he had to deal with the teachers' union demands and budgetary constraints; en-counters with minority parents and the children of Nobel Prize wannabes; the shifting tides of technology and district demographics. These marked the coordinates within which Stefan had to achieve his ideals of "responsible citizenship" and "bringing out the best in people."

A year and a half into his second term on the board, Stefan still spoke to me about it with passion, but also with a touch of reserve in his voice. "I'm not sure what kind of education we're giving out, but I sure know now what kind of education I've gotten here. Life in the service lane is not that slow or easy. I'm sure I care as much about the schools and young people as ever. But my approach, maybe, is too simple, or just naive. 'You have a mission. You know who's responsible for what. You carry it out.' That was our mistake in Vietnam: no clear goals. My philosophy is, you see something wrong, you do something about it, not treat it as today's excuse for whining about the world. But pick your battles. Mine have been to give people a sense of responsibility for their own lives, and—for the students—a feeling of success. I've always had a rather old-fashioned sense of citizenship, a kind of moral calling that should fall on everyone."

He fixed his fingertips in the shape of a steeple. "I have less and less patience with liberals—and conservatives too—ideologues of every stripe. People came over to this country in the first place to get away from taxation. But we're as bad off now as we were back then if you stop to think about it. They say war is too important to be left to the generals?[3] Well, education is too important to be left to the politicians. They turn the school board *into* a war zone. Fighting communists and competitors was easier."

He gave examples by citing people who approached him with good ideas after the election. "This man who does drug education for the state, Frank Ryan, came in about a peer counseling program for young teenagers. And Dr. van Osten, one of our best pediatricians, wanted to do something on reproductive health in the high school. So? Sex! Drugs! 'You left out rock-and-roll,' someone taunted me. Others thought I was crazy, or communist, or racist, or sexist."

He let out a puff of disgust. "Our mission isn't to serve other people's private agendas. Nowadays it's just not the occasional kid like Kenneth who's at risk. We've got whole generations at risk." His index finger poked the cushioned armrest for emphasis. "I've given this over two years of my life so far, and that's been fine. And though I'm no genius, I get things done.

I'm proud of the mentoring program I started, the apprenticeships that brought minorities back into the system—well, at least some of them. But the politics, God, it never leaves you alone to do what you really want."

What pushed Stefan close to thoughts of a second retirement was "small-town life, big-time egos. I want the board to develop its own policies. Stop spending so much money on consultants! They just tell you what you want to hear, what you felt you needed to do all along but didn't have the guts to do on your own authority. If earlier generations made this a safer, more hopeful world, now we have to do that for our communities. Which means taking responsibility, not delegating it. If I can get the board to do that, then maybe I can retire from this too!"

The Voyage Out

Cards had turned up in several places in Carl Withen's life. Score cards. Report cards. Business cards. Playing cards. At present it was poker, a weekly men's game at Carl's house during the months when he was home from his travels. Most of the other regulars were far less mobile: Lester Ulanoff, who had recently retired from a large accounting firm but who stayed close to home caring for his mother and granddaughter; Barney Oleron, still active as a real estate developer; Marv Fishel, Carl's dentist; and Antes (Andy) Marelides, a partner in the law firm that Carl had retired from after 24 years.

In the 30 months since Carl had handed over most of his clients to Andy and another partner, he and his wife Esther had been to Venezuela, Argentina, and Chile for extended periods, with briefer stays in Brazil and Uruguay. Carl had been interested in South America for close to 15 years, but the interest had developed almost incidentally. In the late 1970s his firm began to represent a company with business ties to the mining industry in the southern cone, and Carl, who had that account, began to study Spanish.

"First," he said, "I did it just so that I'd have a bit more ease with some of the people I met. I never intended to do business in the language: even now I can't trust my Spanish enough for that. But it's an 'emerging market' and exciting to be in on, especially now since I make contacts, and negotiate, and draw up papers at my own pace. Twice we've sailed there instead of flying. Those journeys have been voyages out to a new world, not just trips down. In retirement, what's the rush? First I got to love the language, then some of the people, and then the culture—the whole Latin way of living, eating, treating time, even doing business." From the desk in his office, he translated: "Now I'm a pretty 'Type A' character: direct, move quickly, get to the point. So I realized, at some point, that if I loved *their* way of doing things this much, then something in me was being tapped into, some part I didn't know about. That began to work on me. First I was annoyed, then tickled, as if suddenly I'd found I had a Latin for a missing twin brother."[4]

Carl had a real brother and sister, both of whom lived in New England, and an adamantly independent 89-year-old mother who was still in the same home he had grown up in on Long Island. "My workaholic father almost lost that house in his retirement. He ran a very successful bakery business, wholesale. Sold it, then invested in some harebrain real estate scheme with his cronies. They were from the 'old country' like him—'Withen' is what 'Wittenbaum' became on the way here from Germany—and he lost his shirt. I was out of law school then and looked into it. It was pretty airtight. Someone walked away with most of what he'd put into that deal. He also thought his old ties from the bakery world would call him—new opportunities, filling in, putting deals together."

He shook his head. "Unh unh. The phone never rang. He was devastated. Never understood it. Quick oblivion. A success in life"—and, echoes of Alice's dad—"the immigrant dream, but a retirement failure. Fortunately his kids did well, and we've helped my mother, kept her in her home. Other than money, she's been pretty good on her own."

The house Carl spoke of was a secure middle-class anchor, set in a town with just enough diversity so that "you at least knew that everyone in the world didn't grow up hearing just English in their kitchen." He had Italian and Jewish friends he went to the beach with, got in trouble with, swapped baseball cards with. He worked as a soda jerk in his uncle's candy store for several summers to save money for college. Strong, agile, an able student, Carl got an athletic scholarship to Notre Dame, where he made all-conference as a baseball player, and then got recruited by the Chicago White Sox, who signed him to one of their farm teams. "Two seasons. That's what I gave it. By then I figured I'd either make it or not. I'd know if I had it in me. Well," he said, filling his big chest with air, "I was good—but 'good' is not enough in that kind of field. You have to be great. I'd only give myself a B."

Off the field, Carl went to the backup plan he had formulated while in college. Competitive, argumentative, and disciplined, his advisors back then had felt he had the makings of a Jesuit or a lawyer. Law school proved the latter intuition right. He first joined a large firm in Detroit, but then moved to upstate New York, where Esther's family was. He started out with a major firm in Buffalo, and a few years later, after making partner, was asked to establish a branch office in another part of the state—the Shelby region, where computer, genetics, and other high-tech companies were creating a new economic infrastructure.

The new practice offered Carl what baseball had promised but too often withheld: A chance to be in on the action. "My position, from school to the minors to law, has always been, Play me or trade me. Just don't leave me on the bench. I didn't take on life to be a spectator. And the payoff doesn't always have to be the pay: I've been president of the local bar association, and I've done pro bono work for refugees at our church. I just don't want to do the same things I've done before, or get into a retirement rut for the next 15 years."

He stood up to pace. "And I don't mind being thrown into the unknown because that's where I learn who I am. Sailing as a kid on Long Island Sound taught me that. The wind suddenly comes up and turns you every which way. You're thrown back on your own inner compass. It can happen any time in life. Take getting married. How in hell can anyone really know that this is a person they can live with for the next 50 years? You date a lot of girls, and then somehow you just know—this is the one. You have to learn to trust yourself, go with the moral tide." Carl called it "balancing in darkness." He sought it out. "Sometimes I like to *not* know what's going to happen. I feel for direction in the dark, reaching down inside myself to find my own. No, it's not from God. When I'm faced with a choice that logic or law can't dictate, I turn to my 'woman's intuition.' Strange for a man? No. We all have it. That's just what we call it, the part of a man that keeps you on an even keel if you respond to it."

When Carl stepped down from his firm after 24 years at the Shelby office, he felt compelled to assess the losses, the gains, and the quality of his work. "My main worry in leaving was that I'd be bored, miss the people and the action, though truthfully the law didn't challenge me intellectually the way it used to. And I'd seen people who are younger than me die of cancer and heart attacks, especially lawyers." He added that as alumni chair of his college class, he heard about everyone from that group who had died. "That post means being on a kind of death watch. And then there are others who come to reunions, hobbling around. So you learn we're not here in perpetuity. I'd thought about retiring for three or four years, but it was one of those decisions—like marriage—you can't think through too much. You know what you know—*when* you know it. It's that old chemistry thing. So until I felt I was ready, I wasn't going to retire."

One thing Carl did know was how he wanted to feel about himself when he went. The timing was all in the feeling. He had to leave at his peak, before people said, "I wish the old guy would go away." It had to be with head held high, "while I was still on the first team. No second string. Not like a boxer who should have gone before he got so punchy." He bobbed his head fast, then a quick left-right—he still had the moves. "All the cases I gave over to Andy were in good shape, and I felt confident he'd handle them as well as I did. He'll be a good successor, and that matters to my sense of integrity. I kept some of the people I like the best for myself, and so far I find I can handle their business in the months I'm here."

On the rest of the scorecard, Carl got mixed marks. "As a lawyer, I'm pretty sharp—better than I was a left fielder—and given where my talents are, this was a smart choice of career. True, I didn't make the majors, or the Supreme Court, win 20 games, write great decisions, or feed the poor. Still, I was damn good, and had sense enough to know I needn't kill myself trying to be a superstar. I'd rate myself a B+. Luckily I've had a very strong marriage—the one place I've earned an A. Esther and I have raised four children we are proud of." Like others who had moved to upstate, Carl noted that "Shelby was a good choice. It allowed our kids to have a home-town." To which he added, "And our children call us each week. We don't have to call them."

He expanded on the qualities of character and marriage. "One precept I owe to my father: be true to yourself and your principles. Always be able to lay your head on the pillow without worrying who's going to wake you up. Morality is action, not intention. The Ten Commandments? 'Covet not thy neighbor's wife'? Nonsense. I covet a lot of my neighbors' wives. I just don't *do* anything about it. *That* is morality. So you're okay if you can shut your eyes and sleep in peace. And I married a woman who sleeps that way too. Esther, has been a very traditional wife and mother, and that suits us both. She's been active in the Unitarian church for years, their human rights and refugee work. It's what got her interested in Latin America, which is fortunate—and probably not such a coincidence."

Carl leaned closer to me, across the desk where we sat, dropping his voice to the level of a confidence. "The human rights work is fine. It's no-ble. Maybe I'm too much of a cynic to have much faith in it, but it takes us both south and each with a sense of mission. I like the deals; we both love the networking. And while there are some places I can visit in my imagi-nation, others I need to see in the flesh."

There was one more virtue to Carl's voyages out. "You know what I get the biggest kick out of over poker? It's not telling Les and Andy and the others about the food, or the jungles where we've been. It's telling some story that shows how out-of-the-ordinary *I've* been when I'm there. I'm not even sure what to call it. Long Island goes Latin? As if I had to learn Spanish to understand 'know thyself'? Something unusually tolerant or patient in me comes out down there. Something *out of character.* When I travel now, it's to get away from myself. Or, better said, to find some other version of myself. Someone I'd like to get to know better. Someone— maybe someone I wish I'd gotten to know earlier."

The Voyage Back

Carl's reflections resonate with Francis Bacon's idea that knowledge is power.[5] That was true for him whether the form that knowledge took hap-pened to be professional or personal, whether it applied to the law or his hidden Latin character. And perhaps nothing shows more dramatically how powerful knowledge can be than the lengths to which some people will go to exert power *over* knowledge. This was a basic life lesson that Glen McReedy was not taught in medical school. Even the Army, "the birthplace of unreason," where Glen did a residency in nuclear medicine, failed to teach him that singular lesson about power. It took the corporate world, where the politics of profits and research were well joined and well hidden from public view, to show him what his years of training and discipline had overlooked.

Glen's journey to that particular enlightenment took him from coast to coast. He was born in San Francisco, grew up middle class in Seattle, and eventually attended medical school in Boston. During his Army service in the late 1950s, at the height of the Cold War and its atomic obsessions, he was stationed in the Southwest as part of a unit studying the effects of nuclear radiation. The research proved to be far more engrossing than Glen had expected. "The Army itself wasn't exciting, but hell, because of the times, our unit had lots of money and support. I was thrilled to think I was creating knowledge, adding to science, opening up a new world of medicine. For a young doctor, that's pretty heady stuff."

When his Army service ended, Glen had had to strain his imagination to see himself going into straight clinical practice. "It's true I was well-credential by then, and there were good opportunities for internists out there. I had gotten married to Diane ten months before my discharge, and she wanted reasonable things—to start a family soon and have stability in her life. After all, she'd been trailing me around in the service for almost two years."

So Glen joined a practice in Baltimore, started to raise his income and within three years had a son. But despite a seemingly full life, something was missing. "I was not fulfilled. That may sound trite, or self-centered, but it was genuine. Life was very conventional. Now I'm not intentionally *un*conventional"—he swept his hands around the well-furnished living room—"but I needed something more. I felt like an internist who was drying up inside."

When Glen raised the idea of going into research, Diane was not happy with it. The prospect was too risky and uprooting, control too much in the hands of other people. "She was right about the risks, but I felt very confident at the time. I had expertise, some dreams. I wasn't so old that I didn't have some kernel of idealism left too. Not that I was going to save the world, but I hoped I'd find out something it could use. And medical research was expanding then—in government, the universities, the private sector."

It was not blind ambition that took Glen's first marriage under. But even 23 years after it had ended, he could not be sure of the weight his aspirations had carried in its collapse, as compared to the strains put on it by parenthood, and the basic incompatibilities that city life brought out between him and Diane. He didn't actually leave his practice until months after his divorce was final, but then, within a year, he had accepted a research post with Raynor and Coswell, a major pharmaceutical company.

The professional honeymoon was a long one—half as long again as Glen's eight-year first marriage—with projects for R & C on new families of drugs for the treatment of ulcers and diabetes. Re-settled in Virginia, Glen traveled frequently now to corporate and scientific meetings in the United States and abroad. New medicines were approved, patented, and marketed. He got married again and, with his second wife Cassie, started a new family. The sense of growth that Glen felt, both personal and professional, was something that private practice, even at its best, had never been able to give him.

The beginning of the end of the honeymoon—the professional one, that is—was prefigured by the numbers in a report. The document came from a European affiliate of R & C, which was conducting clinical trials of a very promising anti-inflammatory drug. The report indicated generally excellent results but serious renal side effects in a small number of subjects. To Glen, who was now the company's director of research, that suggested extreme caution in further testing and development. He immediately ordered that the trials and licensing applications be suspended, and reported these actions to his superiors. Two days later, called to a summit meeting at national headquarters, he was ordered to suppress the clinical evidence. "They argued that since it came up in tests not required by drug regulations in the States, then the licensing procedure could go forward." Back in his office that night, Glen wrote a blunt memo of refusal, which he telexed along with his medical and ethical reasons for not complying. The next morning, he found his office under guard and all his files under lock and key. Accompanied by two members of the security staff, Glen was given one hour to clean out his personal effects and leave the grounds.

He recalled for me what he looked and felt like when he stood outside that morning, cast adrift with two cardboard boxes at the curb behind his building. In the cartons were a desk set with pens and blotter, a clock, photos of his oldest son, Ian, another of Cassie and their son Josh, his college and medical degrees, some books, and two paintings. "I remember staring into space and thinking, 'Diane was right, but for the wrong reasons.' The risks were there, but they weren't about success and rewards. They were about basic integrity, about taking risks with other people's lives." He shook his head and bit his lip in remembrance. The smile he gave me over his coffee was rueful and wistful. "They bought out my contract, which gave me two years of grace. Cassie, Josh, and I took a long trip to Europe, and then I was back, ready to start something else—wounds licked, lessons learned. One sobered-up medical researcher."

As unfortunate as that chapter in Glen's history was, the timing turned out to be opportune. Venture capital was beginning to discover the possibilities of recombinant DNA and genetic engineering. With the help of contacts he had forged back in his army days, Glen was appointed scientific director at Gro-Plan, the same company that Vincent Armani was to work at. It was a small, energetic, and well-financed firm, and drew on the talent at the colleges and universities in upstate New York. Glen, Cassie, and Josh moved to Shelby, and a few years later, when Josh started middle school, Cassie began a career in catering.

In his new administrative post, Glen found a niche and a set of scientific challenges that would serve him well for the next 12 years. He cited "antiviruses and reengineered bacteria to help plants use soil nutrients"—the new kinds of life forms, in fact, that Ursula Chalfin would field-test 25 miles away at "The Station." Glen was relieved that he had finally stopped being a " 'medical gypsy.' Though I think I also would have gone crazy had I stayed in one branch of the field my whole life." When he did retire at 65, Josh was in college, Cassie was in her professional prime, and Glen himself was being retained as research head for two of the Gro-Plan projects he had helped to start. Leaving his full-time position had not cut him off from either the scientific work he loved or the income he valued—just a lot of the boring meetings and paperwork. Still a professional, and "always a doctor," he felt he now had "just the right amount of control with little of the hassle."

His one regret in retiring, in fact, was that he hadn't done it earlier, be-cause five months before he stepped down to part-time, a worsening case of angina had compelled him to get an angioplasty. The amount of work he had been taking on in the final two years had gotten progressively more burdensome, probably aggravating his condition. But Glen suffered no such regrets over the decision to stay on in Shelby. "I don't like the weather, but Cassie is 13 years younger than me and well into her business here. Neither of us felt the fire to start life over someplace else, making new friends and all that. Also, I wanted to be near my cardiologist, and the real estate market's been so weak that it made no sense to sell our house."

He clinched his case with one academic barb: "Anyway, how could I re-sist this place? We've got Seneca, this world-class college, with some of the brightest faculty there are—or so I've been told. It's true, of course, they all want to teach at Harvard. But the people at Harvard think they'd be more fulfilled and appreciated in Paris. Then the Parisians there want to get out and live in the country—and the peasants really want to visit New York. And the New Yorkers can't wait to leave and buy an old farm in a rural area like this. So sooner or later, it seems everyone in the world really wants to live here. It's just that some of them don't know it yet."

Work, which Glen had amended rather than ended, was neither the be-all or end-all of his retirement. By the time he had pruned back his time at Gro-Plan, he was also volunteering as a board member at ScienceSpace, an education center for children in the local area. And his friend Ed Trayvor had persuaded him to take a paid part-time position on the county's Drug and Alcohol Task Force, where Glen enjoyed pushing his "hard-nosed re-alism" straight at "the bleeding hearts." He explained: "I believe in chal-lenging people, not coaxing them. Make them take responsibility and de-velop some will power—not just some new dependencies. My father was an alcoholic. I broke a 20-year cigarette habit in my 40s. So I clash with the younger task force members on addiction. Maybe it's a generational dif-ference; but I enjoy fighting it out."

His greatest enthusiasm, however, was for a project he had been mulling over for five years but had decided to defer until retirement. It was what he once referred to as "a voyage back over my past," that is, writing his memoirs—but not in the usual way, or for the standard reasons. The twist was that the subject was not really to be, in Glen's mind, Glen himself, but the changing nature of medicine, research and bioethics in the second half of the twentieth century, the Atomic Age.

"Look," he explained to me on his patio, "I'm not a person of such stature that my own life, 'The Glen McReedy Story,' is worth telling in its own right. There are no charismatic people in it, or great discoveries at issue. I'm not a 'historic figure.' But I was a witness to the radiation tests, to what we knew, and suppressed, just a few years after the 'Bomb' became a household word. And then I saw inside the incredible power of the drug companies to help, or harm, or hide. So it's the story of what I saw happen, of what I think people need to know, and of who stopped them from knowing it, and *why*. Now *that* is important."

There was a moral, then, as well as a medical impetus to the whole enterprise. "You're not worth anything if you can't make a contribution, and if you can, you should keep it up as long as possible." He reached back into his own medical past for context. "The most melancholy feeling is to know that you've risked or sacrificed your life for nothing. To know the kind of thing I heard some World War I veterans tell me in the VA Hospital where I worked for a bit. This was long after the Second World War, and they said to me that now they realized they had fought the First World War *not*, as they'd once thought, to make the world safe for democracy, but just to make it safe for World War II. What could they say to their friends, the ones who'd died and lay with the poppies in Flanders fields?"[6]

A year and a half later, with a second angioplasty behind him, Glen was still occupied with both his own health and the state of modern medicine. He had become critical of doctors and scientists who were popularizing concepts of "normal" or "successful" aging by "turning illness and frailty like mine into something like a sin. What they call successful aging's not normal; it's just ideal." Glen's own uncertain condition had brought him and Cassie especially close, and also filled him with a sense of irony that his own health was the main impediment to his passion for writing about the status of medicine. But he had nevertheless made progress on his book.

He fixed me with his eyes over the tops of his reading glasses. "I think it was Hegel who wrote about history showing us the hidden lessons, the trends he called 'the cunning of reason.'[7] But I can't see that far. I have to pin it on people, tie it to who I knew. The government kept secrets from all of us because of politics. The pharmaceutical companies did it for profits. All in the name of medicine. All with *their* cunning reasons. All at the cost of our health. And I was there—even if it was by an accident of history, or at least of *my* history. I don't believe that Americans don't care about the past. They care about what it's done for them—and to them. I'm not inclined to being biblical, but it's the sins of our fathers that we're living with now. Don't you think that's worth telling people? Don't you think it's too important not to try? That, I feel, is the least I can do with what history gave me."

The Bone House

History did not haunt Zoe Leven the way it did Glen, but she did carry with her a sense that its gifts needed to be used. And after a life of carefully chosen disciplines, she had set herself, in retirement, a new one. From childhood through early marriage, there had been dairy farming, with its dawn-to-dusk rituals of responsibility and its warm, comforting sweet-and-sour smells. Later, with her offspring at school, she had parlayed her skill with animals, her milkmaidenly cleanliness, and her native curiosity, into an entry-level job as a lab assistant at TEMCO, a dairy cooperative. She said she "fortunately forgot" to think of her high school degree as a limit on her ambitions. Instead, she treated her "lowly lab post" as an apprenticeship, and taught herself the rudiments of biochemistry, quantitative analysis, and microscopy. Her progress was less of a surprise to her than to her bosses.

TEMCO, an acronym for Taylor, Emerson and Mohegan Counties, monitored the quality and health of dairy products for hundreds of farms in the region. And when its business expanded to two neighboring counties, it kept its old name but moved Zoe up from technician to lab assistant to supervisor. One of the best-kept secrets at TEMCO, a quiet compact between Zoe and her employers, was the modesty of her credentials: these were never mentioned, even when Zoe oversaw Ph.D students. For years, she had alternated between amusement and occasional outbreaks of an "impostor complex," but by her early 50s, she said, "I finally had to accept that I was too smart, too organized, too quick, and, in the end, too old to suffer such doubt."

Besides, she added, the lab was not her only passion, and whatever tested her competency there was irrelevant to her cooking or her carpentry. In an old pantry in the east corner of her house, Zoe showed me the rows of jars holding preserves, vegetables, and fruit that she canned from her garden each year. She had also laid out a small woodworking shop there for herself and her husband Oren. She had no fear, she said, of doing masculine things. "On a farm, everyone does what they can. You're not trying to prove something. You're glad of who you are and you don't waste time envying the other sex." In their shop, Oren made tables, picture frames, and old-style milking stools that he sold along with cheese at the Farmers' Market. Zoe fashioned chairs and benches, and even a pair of stilts for Justin, one of her grandsons. "Whatever talents and inclinations I have, they made me a believer in reincarnation long ago. There were some things I knew when I was too young to have learned them—that I'd be a carpenter of some sort, that I wouldn't want to be a baby-sitting type of grandmother. Now Justin, he thought those stilts were 'cool,' because all his other grandmother ever does is watch soap operas with him. But when he saw that I could walk faster on the stilts than he could, now that was 'way cool'!"

Once retirement freed Zoe to make more things, the most visible signs of her skills were elegant, simple birdhouses, some of which adorned her porch, and her trees, and some sold in Oren's market stall or given to neighbors. Each house was not just a product but part of a learning project about the lives and housing tastes of a different species of bird. If the experiment succeeded, she said, "someone moved in on you."

Zoe met retirement enthusiastically. She had never thought of herself as a career woman, and felt she had been served well by her work rather than seeing herself as serving, in some ill-defined way, a profession. "I'll miss the people, but not the job. I was good at it and grew with it, but it didn't 'do' me; it was never 'who' I was." There was no great concern over who would succeed her. "The place will take care of itself. Sure there'll be mistakes, but I've always argued that failures are good for people to learn from. They teach us more than our successes. It makes us more tolerant of our children and their shortcomings—and ourselves."

When she decided, at 60, to leave the lab, Zoe did so because she "felt ready to. It was satisfaction, not unhappiness. I wanted to leave before it no longer turned me on. I had achieved what I had hoped to there, and wanted to do other things. Also, I'd learned that ambition can so distort a person. In this community there are people determined to go out and do great things, save the world—and I was just doing this basic job. Then I thought, well, if I'm not doing any harm, that should be enough. I mean, what sort of ego do you have to have to know in advance what effect you're going to have on the world? I got to think about life being like a stone cast in the pond: the ripples keep going out and out, and you can't know what your impact will be."

She used an image like Sandra's. "What particularly excited me about retirement was when I began to see it as a new chapter with empty pages, ones that I was free to fill in any way I wanted to. And I didn't realize how stressful the work was until I left it—like you don't know how tight your shoes are till you take them off?" Looking back on that two years of transition, she proclaimed: "I'm so glad I didn't plan anything specific for it, because my plans would only have been based on my past experiences, whereas everything that's happened to me since retiring has been new."

The process turned out to be a matter of time and timing. "Oren and I went off camping for three weeks after I retired. I took a pile of novels, worked through my insecurities, the nostalgia, the blues, doubts, mourning for people. I saw that happiness was a route, not a destination. My last day at work I slipped off my watch and I haven't put it on since. And since then I've been able to do what I want to *when* I want to. I see weeds in the daisy patch and I just get right down there and pull them out—now, not later. I had to get out of the mind-set that you can't do the things you really enjoy till the evening or the weekend. It's the people who make the most of the time they live in now who are timeless." That was why, she explained, "when I left TEMCO, it felt good, the timing was right—to go when you're respected, and can respect yourself. If you'd waited and had to leave on another note, you'd never be able to change that. You'd always hear it somewhere in the back of your mind. You'd talk to yourself about it—at least I would—and never be able to answer. What a conversation!"

Three months after Zoe took off her lab coat she took up *tai chi*. "Now maybe you can't picture anything stranger than some 60–something woman, a bit arthritic and a few pounds over, doing some kind of Asian dance out there next to the cows. And God knows what it must have looked like to Oren's Holsteins. But really," she protested, "they're what got me started." Milking cows as a child, Zoe said, she would rest her head against the animals' flanks, and "listen" to their muscles and organs. Back then "I thought I could hear the milk being made." Much later, through three pregnancies, it was the life of her own body, "trying to reorganize itself, to make some other life, that absolutely absorbed me. Even the lab fed my curiosity in a basic, cellular kind of way."

Sitting in her workshop, Zoe guessed that "all that's hindsight, however, or reading too much into the past, because other than gardening and woodworking, I'd never done any real 'body' work. I hadn't studied biology, or medicine, or even exercised on purpose, other than taking walks." But then a few weeks after retiring, "Sophie Malounek, down the road, brought over this brochure of courses at the Senior Center. 'Painting.' 'Folk Dancing.' 'Quilting'—that's Sophie's thing. 'Personal Finance'? No. Then I saw it: '*tai chi*.'

"Now why *tai chi*? Sort of a coincidence, maybe. I'd read about it. And I'd watched some people demonstrate it in Wheeler Park during Shelby Homecoming one summer. I think I had this intuition I'd find something of myself there. Inside you're always the same person you were, even if your body and abilities change. I've got high blood pressure and a tendency to put on weight now that life's so relaxed. My knees are arthritic, so I groan a bit when I garden. But hey, I walk on stilts now too! You are still 'you' inside. You have to learn to deal with what life gives you. Somehow, when I saw *tai chi* listed in that brochure, I knew it in my bones.

She identified the "it" before I asked. "It's the body's own voice, in voice, in tune." She said of the first classes she took, "I loved the sense of control, the discipline, the quiet. It was like I had moved into a new home—the bone house. Maybe it even reminded me of milking or lab work. But what I actually said to Oren was 'carpentry for the soul.' How did it work? What can I build? Will it change other things about me? What's inside this bone house?"

The questions and the quest were not some kind of self-advertisement, no New Age plea for what she dismissively described as "the disappearing ego that really just wants to be noticed." For a person attuned to the body, she could be merciless on the "touchy-feely" crowd. "Those folks make me think of the kind of stupid lyrics that some Zen cowboy would sing. You know," she obliged with closed eyes: " 'Oh, I've become the kind of person . . . I just can't live without.' "

Zoe was literally too down-to-earth for "that kind of game." Her preference was for the honest humor of those who made fun of PC language by calling the elderly "chronologically gifted." She saw herself as "a very rooted person," someone who "needs to be somewhere to find myself. I couldn't be a nomad." She worked at *tai chi* with the same absorption she had brought to chemistry, canning, child rearing, and birdhouses, rising early each day to practice, traveling every week to take classes. She noticed, months later, how differently she moved now in the kitchen, in the garden, even on walks with Oren in the country. Her chest had "opened up," and her concentration had "deepened." Some "newfound way of being" had entered, or emerged.

A year and a half after, when the basic rhythms of *tai chi* had become second-nature, Zoe decided to do something with it she had secretly dreamed of for decades—to become a teacher. Maybe then she could graduate to a level her own schooling had not ordained her for—and also to lay the "impostor" to rest for good. Her *tai chi* instructor, who was leaving town in the summer, agreed to take her on as an assistant. But there was more at stake, because Zoe also had an element of the true believer in her. "This was exercise that didn't kill you," she wanted me to appreciate. "It didn't hurt or harm. I felt others, especially older women, could really benefit from it— *and* from seeing someone their own age show them how to do it. The mental part, the silence and body-and-soul, make it more than mere working out. I remember how my instructor compared it to the claims for aerobics, which she knew *sounded* great but were 'too true to be good' for old people like us."

For Zoe, *tai chi*'s truth was too good to keep to herself. Eight months later, when I met her downtown, she ventured a kind of cultural *mea culpa* to explain her own decision to teach it and not just practice it. On her way to the Senior Center, to instruct the last session of her very first course, she offered the view that "maybe Americans can't keep things, even talents, to themselves. What they're paying me is nice, but the money's incidental, so what is it that we need so badly?" Her brow furrowed. "Companions, an audience, a mirror? We like to share—and show off. It's an honest enough trade-off, I guess. Look at my birdhouses! Or the ripples we make on a pond. Maybe to live in peace with what we're good at, we have to make it a force that moves others."

The Passions of Maturity

In pursuing the passions of their maturity, these 26 women and men from Shelby had to negotiate tensions between several American values. They had to balance the financial rewards of work versus the fulfillment of unpaid pursuits, the calls upon them made by creativity versus utility, and their roles as child, parent and grandparent. There were the conflicting pulls of self-realization and altruism, pleasure and guilt, material security and moral commitment, art and money, love life and family life, and private and public needs.

Each of the retirees featured here also had to deal with the issue of "succession"; that is, whether they wanted to see the work they had valued being carried on in the future, either by themselves or by the person who would replace them. Their responses were varied, revealing differences in people's attitude toward work itself. Alice and Nonny both hoped for a successor who would further their own priorities. Neither, however, had much control over who that successor would be or how that person would be chosen. Nonny was at least satisfied to know that her influence would continue in the district as a whole. Alice, on the other hand, finally let go of her worries as she became more engaged by her painting. Both she and Zoe, like Ursula, were a bit surprised at how little they came to care about the work that had once absorbed them.

Stefan, Carl, and Glen all wanted to enjoy a form of succession, and each found that fate and colleagues dealt with him in different ways. Carl was able to hand on most of his law cases to a capable partner, while retaining some valued clients for himself. Glen held on to something else that mattered to him, which was a hand in some of the research efforts he cared about; and he was happy to do that part-time in exchange for relief from the everyday headaches of bureaucracy. Stefan was dissatisfied with his successor less because the man did not carry on Stefan's work than because he did not allow Stefan to carry on his own. And he clearly took to heart the lesson of Chesty Puller, a man who had also been the victim of misplaced loyalty, and whose son had been ill-served by the system that his father had placed such faith in.

Both Zoe and Martin were largely indifferent to who would succeed them, but their reasons were quite distinct. Though Zoe had found her job fulfilling, she did not identify with it. Retirement allowed her, as it did Sandra Golecki, to move on without feeling that she was leaving behind some piece of herself. In Martin's case, his greatest enthusiasm had been for the nature of the tasks and the technology he had been been dealing with, rather than with the job per se. He too could move on to new pursuits without a great sense of loss.

These differences in attitude toward succession suggest a fundamental difference in how people view the very nature of their employment histories. Though everyone here worked, only some had "careers," with recognizable titles, such as "teacher," "lawyer," "designer," "doctor," and "hotelier." Jobs, by contrast, just come with job descriptions, which often stood in lieu of a true title. Thus, to be the "supervisor" of a laboratory, or the "director" of a human service organization, tells the world what you do as opposed to who, in a professional sense, you are in the world. But this difference between career and job did not necessarily translate into more or less concern over how one would proceed, or be succeeded, in retirement. Of the job holders, Alice cared about succession and Zoe did not. Among the career professionals, Nonny, Carl, Glen, and Stefan were all concerned about who would come next in line, whereas this issue was of far less weight for Martin.

Virtually every person had held a variety of jobs and positions during the course of their adult life, and even those who stayed primarily in one field had moved around to different parts of it. Carl had been a soda jerk and professional athlete as well as a lawyer. Martin designed appliances before moving on to create their packaging and their promotion. Alice's work life included stints as a teacher, grant-writer, and bookkeeper as well as administrator. Stefan had been a dishwasher, a soldier, and a corporate executive. Zoe had gone from a hands-on farm to a high-tech laboratory, Nonny from a fitness center to the dance floor. And even Glen, who was and always would be a doctor, had shifted—from military research to clinical practice to the pharmaceutical industry to biotechnology.

When people continued some form of their previous work into retirement, the terms, the conditions, and the attitude surrounding their labor changed in profound ways. Glen, for example, was more relaxed at Gro-Plan because there were fewer distractions from his interest in basic science. As a clinician on the task force he felt free to be outspoken because neither his livelihood nor his practice was at stake. In volunteering to help the Y raise funds, Ed Trayvor was doing the same work he had once been paid for, but the knots in his stomach were not there: "What are they going to do," he asked, echoing a sentiment of Sandra's, "fire me?" Carl could pick the clients and the deals he cared the most about, and work with them at the Latin pace he was learning to love. And whether they chose to exercise it or not, these and most of Shelby's other retirees now had a new option: as Sophie realized with her casual appointment at Crown Electronics, when asked to work they could just say no.

What many emphasized was the element of control—that retirement had given them the freedom *to* work, but at their discretion, rather than the freedom *from* work in an absolute sense. Work had become more of a choice and a pleasure than a duty. And as Alice observed in the other areas of her new life, choices could now be based on desire, not necessity.

Retirees often felt called upon to explain their choice of passion even before I raised this as a direct question. Nonny was not only seeking a deeper involvement with her ethnic roots, but also wanted to express how the music of her time had shaped her. Alice needed to test the promise of her artistic talents. Carl had a need for action and a philosophy of life that required a lot of self-testing in new settings. Glen felt that the privilege of what he had experienced in his historical moment could be redeemed by sharing its lessons with others. Stefan's moral creed combined themes of loyalty, service, and duty, and it proved to be a code he could transfer from military to corporate to public sectors. And for Zoe, one of the burdens of each person's gifts was the need to share them with others, which shaped her generosity with both birdhouses and her talent for *tai chi*. For each of them, the "busy ethic" of retirement was truly grounded in a moral commitment to either community life or personal growth.[8]

There were certainly disappointments and anxieties that people found in either their past or their present endeavors. Harriet Trayvor, comparing herself to her college classmates, wished she had been able to "produce, not just reproduce." Alice and Stefan both wondered if they had stayed on at their jobs too long, beyond their own measures of competency. Also Stefan felt let down by a company he had loyally served, and in the aftermath of that he was struggling not to be so "job-identified." For still others, life after work had intimations of mortality. Alan, with high school teaching done, found it hiding in the hopeful piles of papers he could not discard. Felix Davis, who had dreamed of writing a book on environmental ethics after he left Seneca College, once confessed to me that he had not gotten far because the act of writing "dead words" on the page had turned into a flirtation with death itself. "Sometimes I catch myself thinking that it's when I finish this that I'll die." Perhaps, he guessed, it was what his father had felt behind the wheel of his car.

There was also a notable quality of self-deprecation in the way many retirees spoke of their achievements at work. Their statements had a "yes, but" rhythm to them. Carl gave himself decent but far from top grades; yes, he had done some good in the community, but had not starred on either the baseball diamond or the Supreme Court. Glen and Ursula both pointed out that they had conducted useful research—one in medicine, the other in agriculture—but had made no great discoveries. Zoe said she had never intended to be great, wondered about the people who did, and felt you could never know how the "ripples" of your life would affect others. Stefan coupled his claims to moral strength and organizational skill with the caveat that he was no genius. Ed and Harriet Trayvor acknowledged that, for all their contributions to Shelby, they would never rise to the level of Rowena Darman, and Alice said that she could be inspired by but never hope to emulate Rembrandt or Dürer.

This quality of denial was consistent but enigmatic. Were these women and men less invested in their own immortality than mythic heroes, great artists, and corporate CEOs have been shown to be? Was all of this just modesty, or a softened yet sincere way for retirees to take stock of their lives and limitations? For Felix and Alan, the unrealized works before them bespoke the fear of finishing that creative individuals often feel in their final projects. Certainly some of the concerns with succession bordered on a desire for leaving a legacy. The "yes, but" rhetoric also suggests an American habit of qualifying claims with disclaimers and invoking one's personal limits, or the greatness of others, to insure that one's own achievements do not sound too grandiose, or one's own voice too loud.[9]

In a sense, even people who did not work *in* retirement still worked *at* retirement. As the anthropologist Cora DuBois once noted, there is a pervasive quality of earnestness in our culture; Americans work hard even at having fun.[10] The second most frequent piece of advice that Shelby's elders offered, in fact, after "plan your finances and pensions far in advance," was to enter retirement with something to be passionate about, some sense of purpose. They thus parted company with thinkers from Cicero to Schopenhauer who have greeted late life's presumed loss of passion with relief. Instead they seemed to agree implicitly with both Thoreau's warning that you cannot "kill time without injuring eternity" and the philosopher Josef Pieper's observation that when people are too concerned with how they "occupy" their leisure, their free time takes on a rather "*unleisurely* character."[11]

Shelby's elders differed as to whether a life of work had entitled them to be altruistic or artistic, but most felt a moral obligation to use their talents to some end. None of them took what Alan once called "the default option," which was just to live out their days in accord with a routine rather than a sense of some larger purpose. They knew a few people who had done this and were genuinely puzzled by their capacity to "just carry on." In Alan's words, "They've simply built their life around living it."

If work was meant to be profitable, then the women and men featured here felt that retirement, with or without pay, should be meaningful. Certain the metaphors they used to express their search existed in counterpoint: Alice went "looking for the light" while Carl loved "balancing in darkness." The passions that moved them might be long-standing, such as Alice's for art and Nonny's for dancing, or accidental discoveries, as in Martin's sculptures and Stefan's work on the school board. People strove to keep their lives as stimulating, as cognitively complex, as they had been before.[12] And whether meaning took the form of creativity, performance, business, service to others, or self-exploration was less material than simply the presence of some sense of purpose. Despite the urging of spiritual cultures and modern gurus who want people to learn just "to be," in the hills, farms and streets around Shelby, elders still wanted "to do."[13]

The passions and paths noted here contrast sharply with those found in other societies. Irish farmers, and Mesakin and Korongo cattle herders cared about succession, for example, though these traditional peoples differed from Shelby's elders in desiring to pass on their careers as well as their wealth to their own relatives. Like older Abkhasians, Bahamians, and Inuit, Shelby's retirees desired to remain active and productive, and they enjoyed working (and traveling) at a slower pace. But their pursuits often took them in different directions from what their prior work had been. The emphases that Chinese, Irish, and Bahamian seniors placed on the continuity of family and clan roles were echoed in the parental and grandparental ties of Nonny, Zoe, Felix, and their peers, though it was the rare Shelby elder who actually lived with younger kin.

Retirement also carried its own kind of duty. Where Abkhasians fulfilled a sense of purpose by serving on their village's council of elders, their counterparts in rural America could be found on their community's common council or school board. Perhaps it was no accident that board member Stefan Nokalsky, like the Abkhasians, rejected the very word "retirement." On the other hand, though none of Shelby's seniors came close to the spiritual passion of India's *sannyasins,* they were certainly not devoid of religious or moral sensibilities. When they looked behind the mask of age, local retirees still felt they were the same person they had always been, and their pursuits still took classic American form. Stefan saw his core strengths manifested in the military in youth, the hotel business in midlife, and the school board in retirement. Zoe recognized herself "in her bones" as a milkmaid, mother, and *tai chi* teacher. Each, in his or her own way, asked the question posed by Florida Scott-Maxwell in her eighties: "Does the passion in our hearts somehow serve?"[14] In retirement, the paid work that these people had once done was likely to give way either to good works or to art, autobiography, teaching, or some other expressive way to fulfill their duty to their talents, or to a spirit of social obligation. Regardless of their religious background, they all subscribed to some form of a moral calling.

Finally, if retirement strikes some as an anticlimactic end to a fruitful or at least a hopeful life, the stories told here offer a helpful set of correctives. They show the kinds of continuity, novelty, passion, and purpose that are possible in this stage of maturity. In the United States now, there are even consulting companies that well-to-do retirees hire to help them develop a "portfolio of opportunity" for the years after full-time work.[15] But Shelby's elders were able to do this on their own, and they could also draw from their experiences a series of lessons about what motivates, worries, and gives meaning to older people.

- *Passion.* Passion mattered and took many forms, including purely personal as well as professional, political, ethical, expressive, and creative dimensions. It happened in relationships, in art, the self, the community, morality, and commerce. For many older people, the sense of passion underlay the meaning of life, the purpose of art, and the value of work.

- *Succession.* Some people easily let go of the work they had done, and others showed strong feelings about who would succeed them and whether their legacy of concerns and accomplishments would be carried on. Retirees could also be deeply invested in whether they themselves would be able to continue, in some fashion, the kind of work that had mattered to and rewarded them. The extent to which they were or were not invested in these outcomes was not necessarily dependent on whether they felt they had had a career as opposed to a job.

- *Uncertainty.* Women and men approaching retirement were often concerned and uncertain about how they would be perceived at the time they left work. Alice and Stefan, for example, wanted to go before competency became incompetence, and Carl while he was "still on the first team." People also retired with sharp anxieties about how successful they would be at meeting new challenges and finding fulfillment. Most were aware of the disappointments and mistakes of their predecessors and hoped to avoid repeating them. Retirees, as seen earlier with Bruce and Tom, were also curious about how their own peers were doing. Their concern usually expressed itself as a need for reassurance that they themselves were doing at least as well if not better than their age-mates.

- *Moral duty.* In their pursuit of fulfillment, people often got caught on the horns of a particular dilemma: their dual impulse to fulfill a duty to the community and a duty to the self. This conflict played out a classic confrontation between two moral goods in American culture: namely, the altruistic ethic of "giving something back" to society, and the individual's right to the pursuit of happiness—a pursuit that is held to be self-evident not just in the Declaration of Independence but in individual declarations for self-actualization, self-improvement, and personal growth. Zoe made a reflective suggestion connecting these two values, arguing that for Americans to "live in peace" with themselves and what they are good at, their gifts must in some manner be returned to the community by way of example, or teaching, or tangible products.

- *History.* Though Americans are commonly accused of being ignorant of and indifferent toward history, some Shelby retirees did think hard about their own individual past. History became personal and meaningful when they tried to make sense of their own lives, of the good and evil they could be held to account for, and of the way parents, spouses, institutions, children, careers, and social change had shaped the contours and the content of their lives. Glen's book, Nonny's travels to her roots, Sandra's political memorabilia, Bruce's advertising archives, and Stefan's reading of both his own past and of others who had served the military were cases in point. Retirees were not only concerned to "do" something meaningful, then, but also to make sense out of what meaning their lives already had.

A FIFTH CUP

AROUND THE LAKE

At each new stage of life a person dies a little but is then reborn. This is the rhythm dramatized by rites of passage, with their symbolic death and rebirth of the maturing individual. As a person moves to a new identity, the surrounding people may remain the same but their relationship to one another and to the growing individual shift. These transformations of aging and the rituals that mark them resemble the scene inside a kaleidoscope: they mirror the way the shapes and colors of cut glass rearrange themselves as the viewer watches new symmetries fall into place.

This was the image that struck Martin Karler one day when he was shopping for a gift for his daughter Noreen, who had given birth to Robin, her first child and his first grandchild, just three days before. While Martin's wife Inez looked for a sleeper for the baby, he decided it was his "daughter-the-new-mother" whom he wanted to honor. When Martin picked up a kaleidoscope in the toy store and looked through the lens, he recalled giving one to Noreen as a child, and smiled at the new symmetry of giving her another now as a newborn's parent.

The links of memory with toy, of shape and shift with pattern, were more than coincidence. Until his retirement seven months ago, Martin had worked as an industrial and graphic designer for three decades. For half that time he and Inez had run their own agency, developing home products for appliance manufacturers. Then Martin, tired of the cycles and details of the business end, went to work for Crown Electronics. The income at first was less, but so were the worries, and it was more than a welcome trade-off.

Inez, out from under the burdens of bookkeeping and running their office, had turned to human services, working first for a Head Start program and then for the local outreach project of the Economic Opportunities Commission. She was scheduled to retire five months later than Martin, and that impending event was momentarily overshadowed for Inez by grandparenthood. The end of work left her so relaxed that when she went to help Noreen, she cleaned the windows as well as changed the baby. "It's different," Inez explained, "when they're not your windows." But what really put retirement into perspective for her, more in a visceral than a visual way, was a sense of having her life, her things, and especially her people settled in place: two sons were married; Noreen a new mother; Martin's enlarged prostate still benign; a pension in the offing for herself; and the mortgage paid off. Even the level of the lake was good this year.

The lake was important to Inez and Martin. It's water defined, protected, and clarified their lives. Their house was on an island in a lake in the heart of the country 12 miles from Shelby. From their front porch, having coffee in the autumn sunlight, we watched wild ducks circle, land, and refuel on their journey south. There were hills on two sides whose runoff fed into the lake, a dirt road and stream bed snaking away to the east, and the remnants of a flood plain to the west. To visit the Karlers, you parked at the end of a thin spit of land that tongued out from the northern shore and walked over a long narrow boardwalk, two planks wide, which stood propped up on squat pilings. Their clapboard home, with gabled bedrooms on the second floor, stood behind a screen of evergreens; the ends of the house were framed by giant weeping willows that draped their limbs over a shingled beach.

The calm of the lake had not been able to dissipate the uncertainties the Karlers went through in reaching their decisions about when and how to retire. They both were in reasonably good health, but the sudden death and decline of several friends and neighbors pushed their plans ahead. They had originally intended to wait till age 65 to get the maximum in Social Security. But then, as Inez put it, shortly after they had both turned 60 "the bells began to toll."

First it was Gerry Rudman, a co-worker and acquaintance of Martin's, who died during an angiogram. Four months later, on the day before Christmas, one of their oldest friends was diagnosed with brain cancer; at 58, Joan learned suddenly she had less than a year to live. "She and Hank had struggled together," said Inez. "They married right out of high school. 'Too young,' people said. 'Foolish. It'll never last.' But 40 years later there they were. They'd raised their kids, finally reached a point where they could start doing what they wanted to, 'stretch out.' He was with her every minute those last months." Martin added, "Noreen was here at the house on Good Friday to tell us she was pregnant. Then the phone rang, and Hank told us Joan had just passed away. She was Noreen's godmother."

Martin leaned his head to one side but kept his eyes on mine. "It made a lot of people in our circle stop and think: what are we living for? I told Inez we should spend more time visiting old friends and family. Because if you don't, you're always going to regret you didn't."

There were lessons from the living as well. Two coves up the lake were elderly neighbors, Don and Frannie Timbro, 79 and 75, whom the Karlers were cooking occasional meals for. Frannie was laid up after a hip replacement, the Timbros had no children, and Don totally lacked kitchen skills. "It bothers them not to be independent," Inez said, "and they don't like strangers in their house. Though we have family, it's terrifying to imagine that someday that could be us."

Until the fates of Gerry, Joan, Don, and Frannie hit home, the Karlers had been thinking of relocating to a warmer climate, at least for the winter months. But as the messages accumulated, they started to rethink things. They moved their own retirements up to their 62nd birthdays the following winter. Quietly, they forgot about inquiries they had made about the Peace Corps. And the dream of Costa Rica, a haven they had fallen in love with on vacation, was also put to rest. Even the thought of the South, where they had happily traveled and camped over the years, gave way to Martin's feeling that "we are too family-oriented to be that far away." Another truth, according to Inez, was that "Martin gets homesick when he's gone for more than two weeks anyway. We met a real estate agent once in the Carolinas who told us that 'down here you'll have more bad hair days than snow days.' Fair enough. But even though we've got more home now than we need, and everything that goes in and out has to come across that footbridge, we just don't want to be that distant from our children—or the grandchildren."

What had frightened them about the Timbros was turned to practical advantage. Martin called it a "sex change": they started to train one another to do the basic tasks that the other usually performed. Martin began to clean the house and cook, and by the time he formally retired he had built up a small library of recipes, an intimate knowledge of garlic, and a habit of turning on the late afternoon food shows normally watched by women. Inez learned how to use the caulking gun, the boat lift, and, to a degree, Martin's idiosyncratic system for filing bills and papers. Their goal, partly fulfilled, was for each of them to become reasonably self-sufficient, to "not be needing meals or help simply because of ignorance."

Once they had decided to retire earlier and stay put, the Karlers indulged in a small buying spree. Inez's sister, five years older, had advised her that "when you're getting ready to retire, make sure your refrigerator is in good shape. If you can, buy a new car and appliances *before* your paychecks stop. Get your teeth fixed. Everything starts breaking the day after you finish work." So they bought a washer and fridge and a newer used car after Lazslo gave up on the one the deer had redesigned. Inez actually did get a bridge put on her lower teeth. "And I changed my will," Martin claimed. "Now I'm going to be buried with my freezer."

He and Inez teased one another about time. "What I like the best about retirement," Martin claimed, "is being able to start a project, like fixing something or designing a sculpture, and complete it without interruption." "No way," Inez said, "we were better at finishing things when we were still working. Then, they had to be done by the end of the day or the weekend, whereas now you drag them out—like recaulking the windows, remember?—because you've got all kinds of time and excuses."

The banter had a well-worn quality, a smooth dip in an old oak floor, and its grace came out of the Karlers' deep history together. Other than their love of travel, their lifestyle was modest because, Inez felt, their tastes were simple. And they led one life rather than two. "We both like the same things: a walk, a canoe ride, camping. Not bars, resorts, clothes. When we were both finally finished with our jobs, we went on a slow trip down the Skyline Drive in Virginia and Tennessee—it was the same route we'd taken the first month we were married, full of plans. It was like a retrospective. We saw we have a lot of pride in our kids, and what we've done so far with our lives. It's amazing to think what you don't know about marriage when you get married. Fifty-percent divorce rate? It's a wonder *any* survive."

Inez recalled that a colleague had asked, at her retirement party, "How can the two of you stand being together so much—out on that island, no less?!" Martin laughed and said "Can it last? Can we? The doctors now are all very junior to us. They look awfully young to figure out how to keep people like us going. We teased our children that because there were three of them, we'd do the *King Lear* routine: give up the house, spend a third of the year with each of them.[1] "They didn't get it, though. They thought *Lear* had something to do with jet planes." He rolled his eyes. "Because we live on a lake, our kids call us 'Norman' and 'Ethel' from *Golden Pond*.[2] So now, whenever they're here, we purposely call one another by the wrong names, and talk about 'our president, Mr. Roosevelt.' Then they get these worried looks and discuss what to do with us in 'eventualities.' Not to worry. They've adopted the Eskimo custom: they say they'll put us into the lake on an ice flow."

If there was ever an image to express the insularity of the American nuclear family, the Karler's tight little island was it. But the metaphor did not really fit, for friendship and kinship connected them to a wide body of people. The house and the island had been in Inez's family for two generations, and a network of her relatives could be found in the surrounding area. A widowed aunt lived across on the lake's east shore, and three cousins made their homes within 25 miles of the valley. Inez's brother and wife lived right down the road. "They are just like our own children," she said. "They were still young when our kids went away to school, so we've kind of adopted them and spent a lot of time together." It was true that Martin's East Philadelphia family was more scattered and, by his account, "much less wholesome." But he had a married sister he was fond of about 130 miles away in the coal hills of Pennsylvania.

Of the Karlers' three children, Noreen was a two-hour drive to the west, in the farm lands along the Genesee River. Her brother Richard, three years older, ran an insurance agency in Cooperstown with his second wife, and his visits to clients occasionally brought him to the family homestead for a meal. Only Martin and Inez's youngest son, Tod, had moved far away—or rather been moved by the army. When Tod's college forays into business and accounting failed to enlist his enthusiasm, he had instead enlisted in the service and, finally, "found himself" in mechanics and engineering. He was stationed in North Carolina. "He really loves it," said Martin, "and it's another reason for us to go camping in the Smoky Mountains."

Having a son in the military was nevertheless a deep irony for the Karlers, who described themselves, with a touch of weariness, as "60s liberals and garden-variety pacifists. We were ready to go to Canada during the Vietnam War." But what Martin jokingly called Tod's "desertion *to* the army" was not the only surprise that midlife had brought them. Inez said, "I don't think we ever expected to get quite so connected to some of the other people who live around here, the ones who are not just family. You'd think a lake separates people by spreading them out, but it seems to work more like a magnet, an old-fashioned village green. It makes people aware of one another. The lake may not be a 'commons,' but it is something that people have 'in common.' They feel tied together, as if the lake were a fate they shared."

What also surprised the Karlers was their sense of responsibility for some of those around them—Hank, the Timbros, others they felt bound to by proximity and neighborliness rather than blood. Even without the element of kinship, consciousness and conscience fostered some of the "mystical interdependence" that ties the members of African age-villages together. "There are some weeks," Martin reflected, three years into retirement, "where I look back on who I've helped out or been thinking about, and I have to conclude that while we've got two wonderful grandchildren now, sometimes lake water is thicker than blood. The picture changes—like that kaleidoscope I once showed you—but the circle still holds it all together. When you've traded tools and gossip with friends for enough years," he explained, "or run enough errands for one another, or put in appearances at holiday parties and hospital beds, and when you've watched one another's kids grow up—in your own yard, sometimes under your own roof, having sleep-overs and squabbles—you find you've bought into some sort of social contract. I couldn't quite tell you what its terms are, or even how it got drawn up. Given enough time, though, you just know you've signed on, and for as long as you live here you're obliged to one another."

"It's funny how being retired brings those bonds more into focus," said Inez. "You have more time and so you think about them more, you're more conscious of them. We didn't plan a lot of specific things for retirement—why commit in advance to something you may not like? Once in a while my old office calls me up to work for a few days, and it's okay because I can say 'no thanks' if I want, so my life still feels very controlled, very retired. But most days I sit over my coffee in the morning instead of rushing off to work, and when I look out the window I see some of their houses, the people we've known all these years, and I think about them. I guess we've always had our own 'good neighbor policy.' It's just that now—like when Martin helped the Tautleens shore up their dock, or cooked for the Timbros, or when I gave old Mrs. Queller a ride to the doctor last week—it's that we have more time and energy to *be* neighbors. I don't know whether it's coincidence that some of them need more at the very time we're around more. But it's just like what's happened with Noreen and Richard these last couple of years: we have more time to *be* grandparents right when we're called on to *become* grandparents. Maybe I'm paranoid," she laughed, "but it seems like a conspiracy."

CHAPTER 5

THE KALEIDOSCOPE AND THE CONSPIRATORS

KINSHIP, FRIENDSHIP, AND MEANING AMONG ELDERS

Every culture and every faith has its favored metaphors for making sense of the world. As the American archetypes of cowboy and settler show, some people think in dualities, calling upon the balance, or the struggle, between such forces as good and evil, God and the Devil, yin and yang to explain the nature of life. Others invoke a circular view of life involving the endless cycles of birth, death, and reincarnation that affect both individuals and the cosmos itself. And groups as different as animists and ecologists see all of creation as alive in spirit, a great organic whole, whose fate depends on thoughtful human action.

When it comes to making sense of the political and the personal, however, Americans often show a penchant for conspiracy theories. The death of presidents, the rise of communism, the decline of the West, or the collapse of a marriage or business may all be explained in this way. When Inez invoked a "conspiracy" to explain the unexpected shape her life had taken, she was making a serious joke. It did feel that the Karlers' lives had been orchestrated to connect and make them responsible to a wide circle of people just at the point when retirement had given them the "freedom" to take all that on.

If Inez's intuition was correct, then the "conspirators" she implicated would include her own culture, which had invented retirement out of an aging work force, a changed labor market, and the modern financing of longevity. Martin's words spoke to a related aspect of their experience. His playful metaphor of the kaleidoscope suggests the dynamic process of social transformation, which reconfigures people into new patterns of relationship as retirement unfolds.

These home-grown figures of speech point to fundamental issues confronting virtually all women and men when they enter this stage of life. How does the passage into this period of maturity affect their ties to spouses, partners, relatives, neighbors, and friends? Do retirees' expectations about these relationships change in concert with the new rhythm of their lives? How do gender and marital status affect people's experience of retirement? And does the overall importance of kinship and friendship increase or decrease as the centrality of work recedes?

Among Shelby's retirees there was a great diversity of personal circumstances, including individuals in long-term marriages, those who had never married or were divorced, and those who had remarried or were living with a partner, or a married child, or were living alone. Their circles of friends ranged from handfuls to dozens of people. Some were childless, others had grown children and grandchildren. And about half had elderly parents or in-laws whom they were in touch with and, in some cases, helping to care for.

This variety is clear in the three stories that follow, about:

- Johanna Alexander, a retired bank employee, who discovered, in a special friendship, what she had long missed in her marriage;
- Lester Ulanoff, a divorced accountant, who counted his ties to his elderly relatives and married daughter to be the most meaningful and demanding of his retirement; and
- Donna Younger, a college administrator, whose status as a single woman brought into sharp relief the fragile nature of family ties and the enduring value of friendship and community.

Along with the "kaleidoscopic" and "conspiratorial" views of Martin and Inez, the experiences of these people point to some common threads in retired life. Besides the themes of freedom, responsibility, planning, timing, succession, passion, and role modeling already considered, their accounts show, first, *how the fact or quality of marriage affects the manner in which men and women approach retirement*; second, *how the way people take on grandparenting varies with circumstance and character*; third, *how caregiving enters into the fabric of daily life and moral reflection;* and fourth, *how the importance of friendship fluctuates with the gains and losses that retirement inevitably entails.*

Inner and Outer Space

People are born into families, but they have to grow into relationships. And few relationships are as variable as marriage. Johanna Alexander once guessed that by the time women and men reach retirement "their marriages have either fallen into a pattern or they have fallen apart." American conventional wisdom, at least its sardonic side, stresses the added burden that a retired partner can place on a relationship. The standard joke is a one-liner told by countless retirees from coast to coast. Usually it is put in the mouth of a harried wife suffering the daily presence of a meddling, recently retired husband: "Look, I married him for rich or for poor—but not for lunch."[1]

That joke was unlikely to pass the lips of a person like Johanna. It was not that she lacked a sense of humor. On the contrary, she had a wonderful smile, and a wry if understated way with words. But she was a very private person, reticent about her inner life and her marriage. Even more to the point, however, the joke—like the image of the Karlers' island life as one of isolation—did not fit Johanna's personal life. She had been married in her early twenties, a few years after finishing high school, and soon had the first of her three children. Deferring her dream of returning to school, Johanna held part-time secretarial jobs while her husband Art worked his way up from sales positions to the purchase of his own clothing store.

The family grew, but the marriage slowly grew apart. The business of busyness, Art's drinking, and a golf-and-country-club-set that Johanna could never quite fathom or get comfortable with interposed themselves; they constituted a kind of alien landscape that she stepped around the edges of in a new choreography which kept her and Art at a safe distance from one another. When their third child Brad entered high school, Johanna—hungry for what had passed her by, embarrassed at the prospect that her youngest offspring would soon surpass her own education—started taking evening classes at a community college. One course was "The American West," another "The Faiths of the Far East." During the same period, her diligence as a worker earned her promotions at Evergreen Savings and Loan from part-time file clerk to teller to administrative assistant in the bank's planning division.

But returning to school and moving up at work were only part of the movement in Johanna's life at this time. She also traveled further inside herself, and deeper into a world of books. The religious volumes and the histories her teachers urged her to read slowly displaced the cloth and thread on the shelves of what had once been her sewing room at home. Texts and textiles created what Johanna called her "inner and outer space."

She had picked up the metaphor, and some of the books, at the Sitting Room, a study-and-meditation center she often stopped at on her free hours between work and class. "The Room" had been added as a second-floor annex to Tao Jones, Shelby's only spiritual bookshop, which Johanna had first visited in search of a volume on Buddhism. The Sitting Room served coffee and tea, and there were comfortable couches. You could buy incense, cards, CDs, or you could just browse. It was where Johanna and I usually met to talk. There was "mood" music too, sometimes classical, occasionally Japanese, but mostly Indian. She was bemused by how "carefully timed it was: morning ragas before lunch, evening ones after tea."

Johanna had unintentionally laid the groundwork for her retirement even before it began. With the sewing room at home and the Sitting Room downtown, she joked she had "gone beyond Virginia Woolf" to make not one but "*two* rooms of my own."[2] Neither was a denial of family or a rejection of marriage, but each gave an alternative to sheer domesticity and office life. And both proved to be harbingers of other things—and people—to come.

Art Alexander was almost exactly Johanna's age, but he ended up retiring well before she did. Neither had expected that. A self-employed businessman, Art had intended to run his clothing store "until he 'ran out of steam,' " hoping that one of his children would take it over. But neither Brad nor his sisters showed any interest, and then Art had a heart attack at 60. Anxious, resentful, he grudgingly arranged to sell the business a few months shy of 62. If retiring this way was a disappointment, however, Art also found it surprisingly easy to get used to. "Unlike his heart," Johanna said with a note of admiration and envy, "his life hardly skipped a beat. He had his golf buddies, with their daily coffee, and he became the main organizer of their tournaments. It's funny, I never thought of him as a good candidate for retirement. Maybe after all those years I knew him as little as he knew me."

Johanna would smile with resignation when describing the "separate but equal" lives they had come to lead. She felt that "Art's drinking was the hardest and saddest part, which he'd never admit to, the part that wasn't there at the start." And then there was his family. "No—not what you'd guess. I *loved* them. His parents and his sisters were wonderful to me. When we first got married, spending time with them was one of my great pleasures. Truly. They made me so welcome. I'd found a second family. And then Art started to pull away from them. And I could never understand why, unless it was the start of his drinking, but I couldn't keep us connected by myself. I felt such a loss. I felt sorry for him, but sorrier for myself, and I blamed him too."

By middle age, Johanne's "separate" life kept her involved with her children—Brad still in high school, Elaine and Peggy married, each a few hours away—but it also kept her education on track, from course to course and from community college to a nearby state university. A persistent part-timer, she laid up credits year by year, finally earning her degree in religion and history just as Brad finished his junior year at the same school.

The degree freed Johanna, but more in an emotional than an economic way. The long college project was over. Her family was proud of her, but she had done it more for herself than for anyone or anything else. There was no dream of a profession that drew her on. She kept the same job. She had only a few more years before she expected to retire, and no great goals there. Her four grandchildren, the reading she had set herself, and a few friends she had made at the Sitting Room were far more of a "growth" area in her private life. Johanna particularly loved the Sunday dinners with Peggy's family when they drove down from Buffalo—especially the company of eight-year-old grandson Soren, who shared her enthusiasm for books and bragged about his grandmother "the coed." When she could, Johanna loved being with one grandchild at a time so that each one felt special. Once she even tried teaching Soren to meditate, but "we ended up in hysterics, not nirvana."

What happened next in Johanna's work life, however, was no laughing matter. When Evergreen Savings was bought by a larger institution, her boss Walter Baylen was pushed into an early retirement. Johanna felt that her own presence was no longer assumed by the new administration. There were hints of being downgraded and shifted to another office. She thought she could "read the message between the lines. And it didn't say 'Smile' or 'Have a Happy Day.' It said, 'You're next.' I didn't think I'd actually lose my job because I had some seniority. But did I need to go through this? Adjust to a new boss? Learn another company's routines—and computers?! No. It was just a job. A nice one. But still just a job. I was 64, and had my pension and Social Security waiting. So though I'd planned to stay on longer, I gave my notice, and Walter and I retired together. I remember saying to myself: Nancy Reagan got it right for the wrong reasons. Work's the place where you should 'just say no.' "[3]

Later, Johanna would admit that the "no" was more from her head than her heart. Six months after retiring, she told me she could remember asking herself, back at her old office: 'Why me? I'm not ready for it. I usually didn't think about age at all at work. But sometimes, at coffee breaks, I'd look around and suddenly realize I was just about the oldest person there, and I'd wonder: How do these younger people see me? As an old woman? Those were the only moments I ever got self-conscious about age, realizing how unfriendly this society sometimes is about it. My predecessor, she worked until she was 70, and if things hadn't changed there, I'd imagined I would too. Maybe because I was in planning I got to think I had all this control. For a 60–something I was pretty naive."

A year later, Johanna was ready to pronounce on society's own naive stereotypes of retirees. "Either we are seen as suddenly bored, aimless, and falling apart, or people think we're immediately blessed with purpose and focus, and have fulfilling lives. But neither is generally true. Most of us fall in between those extremes."

Placing herself on the spectrum between "the fallen" and "the fulfilled," Johanna said that retirement had first struck her as being "like a long weekend, one that keeps getting extended, where you can finally get beyond basic chores and stop being what my friend Malvina calls a 'weekend warrior.' At the start I was insecure, and I'd make dates to make my calendar and life look full. But now days open that are no longer just marked with errands and lunches. I have three or four things on my calendar most weeks, which is good, but what I really welcome is a blank day when I do my own things, or let them discover me. Retirement's different from a vacation, which is a break *from* work so that you can go back *to* work. No. This is a break *with* work. And for me the goal has been one of balance: finding the way to feed my spirit, my intellect, my ties to the people I care about."

Of those priorities, Johanna gave the greatest moral weight to her family. "The meaning of my life, I guess, has been my children, and what they will do to make this a better world. They're the kind of people who *can* make a difference. Like Peggy, my oldest, Soren's mom, she teaches high school in the prison at Ardley. She relates so well to those men because she had an alcoholic father and husband, and she came up out of that instead of having it all pull her down."

But even with the pride she took in her children, the balance that Johanna sought for herself was in question because of her own doubts about whether the person she *was* matched the person she thought she *should be*. That double vision was there in her alter egos—as volunteer, reader, and would-be hermit.

- Volunteer: "I took the training to volunteer at the hospital, the oncology unit. I've only worked with two families so far, but I felt I had to give something back. In the past, I admit it, I've been shy and lazy. I didn't want to be bothered in that way."
- Reader: "I would have been happy being a perpetual student. I always used to make my sister 'play school' with me, even during the summer. Later, going back to college had nothing to do with ambition. I just wanted it to pry open my mind. When I first learned to read, I thought it was the greatest thing that had ever been invented. Now that I don't have to be at work, if I'm reading something interesting I'll sit there and go through the whole article. Or just finish the book. I've also been rereading novels I read long ago, which means I revisit other times in my life. One night I realized how dangerous that is. Remembering is just going back in your mind to an unchanged place, the 'old' you. But rereading is risky because it's reliving things. And maybe the place, or

the book, or *you,* have changed. You can't go home again when you do it this way. The home isn't the same. Neither are you."

- Hermit: "I could easily live as a hermit. Unlike my husband, I really don't need people that much. He can sit with his friends in a coffee shop, down at the Clockworks, and talk for hours. I don't know what the same people can talk about every day of their lives, especially when they haven't been doing very much *with* their lives. Me? I'm very happy by myself. My own things, thinking my own thoughts. Like I can sit half a morning and wonder what the next stage of technology will be. It's so hard to imagine now because computers feel like the ultimate. But that way of thinking's always been true. Television seemed like the ultimate when it came in. Nothing could surpass that! People must have felt the same way about the wheel, or the steam engine. Our imaginations are so limited by the technology we inhabit. You see?—I can go on and on like that in my mind. But I don't think that's very healthy. So I knew, when I retired, I'd just have to force myself to get out and do things. That led to the hospital. And I just started *tai chi* with this woman Zoe at the Senior Center, and these courses on spirituality down at Tao Jones. I think I made a new friend there too."

Nearly two years later, from the vantage point of a retirement that had now been tried, tested, played with, and reconfigured, Johanna picked out four defining moments in the first three-year phase of her new life. Each involved a decision, each concerned a significant person—her husband, a daughter, a guide, and the new friend. The first encounter was with Art, and it turned the joke about not marrying for lunch inside out.

To Johanna, the encounter, like the joke, was not funny. When Art had retired and she was still working, he had expected her to continue as the chief cook, cleaner, and provider of domestic services. Johanna quickly "clarified" that, insisting he take charge of food shopping, minor house repairs, occasional errands. But when she left the bank, Art assumed that their married life would return to the preretirement status quo. During Johanna's first week home, Art casually told her what he wanted at the market. Whether it was being degreed and retired, or 64 and a grandmother, or maybe better read and more centered, some quiet courage came out of

Johanna's recent history and she said, again, "No." Not to responsibility, but to regression, to going back to being the kind of homemaker she had been before she and Art passed the watershed of work's end.

That first defining moment was meant to protect Johanna from becoming tied to home. The second and third ones took her away from it. Both were journeys, and the farther of the two took her to Greece. It was liberating, a literal and moral breath of fresh air, but it was not what the doctor had ordered. Johanna's physican had, in fact, warned her against the trip, feeling that her asthma was too serious to risk the confinement of a ship's cabin, the pollution of Athens, and steep climbs up temple steps and ancient mountains. But Johanna had already been so inspired by her teachers' passions for the classics that she insisted on going, even if it had to be with her inhaler and her husband.

The leader of the tour was a young woman, an archaeologist, whose energy and enthusiasm overshadowed the passivity of Art and most of the other tour members. "Her name was Nancy Baker, rather plain for someone doing such exciting work—along with shepherding 20 seniors through the islands, the mainland, the Peloponnesus. She had this knack for turning stones and words into something worshipful. Once, she got so emotional at Delphi that she asked the three of us who'd made the climb with her: 'Do you know where *"enthusiasm"* comes from? It means to be filled with the spirit of God.' Then we all four just walked through those ruins in silence. Something changed. Maybe it was in the air, but I climbed those mountains almost without thinking about the effort. I was never short of breath! Honestly, I don't know what happened to me. And the whole year since then I've been fine. I've never had to use my inhaler."

There were other places she wanted to see, but nothing she could come up with filled Art with enthusiasm. He had actually enjoyed the trip to Greece in a quiet way, but she said she would feel guilty using their money to make trips that only she was truly excited by. And there were other asymmetries to keep her company when Art would not. Aside from her asthma, Johanna was in far better health than her husband, and so the family thought of her as being responsible for him. "They expect me to watch over him. But I think married people should not be so dependent on one another. He could take better care of himself—his drinking, his diet—so his heart wouldn't be such a worry to others."

Talking of Art's passivity, Johanna shook her head, pushing the incense in the Sitting Room air. "As time goes on, my health gets better and our marriage gets worse. I went back to ALANON meetings, but I find those hard because everyone there has something truly horrible going on—whereas I'm just watching my husband slowly destroy himself. I feel guilty not having problems as terrible as theirs, yet the group's so small that I feel called on to talk more than I want to."

Though Johanna's *moira*, her fate, seemed to preclude a repeat of her Greek adventure, a much more modest journey proved of equal significance. This was a trip to Maryland, to her middle child Elaine and her three-month old granddaughter Renée, whom Johanna had not seen since the baby's birth. That first visit had been in the dark days of February—in the winter after Greece, in the second year of retirement—when Johanna and Art had driven the six hours to Baltimore. But now, with spring golfing under way for her husband, Johanna fixed on something doubly unprecedented: to make the trip herself, and to go by bus.

The decision was unpremeditated. It "just announced itself one day" over tea with Malvina, Johanna's friend from the Sitting Room. They had gone out for a cup after a confusing lecture on "Money and Buddhism." When Malvina asked about the baby, Johanna found herself showing pictures of Renée and talking about how much she missed her daughter. Malvina had said: " 'You're free now. You're retired. Why don't you just go see her?' Suddenly," Johanna told me, "I realized she was right. So why didn't I see that myself?"

The memory of that moment drew Johanna's shoulders into a shrug. "What I really saw was that I was still thinking of myself in the old way—bound by routine, as if most of my week was already accounted for. In fact, it wasn't. Once or twice a week I do go out to Jackson's, the trailer park, to take my mother shopping or to the doctor or her hairdresser. She can't drive any more. Or maybe we just have lunch. My sister used to do most of that when I was working, but now we share it. And though my mother and I are not the easiest companions, she needs it—and expects it. Otherwise I'm really free. Still, that idea hadn't really taken hold for me.

"Anyway, I remember staring at Malvina: my eyes must have been quite wide with amazement—amazement at myself—and I said: 'I'm going to do it.' And when she asked when, I thought for just a second or two—I knew I had a doctor's appointment the following Tuesday—and I said: 'The week after next. And you know, I think I'll go by bus.' Just like that! I don't know where it came from, being so sure about what, when, and how I was going to do this. Maybe we both just felt a bit giddy because of that lecture. But I think, at that moment, with a good friend to talk to, I suddenly discovered something new about being retired. It was not that I was free *of* ties. It was that I was free to act *on* them."

Downstairs at Tao Jones, someone had put on another CD. Johanna listened to a few bars, Haydn this time, and then told me about her journey. "The trip was amazing. Not just seeing Elaine and Warren and the baby. But the trip itself. I know this will sound silly to an anthropologist, but for me, getting on that bus myself was scary. I had to change in Harrisburg and wait there for over half an hour. There was a drivers' strike on, and some people got angry—and others just bonded. Bus stations are so strange, real way stations, with the kind of people you, or at least I, would not usually be with in life. I struck up conversations—which is not like me. And then I sat next to a black woman, a lovely grandmother from Washington, D.C., on the second bus. We each pulled out baby photos. Then I suddenly realized I was one of the few passengers on the bus who was white! For one long stretch of US 83, I was a minority. The whole experience was such an adventure for me. I decided everyone should ride the buses at least once a year, just to see what the rest of the world is like. I felt free, new, as new as this newborn I was going to hold again."

The friendship which had made this journey possible, which had helped remake the meaning of retirement, was the fourth defining experience in Johanna's new life. Malvina was almost 25 years younger, a real estate agent, recently divorced, with one school-age child. But the generational, marital, and occupational differences between them did not seem to matter much. Both were drawn to Tao Jones and the Sitting Room, partly by the same sort of spiritual curiosity. But what also brought them to one another was, in large part, the empty spaces in their own lives. And their laughter. At the talks they attended, each noticed that they both laughed at the same moments of excess, and that often it was just the two of them who saw humor in what others thought profound.

After one such evening's encounter, months before Renée's birth, Malvina had asked Johanna if she would like to go for "a cup of something," and over tea they arranged to meet for a weekend hike. It was November, and most of the leaves were down. So they went up along the creek bed of one of the deep, meandering gorges that fed water down to Allegany Lake. They pulled small fossils out from the shale walls, examined their marriages, and breathed in large draughts of moist autumn air.

Two such walks were sufficient to start a friendship. Whatever was found by these two women in the larger world of books, Buddhism, and workshops, they also recognized a kind of common ground—a kinship compounded of a shared sense of loss, frailty, and hope. Johanna knew that here too there were blatant asymmetries, that unlike her own life, much of Malvina's was consumed with work, money worries, and child care. But that was all right. The two exchanged companionship, compassion, and laughter. The only other person Johanna had felt that close to in years—other than her children—had been Soren, who was now in boarding school, and too far away to be part of her weekly life. When Johanna spoke now about what retirement had brought her, then, she always mentioned her "special friend." "I really like that phrase," she once explained. "Saying it, just like saying, 'Yes, I'll take that trip,' helps to make things happen. Greece, and Buddhism, taught me about silence. But I never knew language itself had such power."

The Most Taxing Season

By the time of retirement, as Johanna came to realize, "home" and "family" are no longer synonymous. In her version of this American experience, when grown children and grandchildren relocate, their elders are left to redefine the nature of domestic tranquillity and social life itself. But while Johanna, Martin, and Inez, just like Alice, each entered a world where "family" was no longer synonymous with "home" for Lester Ulanoff they were still one and the same. He was fond, in fact, of describing himself as a "homebody" and a "family man." And he was, but in a most unlikely way. Especially for a divorced, retired male of 62.

Les, whose accounting firm did the books and taxes for Art Alexander's store and Carl Withen's law firm, had been a fixture of Shelby's business scene for just over three decades. When he retired, the financial and practical details of his life had been carefully worked out, including a part-time return to his office each year during income tax season. It was the rest of his life that had not gone according to plan. The irony did not escape Les, who was a self-described conservative, "the kind of accountant who always advised clients to plan in advance, follow the rules, cover your bets, expect the unexpected."

But Les himself had been caught unawares when, a decade and a half before retiring, his wife of 23 years had left him and their children. Though he had followed "the rules" and kept all his affairs "in order," suddenly his life was "in disarray." A teenage son and daughter were still at home with him, and his mother—74, ailing, and widowed two years previously—was being watched over by Les in her own home across town. Les's children were soon "acting out in classic style" over the divorce; it was a roller coaster of "sullenness, guilt, bad grades, tantrums, blaming." On a rare night out that year, sitting over a beer with Carl Withen and Earl Blankowsky, an old football buddy from his Seneca College days, Les realized that he was "full-time three times over: accountant, single parent, and caregiver."

The next few years were a harrowing, painful "coming of age in middle age" for Les. Without mentioning his wife or the word "divorce," he admitted that "how some things happen the way they do in this world I'll never know. It sometimes shakes my faith in people—but not my values. I worked hard at keeping my family, and myself, together. A lot of the time I didn't know what I was doing, and it was hard with my son. I know I fumbled a lot of things. I told Earl once, 'In college, you know, I was a tackle, not a back. I didn't have to run all that much—hold my ground, take some hits, and get in there to do my job.' Well now I had to hold my ground, but I also had to run—all over town, build up my lungs, this emotional stamina too. I tell you, this was not what I had trained for."

It is easy to mock the use of sports metaphors; in modern American life they have been nearly battered to death by politicians and preachers. But with Les they came out in an unaffected, aptly autobiographical way. "Some teams hit their stride, get momentum, keep drawing on everyone's talent. Then, at some point, the key people move on and those good seasons pass. You go into what coaches call a 'period of rebuilding.' Well, I'd had a long run of smooth years, and then that winter came along when my wife went off—the most 'taxing season' I've ever had—and I looked at my desk, this pile of paper, and the people I was responsible for, and I said to the mirror in my office, 'Les, it's time to rebuild yourself.' "

When high school ended for Les's son, it was a mercy for both of them. A year away at college softened and dissipated Ben's anger. Meeting other students who had been pawns in their parents' divorces even engendered some compassion and respect for his father. Les could turn more of his attention to his daughter Becky, 22, who had been "marking time" as a waitress at the Stonemill Inn. He encouraged her to think about college, and they "compromised" on a nursing program. For the first, intensely demanding months of classes, it was nearly a disaster. Academics had never been Becky's great love, but from early adolescence her own doctor, Petra van Osten, had been encouraging Becky to think about nursing. In Becky's first semester at community college, Petra had periodically called her to give some moral if not technical support. When the program finally turned from classroom to practice and Becky got the chance to deal with patients, she was transformed.

After graduating Becky worked for a year in a hospital in Corning, but that soon grew routine. In Les's words, "She needed more than just a job, because with nursing she'd found a mission, not just work." Twelve months later Becky was on her way to El Salvador with the Peace Corps.

Her sojourn in Central America changed Becky's life and, ultimately, the shape of her father's retirement. In El Salvador the political climate proved to be just as troubling as delivering basic medical services. Alternately engaged and appalled, Becky stayed on after her Peace Corps commitment to help plan a regional health service. And she married Agustín Pintero, a Salvadoran community organizer whom she had met in her work. A year and a half later, after the birth of their daughter Rosa and renewed waves of right-wing rural terrorism, Becky and Agustín were forced to leave the country. They arrived back in the United States with Rosa, jobless and homeless, and moved in with Les.

They were not the only new arrivals under his roof. During Becky's time abroad, Les had moved his mother into the house, refitting a ground floor room for her with wheelchair access and a separate entrance for privacy. Ben, who had graduated college and gone to work in Boston, came back to visit periodically. Another year passed, and by the time Les went into semiretirement, Becky had taken a job under Anne Freudenberg at Elmwood Grove Nursing Home.

Other threads tied the family to Shelby's fabric. Rosa was getting her check-ups from Petra van Osten, Becky's mentor, who spoke with pride and surprise now about the political turn her former patient's life had taken. Agustín had learned enough English to begin attending Seneca College, where Felix Davis took him under his wing. And though Rosa was now in day care part-time, it was Les who still had charge of her, and his mother, for a good portion of each week—except at tax time.

Retirement, then, began with what Les called "a full house." It was "not a bad hand to be dealt" but, being an indifferent poker player, he did not really pursue that metaphor too much. "Accountants are bad gamblers," he claimed. "They're better parents." Instead of seeing his life laid out in the cards, he chose to relate his fate to his character, and to some self-evident truths. "I am not a great dreamer, or schemer, or traveler. Sure, I take vacations. I like to go to Florida or the Southwest once a year. But my life's never been built around some grand design or great drama. Two years with the army in Korea was enough of that for me. My job and my family—they've always been where my life was centered. That's why, like my Dad did, I've started giving some of my money to my kids—now, when they need it, not after I'm dead."

Les once confided that "sometimes I think I'm letting my mind rest too much. I watch my granddaughter, and help my mother, and I look after the finances of some old friends we have, gratis—but I'm not saving the world. There are times I feel I should go out and do more. This world Rosa came into is not a very pretty place: look what happened to her parents!" He tapped his chin. "Don't misunderstand, it's not all worry. Like the last few years—I've had a female friend, a retired woman, who I see two or three times a week. But she also cares for a grandchild. So it's basically family-oriented. That's what things comes down to. See, I don't feel I've led a very exciting life, but I can't say that I'm sorry. I made my choices. Without doing much, I find plenty to do. The responsibilities don't tax me the way they once did."

Les took the measure of desire and found it muted by time. "Age is no *Golden Pond*," he said argued, playing with popular culture the way the

Karlers did. "If I could have retired at 35 or 40, thinking how much more involved I was then, that would have been great. Maybe in your wildest dreams you say now, How can I recapture, what can I do to . . . that sort of fantasy. But you can't recreate that, or who you were then. The drives and reasons of 45 are no longer there."

He warned, "You can have a positive outlook on retirement, but don't fool yourself into thinking that at 65 you can actually live out the dreams that were vivid when you were 30 years younger. Retirement *now* is not as thrilling as it might have been two or three decades ago. When you've lived that much more of your life, it's difficult, or at least different, because there are a lot of memories, a lot of history. You carry all that with you. Thank God I still have my family, and this home, and my friends. Believe me, just having hobbies wouldn't be sufficient to build a life around. If that's all you can do, you might as well have stayed at work."

The quality of retirement that Les loved the most was "the freedom of being in charge of your own time." He felt he had this, even with caregiving responsibilities for a mother and granddaughter. Yet at work, he told me, the period he had hated most was not "the frantic run-up to income tax day, but the 'easy' October-December stretch; that was the deadest part of the year, and it was hard to fill my days. In the other months, yes, there were always other kinds of grief. Every time the phone rang, it was not someone calling to wish you a happy birthday. Usually there was a fire to put out. Since leaving," he said candidly, "it's also a relief not to be worrying about how you speak to people—that someone'd hear a slip of the tongue, or a joke, as sexual harrassment or an antigay remark."

Recovering the right to jest was up there for Les with his newfound daily freedom. But even the latter quality was a qualified virtue. "Retirement's a prolonged vacation. What makes a vacation special is that it's not prolonged. That's the bitter and the sweet of it. When I didn't get my first paycheck in over 30 years, the 'finality' of retirement really hit me. I guess you could say I'm on sabbatic now; it just took a long time, and it's unpaid. Maybe I should get a grant from the college!"

Les indulged some of Shelby's animus toward the college. "When I went to Seneca, there was talk of changing it to a university, and it seemed the teachers were always away, playing paid 'expert' for someone else. Now it's the students who play. My house is downhill from the main campus, and half the homes around us have been cut up into student apartments. They parade through our streets on weekend nights—drunk, urinating, shouting obscenities at one another, the women as well as the men!" He shook his head and tapped his fingers in rhythm. "Believe me, we were not that disrespectful in my day. A trustee, an old teammmate in fact, asked me to donate money as an alum. I told him, 'Given how students act and talk now, I'd only think about it if you'd first change the school's name—you know, use their favorite expression. Change it from Seneca College to "Fuck U." ' "

Jokes about sabbatics and students had an edge with Les because he was so conscious of having stayed in one place. "I haven't wandered far from home, except for Korea. I grew up, went to school, and settled here. I worked in the same firm for 33 years, and I'm still there in retirement. Some clients would have left the firm if I hadn't stayed on. In the off-season I keep track of their accounts and stay in touch on the computer at home. So I'm even there when I'm not there, doing the bosses a favor. Really, I think they owe me. When I had a heart attack four years ago, I hardly took sick time, and was back in a month. That's when something that Carl said really hit me. He claimed that 'accountants are notorious for not following their own advice.' It was true. For years, I'd been trying to get the firm to set up a pension plan, and they wouldn't. At least the partners did generate what's called a 'rabbi trust' for me. That's what congregations do when they don't want to create a pension fund for just one person; instead they give you deferred income to draw on in retirement."

Though still an accountant in name and practice, the phrase that Les liked best to describe himself was "single parent retired." The house he shared with Becky's family was the same one he had lived in for 50 years. Three decades ago his grandmother had died in his arms there, in the room next to the one we were sitting in as his third retired year was drawing to a close. "I watched my mother care for that grandmother. So I know how much it can take out of a person to do that. And there are strains in living the way I do now," he admitted. "Arguments, questions of discipline for Rosa. But it's worth it. I've come to think of this place now as the 'Salvadoran Embassy' because anyone from there who comes to Shelby stays with us."

Les had one other way of accounting for his life. "I put in 39 'kid-years' here raising Ben and Becky. Now I'm accumulating 'grand-kid years.' When I think of where it will all end, you know what I've decided? I want to be cremated and put in Allegany Lake. My kids don't know where anyone in the family is buried anyway, and they don't care to learn. But I love the lake—and I think all the cemeteries will probably be condos one day. So this way, at least the people who know will be able to look at the lake every time and say, 'Hey, there's Les!' "

He smiled, shrugged, dropped his shoulders. "After my wife left, it was me and my children. Later, they were gone too. I was here alone, some aimless thing in this empty house. Now there are four generations here: my mother, me, my daughter, my granddaughter. Everybody needed a home. I had one. These people were part of a family. That family was me. That I had no wife, and my children's mother was gone, was regrettable and, after a point, beside the point. Something had to be done. Someone had to be there. This house was 'there,' and that 'someone' was me. I no longer argue with the gods about that. Maybe I should thank them."

Orphaned at 63

Some might think of Les's life as having a tragic quality. But he honestly did not see it that way. When I suggested that interpretation, his reply was, "No. A tragedy's a situation where you have to choose between two rights, so whatever you do, you're destined to fail someone. I didn't have that kind of choice. Other than walking away from my own mother, or children, or grandchild"—options that needed no comment—"I knew what I had to do. One thing led to another: first the divorce, then mother, then Becky's family. Except for realizing, finally, that retirement was not going to be what I'd imagined, I didn't think about it much. I just did it when the time came. Just as I dealt with those other things."

Implicit in Les's experience is a view of retirement as a set of choices and circumstances over which people can exercise, at best, a degree of control and foresight. In his story, gender, marriage, morals, family ties, and finances each played a role. These same factors also affected Donna Younger, but they shaped a very different outcome for her. When she retired at 63 as vice president of Seneca College, she was a single person with a long and remarkably successful career. For a woman of her generation and background to have reached a place of such power and professional regard seemed almost fictional. When she joked about how others liked to tell their own version of her "success story," she was fond of recalling how her father once described her as "a woman out of Willa Cather."[4]

Donna liked Cather's work and appreciated the compliment, but she pointed out the difference. "Sure, those women in her books were creatures of the Midwest like me. They were Nebraska, I was Iowan by birth. We grew up on farms. But they stayed for good, and I left for college—and when I left it turned out to be for good. I did travel back home to visit a lot, but in other ways I never looked back. I never gave the land a chance to beat me down or mold me in its image. It wasn't a conscious escape *from* anything, though. Iowa never oppressed me, and I've always been fond of where I grew up. It's just that early on I discovered something else I wanted to do, and it was quite intellectual. Maybe my father was half-right, but I guess I'm more Jim Burden than Ántonia Shimerda."

The names were fiction, Cather's masterful creations from *My Ántonia*, but they served Donna's purpose of capturing a central aspect of her own life through someone else's characters. Ántonia was Cather's immigrant girl, a weathered flower who plants her Bohemian soul deep into the soil, and stays rooted there throughout a long life of toil, loss, and childbearing. Her childhood friend Jim Burden is American-born but orphaned early in youth. Raised by his grandparents, he grows away from the prairies and small-town life to become a college-educated Eastern lawyer—a man of the larger world who nevertheless remains wistful about the homegrown world and girl he left behind, and inexplicably reticent about the marriage and family he himself never found a place for.

In Cather's work, Jim narrates Ántonia's story. In Donna's story, she had her own words, plus a wall of memorabilia, to mark and measure her progress. When I first met her in her office, a term before retiring, every paper, ornament, and file was placed with precision. Though it would all be moved in a few months, nothing in Donna's attitude made a concession to the impermanence of what was around her. Her life's work as an educator, historian, and innovator would be more lasting than the presence of her body or books in an ivy-covered building. She explained with a bit of personal history.

"My roommate Tessa from Smith, who I see faithfully every year, once broke up with a boyfriend. And I've always remembered a slip of the tongue she made when she came back to our dorm furious and heartbroken. 'He'll know what he lost till the day he dies,' she cried, 'because I'll still be around, and he'll live his life with such regret. I'll outlove him,' she sobbed. Now, she'd meant to say 'outlive' him. But I've always thought she probably felt both those things." Looking around her, at the Cornell doctorate, the awards, the well-framed photographs, Donna calmly put her hand down on a neat pile of reports, and tied her own life to Tessa's story. "This office, these papers and objects, will undoubtedly be here, or somewhere, long after I'm gone. Well, I'll be outlived but not outloved by them." She fixed me with her eyes. "Like Tessa, I've had my passions in life, though they're pretty unrecognized and unremarked on by most of the people around me here." She smiled a knowing smile. "No matter. I know who and what I've lived for, and mostly I've loved it."

Donna's account of her passions sounded, to my ear at first, more professional than personal. Then I came to realize how much the life of her work really was the heart of her life. She told me, with mounting ardor, about the years of teaching, her love of history, her dedication to standards, and the agony she went through over her first invitation to enter administration. She turned that offer down, knowing that she was perhaps only a year away, maybe two, from finishing a manuscript on women in the ancient world. But when the book was done, and praised, and the call came again, she found herself more defenseless and uncertain about it. Her sense of self was momentarily unsettled; was she tempted more by vanity or real opportunity? She talked it over endlessly with colleagues, her brother, local friends, and Tessa. What finally swayed her to say yes was the conviction that as a dean she could become an instrument of history, not just a student of it.

Her second career as an administrator took her to two other schools and up several rungs of the academic ladder. As she moved up, she found some of what she had hoped for and some of what she feared. "There are certainly a lot of small minds in big places, but I found some people of vision too." At the center of Donna's own "quiet agenda" was the desire to create more opportunities for women. "To prove by example as well as by creating programs." To show that "a broad and deep education" was not just for the benefit of students; "it also served the common good."

In her two mid-career moves, Donna raised scholarship funds for women, brought on more female faculty, and helped create a women's studies program. "I also mentored a number of young scholars, a few of whom went on to become leaders in their fields. Since Seneca doesn't give me much of a voice in who my successor will be, I guess it's the women and men I guided who are my real 'successors' in life. For the rest," she said, "to run a good school, you just have to take a strong hand with the politics and the trivia. You have to respect what you want to do, even if others don't always respect you for wanting it. I stepped in here when I got fed up with the way history itself was being taught by certain faculty, the masquerade that some passed off as scholarship—what this British historian, E. H. Carr, calls the modern weakness for 'knowing more and more about less and less.'[5] Sometimes, being at or near the top was not the best place to do what I wanted. The trick was to find a post where I had maximum flexibility. Being a vice president could actually be more advantageous than being a president or provost. You can do a lot when everyone's eyes aren't on you all the time."

Though Donna's goals focused on the value for women, of what she called "the liberating arts," one of the role models who loomed largest in her late career was a man. George Mulhany had been the chair of the first department she had taught in, a person who shared all her values except religion, who encouraged her ambitions, and fostered her progress. He himself had gone on to become a dean, but his example later became more a caution than a model. He had stayed "past his moment. He lost his sharpness. From what people at Jefferson State told me, his memory was showing signs of—you know. You have to leave while you're good at what you're doing, go with grace even if, like George, you can't go with God."

When Donna decided to leave Seneca at 63, then, she mentally took George home with her to the neat gingerbread house on a country hillside that she shared with Reggie. Well on in age himself, Reggie had been her companion for 14 years. He was compact, handsome, and well-proportioned, and he stood out clearly against the dark background of woods. Reggie was a white poodle.

Donna knew the joke about not for lunch, and observed wryly that even if Reggie's English had been better, the point of the joke would have been wasted on him. He *liked* having her around more. "In fact, he thinks the reason I'm home more now is for *him*—that I should feed him more, take him for more walks, pay more attention to him." It was a point Johanna would have easily grasped.

When retirement formally began for Donna, she reveled in it—and then got lost in it. She referred to it at first, as did others, as a "permanent vacation." There was "the luxury of time" and "the freedom to set your own agenda." She described going to a conference and realizing that she no longer had to attend the formal sessions; she could just gossip with the people she had really gone there to see. Or she would stop by the college, where she kept an office—"a very nice perk, to have a home away from home"—and feel "graced with the knowledge that I did not have to solve any of the problems there."

But then, she told me, "as time went on, there was more than I could handle; I became a procrastinator." She postponed whatever was not pressing until tomorrow, and then found that she was losing track of time itself. Her e-mail piled up, and what had once been a great electronic convenience became an occasional embarrassment. She forgot to go to a meeting. She became casual about buying food, and discovered once that she didn't have enough in the house for dinner. A niece's birthday came and went, and Donna, who never overlooked dates, realized too late that she had never gotten around to sending the gift that had been sitting in her own closet for a month.

So "by the end of year one" she began to create what Stefan Nokalsky had built into his retirement—"a structure for the day." Donna's alarm went off at 7 A.M.; she breakfasted with a news broadcast; did her back exercises; took Reggie for a walk; dealt with letters and e-mail; devoted the afternoons to readings and meetings, and the evenings to writing and culture. Her greatest concession to the "casual culture" of retirement was her clothes. Formerly known for how well she dressed, Donna came to terms with the virtue of slacks and the comfort of flannel shirts. Once she proudly showed herself off to me in her "retirement sweater"—a roomy cardigan with several deep pockets housing pens, notes, tissues, reading glasses—the wherewithal to get through much of a day without wondering where the necessities were.

Other than the casual clothes, the strategic way Donna had approached her career carried over into her retirement. Both work and its aftermath had to be carefully plotted, she argued, because she had been so willfully out of step with her times. "I grew up," she explained, "belonging to a gender and a generation whose whole life had been laid out in advance. The choices we had are what I call 'three things and a husband': you could be a school teacher, social worker, or nurse, and then you were supposed to get married. But those were never serious options for me."

Donna had guessed, early in maturity, that her life would largely be a solo endeavor, and that if indeed that turned out to be the case, she would have to plan a lot of things a long way in advance. So she chose Shelby for her last professional move because she thought it would be a good place to retire in. Once she knew she liked it enough to stay on, she began to cultivate people and pursuits so that they would be able to sustain her later on. "Then," Donna felt, "the end of work wouldn't be the end of everything you've done." The Unitarian church soon became one of the mainstays of both her social and her spiritual life. She got to know Carl Withen's wife and Alice Armani there, served on several committees, and took a leadership role in governance. "It seems sometimes we talk everything to death there. Alice once called it the 'Conversational church.' "

Along with the Protestant ethic, a spirit of prudent capitalism also moved Donna. Years before, on the first rung of the academic ladder, she had joined TIAA, the national pension plan for college teachers, and had made sizable investments in it for decades. At mid-career, when it was a relatively inexpensive purchase, she had bought long-term care insurance. She felt there would be no one to care for her if she ever became frail, and she was banking on being at least financially self-sufficient if other dependencies came her way.

Donna also knew, as the end of her career was drawing near, that eventually she would have to leave her home, which was more house than she cared to care for. Anticipating that age, her back, and her arthritis would make it harder for her to clean, rake, shovel, and repair things, she decided to search for something simpler and smaller. Eighteen months after leaving her post, she put her home on the market and began sorting through the local housing possibilities. Her desires were based on lifestyle and location, not luxury; she treasured privacy, hated asking others to do things for her, and wanted to be close enough to stores and people so she could shop and be social without depending on a car or worrying about the weather.

Studying the area's apartments and developments with a researcher's skills, Donna finally decided on Orchard Hill. It was a condominium community on the edge of Shelby with bus service, landscaped grounds, and older residents, several of whom were retired colleagues. Orchard Hill was the fine and quiet place Donna had wanted. She made a deposit on a two-bedroom unit that looked out on a tree-lined abandoned railroad right-of-way, a view reminiscent of the one she and Reggie enjoyed in the country. There would be room for guests and Donna's piano, a crew to mow the lawn, clear it of fall leaves, and plow the winter walkways, plus an enclosed yard for Reggie to chase rabbits in.

It turned out that Donna's sense of timing for the move was both good and bad. But she could take neither full credit nor even partial blame for what happened next. On the fortunate side, her house sold for a decent price just months before the real estate market (and the economy) plunged. After paying her taxes and the down payment on the condo, Donna still had cleared close to $50,000 to add to her retirement investments. What she could not foresee was the touch of winter and the hand of death.

Her misfortunes began with a severe cold spell three weeks before the scheduled closings on the two properties. The occupants at Orchard Hill had vacated Donna's new unit early, leaving the condo empty, the final papers in the hands of their attorney. But one night the subzero weather burst a pipe in the laundry room there, and when the thaw came two days later, water spewed out the crack, down the sheetrock, and across the floors and rugs of the kitchen and guest room. Donna, her belongings all packed and ready at her house, had gone home to Iowa to visit her widowed father for Christmas, and only heard of the flood when she returned. Then it was lawyers, insurance adjustors, carpenters, carpet layers, painters, plumbers—every homeowner's nightmare. The condo closing was postponed, the possessions went into storage, and Donna herself went to her friend Alice Armani's house.

The insurance company had offered to get Donna a motel room for the two weeks the basic repairs would take, and she was momentarily tempted. But in the end, her sense of dislocation and unease, of burden and betrayal and isolation, was too unrelenting to hold at bay alone. Alice's offer to move in was too comforting to resist.

The two women had known one another for years, and were drawn together by coincidence, by election, and by difference. Alice, the community leader and would-be artist, was the more visible and audible in the local world. When they first met, Alice had just become head of Homebase; she had survived the publicity of a midlife divorce; and she had then gone right on with her public life, agitating, advocating, and speaking to the newspapers about county budgets, displaced women, and vulnerable youth. When her agency's board needed new members and a stronger tie to the college, Donna had been nominated by a man who belonged to her church. He noted that she was both a "doer" and a "voice of reason." Three years later, Donna was the board's secretary.

In those human relationships where the emotional seems to rule—in the bonds between lovers, for example, or in those between mentor and student, therapist and client, guru and follower—there is a kind of unexamined chemistry, one that can sometimes turn work ties, too, into friendships. It happened for Donna and Alice, despite the fact that as board secretary and agency director their relation was not one of equals. That Alice was technically accountable to Donna hardly mattered to them. Nor did the truth that each had reached her midlife status as "single woman" by a very different route.

They both respected what Alice called the other's "way in the world," and those distinctions of career and temperament subsumed what Donna called "a kind of moral kinship," the shared purpose of "making institutions serve *people,* instead of making people serve *them.*" She and Alice had seen one another practice what others only preached in their separate efforts at college, in church, and at the agency. It was Donna's regard for this that overcame her reserve when Alice offered her sanctuary in the midst of her housing crisis. Donna and Reggie arrived worn out and humbled by being thrown on the mercy of the world. Months later, still shaken by that memory, Donna said, "The greatest indulgence I've ever allowed myself, other than living my life the way *I* wanted to, was to let myself fall apart the one time my life seemed to be doing the same."

Five weeks later, her condo repaired, Donna's life fell apart again. Surrounded by comforting, familiar things, she was deep in the pleasure of unpacking books when the phone rang. It was Henry, her brother, calling from Iowa. His calm voice inflected just enough unease to give Donna a half minute's warning. Their father Quentin, 87, had died of a coronary an hour ago—on Main Street, just outside his favorite coffee shop. By the time the ambulance arrived, even by the time a waitress had finished her call to the hospital, his life was over, his movement stilled by a long, cold spasm. Twenty minutes after Henry broke the news, Donna said goodbye and cradled the receiver. The call over, the funeral arrangements sketched in, she sat on the edge of a hassock, rocking herself in her arms, staring at Reggie and the piles of other people's history on the floor.

Frozen pipes. Frozen heart. A week later, sitting in the Iowa home she had left 44 years ago, the weight of her father's death that had lodged in Donna's own heart finally fell into her belly and exploded. "It spread through me like a cloud, and my whole body, my whole self knew then that I was homeless again in this other way. More truly this time." She paused, staring past me. "I won't lie to you, though I feel a bit foolish saying this. When I heard the voices of the visitors in the next room, waiting for me, my father's youngest child, the thought took hold of me: I've been orphaned at 63."

She twisted her head back and forth as if shaking that memory loose. "I thought the world had shifted. But it was my stomach, the top and bottom rolling over and changing places. A boat capsizing. I thought, 'the end of an era.' That wasn't very imaginative for a historian. But when my father went it *was* the end of a generation in my family, and it made my generation into something else—but what? Maybe we'd graduated. We were now the 'elders.' "

Another twist of her head. "It's still too abstract for me. I don't have a generational identity. The Lost Generation. The Beat Generation. Children of the '60s. Boomers. Generation X. That way of thinking has always struck me as too pat, too convenient. It papers over all the complexity of people's lives; it's bad journalism and worse history."

She made her irritation personal. "I've always been sensitive to how easily others see me in the wrong way. Because I'm a woman, I can't lead. Or because I'm single, I must feel bereft. Or being old, I'm somehow frail." With an edge of defiance, Donna explained, "I'm arthritic, not crippled. I'm alone, not lonely."

We looked around the temporary disorder of her new living room, the boxes from her office, some half-empty now, finally getting sorted through. There were also files of papers and photos from her father that needed to be organized and "cataloged for some other chronicler." "This is good timing," she observed. "It's almost meditative to go through these. My life and his." She waved a folder from the college. "My one consulting job since retiring. A case of academic malpractice or revenge, missing funds in Wisconsin—I was asked to investigate it. The first time I've gotten paid extra for being highly ethical!" She showed me two major awards given to her at professional meetings since leaving Seneca. Both honored Donna's work as a woman working on behalf of women.

She paused, reaching for context. "The college, this community, my church—they are places where good things happen. Being retired is giving me a chance to appreciate that all over again. And read history—*and* brush up my Latin. What a joy *that* is. Besides, and more to the point, I do have a family and wonderful friends—Tessa out there, and Alice right here, among them—and those friends have been part of my life for a lot longer than many marriages last today. I'll tell you, maybe it's easier to be understood when you live by yourself. Then there's no one around to misrepresent you."

Re-imagining the World

In Donna's wondering how reliably one person can represent the life of someone else, there was the hint of the antihistorian, an interpreter of the past questioning the credibility of her own profession. Some of the other retirees raised questions about how well they could narrate, or anticipate, even their own lives. For example, several invoked the idea of a "vacation" as the metaphor for retirement only to reject it upon further reflection, and they criticized the concept of the weekend as a model or a reward for good behavior. And when it came to such personal domains as kinship and friendship, Martin, Inez, Johanna, Les, and Donna were sometimes genuinely surprised at how things had turned out for them. They struggled with the balance between family and friends, duty to others and personal fulfillment, freedom and responsibility, a sense of mission and the grace of respectability.

By invoking the metaphors of the kaleidoscope and the conspirators, for example, Inez and Martin reflected on the way relationships and moral commitments shift over time. In later life, home and family may not be in the same place or comprise the same people. To a notable degree they did remain congruent for Les, but not for Johanna, or Donna, or the Karlers. Inez and Martin found themselves in the midst of a process of consolidating and reimagining the world; they were doing it not only in the wide circle that encompassed their children and grandchildren, but also within the microcosm of their island's lakeshore neighbors.[6]

The weight of the Karlers' partnership, however, was not replicated in some other retirees' lives. For Johanna Alexander, marriage had been a disappointment. Retirement did not reveal its weaknesses, as it sometimes does for others, for she had been aware of her marriage's shortcomings for years; but leaving the work force brought home to her the realization that she could become trapped again in domesticity, and she made a conscious if uneasy decision to avoid that. The movement between sewing room and Sitting Room, and her discovery of friendship as a medium for self-discovery, shaped the spirit of her early retirement. As long as she could continue to grow in these other ways, her sense of integrity was intact.

The vulnerability and durability of family ties had been long-term issues for Les Ulanoff, and they predated his retirement by many years. His wife's unexpected decision to leave her family had placed him in a position of great and unaccustomed responsibility. By the time he did retire, Les's commitments as a caregiver had grown rather than diminished. He had "come of age in middle age," ending as the head of a four-generation household. This role surprised, taxed, and affirmed him all at once, providing a moral focus for his sense of self and his vision of life.

Across town, on Orchard Hill, Donna Younger struggled with a different set of dilemmas. Resisting the tendency of others to misrepresent or merge her into some generational caricature, she remained deeply committed to her autonomous life. But age also showed how loss could, at least momentarily, shake one's self-image and faith in one's own control. Though living alone, she insisted she did not feel lonely because she enjoyed the refuge of friends, the companionship of Reggie, her passion for learning, and the sustaining sense of her own achievements.

The relationships that dominate people's lives at any stage are deeply influenced by who and what their culture teaches them to value. And American retirees differ from other societies' elders in how they deal with this aspect of the human condition. In virtually all nine of the non-American cultures we have been considering, marriage is the norm, and close ties to kin remain central in later life. To the older people of Abkhasia, China, Ireland, and India, and among the Inuit, Korongo, and Mesakin, a basic concern is family continuity and a succession in which appropriate members of the next generation assume control of the household, the kin group, and its resources. Except for India's *sannyasins*, elders continue to live with or near their kin, and they count on being cared for if the need develops. To Indians and Inuit, continuity will eventually also take the form of reincarnation. More focused on the present, older Bahamians serve not just as child care providers but in true *loco parentis* as the prime rearers of their grandchildren.

Of the five people featured in this section, Les came the closest to that Caribbean way of being as what he called a "club sandwich generation" caregiver. Martin and Inez actually invoked an Inuit ice-flow image for themselves, but were really more like Abkhasians in their active lives, and like the Irish in keeping to their home turf. None of these five individuals left their families to become American versions of the *sannyasin*, though Johanna took a page from their Hindu search by finding, in her journeys, a source of transcendence. In her switch from bank duty to a search for the self, she even seemed to accept, implicitly, the Chinese maxim, "a Confucian in office, a Taoist in retirement."[7] Only her husband Art recalls the Korongo and Mesakin in his desire for a family succession in business, whereas Les measured his life not in cattle but in kid- and grandkid-years.

These and other retirees expressed a variety of feelings about their experiences with family and friends. There was gratitude for the ailing mother who drew Ursula to Georgia and for the flexible partner who eased her departure from Shelby; the special delight that Felix and Teri took in their new roles and names as "Grandbird" and "Grandflower"; the Trayvors' sense of irony at their role reversal, stepping in for their children to create some discipline in their grandchildren's lives; and the Ellmans' feelings of wonder over the grown children and friends who kept them in town and helped them during their medical crisis. For Alice, kinship itself became something new: it was her friends who now constituted "the true, the spiritual family."

The influences on social ties in retirement were varied. They included the examples set by others, the timing of life events, the presence or absence of a partner, and people's styles of caregiving and grandparenting. Role models, for example, often had a critical impact on how retirees acted either on their own behalf or toward their elders. Donna was one of many who approached retirement in reaction to the negative example set by a mentor or parent. Caregivers also had genealogies, though these were often more positive. In their childhoods, both Les and Ursula had watched their mothers care for a grandmother in their own homes, setting a precedent for what they themselves would do a half century later. But when Rita nursed her husband Tom, and Nonny made "command visits" to her mother, and Inez and Martin fulfilled their "social contract," there was no denying the simple fact of duty itself that went with being a spouse, a child, or a neighbor. These commitments were as much a part of their moral biographies as what they gave to their community.

Some people struggled in their relationships with their children, their grandchildren, and their partners. Bruce and Nikka were not alone in their concern over a grown offspring who had still not found himself in the world. Sophie had an injured and unemployed son who occupied a lot of her thoughts, and Alan and Anne Freudenberg wrestled over how much support to give their adult children. But there were often elements of humor as well as worry. Alice loved to tell the story of turning the tables by telling her son to "get a life." Ed Trayvor once shared with me a Father's Day card one of his daughters had sent him. The front read: "Dad, thank you so much. You've made me all I am today by the advice you gave me." The inside said: " 'Go ask your mother.' " Frank Ryan, a 78 year-old retiree whose drug education programs had once inspired Stefan Nokalsky, showed me a new bumper sticker he had bought to celebrate his recent birthday. "Get Even," it said. "Live Long Enough to Be a Problem to Your Children."

When it came to grandchildren, several—like Johanna—expressed a preference to be with just one at a time so that each child could remain special. Only Les actually lived with a grown child and grandchild, though issues of discipline, order, and propriety came up for the Trayvors and Nonny too. And they and Les were not alone in their concern about the kind of world they were leaving their grandchildren to grow up in.

For all those entering retirement, intimacy was also an issue. Martin and Inez retired "in sync" with one another, whereas Johanna and Art did not. Yet in both instances the nature of their marriages had far more of a bearing on where their relationships went than whether or not they retired together. Timing was also less critical than quality for other people. Teri and Felix, Nonny and Ernie, the Palanoses, and the Trayvors retired purposely and smoothly at the same time as their partners, whereas Sophie and Herb, Rita and Tom, and Alan and Anne, did not. But where the Ellmans and Freudenbergs were untroubled by this disjuncture, Sophie had to turn elsewhere for meaningful companionship, just as did Johanna. The joke about not marrying for lunch only applied in some cases, as did the claims of psychologists that long-term marriages convey a benefit in adapting to later life. For people such as Johanna and Sophie, what helped their adjustment instead was the stimulation of new travel, personal interests, and friendships.[8]

Among those who retired without a permanent, live-in partner, the focus of intimacy lay elsewhere. For Les that bond was still under his roof with relatives. For Ursula it took the form of a seasonal commuter relationship, whereas Sandra had it in a weekend marriage. For Donna it was at church, with friends, and with Reggie. And for Alice it was situated in a long-distance romance and, locally, with her fellow artists. In summary, kinship, gender, friendship, values, religion, creativity, health, and chance each played a role in making the relationships of retirees meaningful.

The stories told here each have a distinctive voice, but they also express a set of concerns about human bonds that are common in the retirement experience. Five themes in particular stand out from these and the preceding accounts.

- *Marriage.* Later life casts the strengths and weaknesses of marriage and partnership into bold relief. Go ask Alice, or Johanna, Les, and the Karlers, or the Trayvors, the Levens, the Freudenbergs, Nonny and Ernie, and Felix and Teri. People may be thrown together more; their roles redefined; their relationship reexamined; and their goals reassessed. Whether or not the lives and careers of partners are "in sync" may be a critical factor, but the basic quality of a relationship is even more fundamental to its fate in the years after work.

- *Grandparenting*. Elders who are grandparents play that role in diverse ways, and retirement opens up both demands and opportunities. Les, Harriet and Ed Trayvor, Zoe Leven, Felix, Teri, and Nonny Schein showed that though some look forward to indulging their grandchildren, others feel called on to serve the young best by setting limits or setting examples for them. Retirees may have a special bond with grandchildren that bestows a unique form of gratification, but some find that they must circumvent the values and surveillance of their own children to achieve this.

- *Caregiving*. Though life after work is often associated with freedom, many retirees are confronted with heavy responsibilities as caregivers. Les, Johanna, Martin, Inez, Nonny, Alice, Sophie, Rita, Sandra, and Alan each experienced this in a literal, an emotional, or a financial sense. They cared for a parent, a partner, a child, a grandchild, a friend, or neighbor. While it is a truism to speak of the mix of burdens and rewards in caregiving, there is also a cultural element involved: many people in the so-called club sandwich generations must contend with the coincidence (or the conspiracy) that these demands come at a time when society has promised them the opportunity to finally indulge the self rather than be responsible for others.

- *Friendship*. In American society's stress on family values and the sanctity of home, the meaning of friendship often gets overlooked. That may be why some retirees, especially women such as Donna, Johanna, and Alice, are so surprised and grateful to discover friendship's special rewards at their stage of life. Although several studies suggest that retirees continue to enjoy the support of friends made on the job, and that older people, particularly women, suffer from the lack of work-related ties when they retire, neither was generally true in Shelby. Some people initially experienced what essayist Carl Klaus calls the retiree's "desire to be missed," but they soon passed beyond this.[9] Former co-workers usually receded in significance as retirement proceeded and people found other ties moving to the forefront, occasionally with neighbors or pets but more often with friends. The latter served as surrogate kin in some cases; in others they supplemented ties already there by offering new kinds of growth.

- *Gender*. Retirement was distinctive for women. It shaped Harriet's regrets, Alice's worries, Johanna's search, Donna's sense of identity, Nikka's maternal anxiety, and the caregiving of Rita, Ursula and Nonny. Men were not specifically spared any of these concerns, but their roles, and their greater material and social security, made them far less subject to these uncertainties and demands.

Kinship, friendship, partnership, caregiving, neighboring, and grandparenthood are not unique to retirement, but this life stage lends each of these some unique, often unexpected qualities. The spectrum of ties revealed here also reflects on the moral imaginations of Americans—imaginations that rest on the ability of people to see the value of others, and their own responsibilities to them, be they next-of-kin or the person next door. Though some find these connections burdens, others feel that what retirement has given them is the freedom to act on their sense of commitment to those ties. People's experience may please or dismay them, but they indicate that in life after work, not only do women and men have to work at retirement, but they still have to work at their relationships.

A SIXTH CUP

THE INCOMPLEAT FATALIST

In the end, Frank Ryan argued, it is "the unavoidable" that preoccupies us, "even if mostly we're trying to avoid it." When I asked what "*it*" is, he leaned across our cups to explain: "It's what doesn't change and won't go away. It's death and taxes."

He gave a short, sharp laugh. We were sitting over coffee in the Clockworks, Frank's favorite breakfast stop, a spacious cafeteria where he and a half dozen of his "cronies" liked to gather to "solve the world's problems." A year before, on the first morning I met him there with five of his friends, he had told me: "It's a mystery. I don't know why things are in such bad shape." Between the six of us, we've really got all the answers. Do you think no one's listening?"

The cafeteria was a perfect place to talk and muse, and the casualness of the decor and the staff gave unambiguous permission to take your time. Shelby's elders used it as a drop-in center, turning up with grandchildren in tow, crowding the aisles with shopping carts and strollers. The Clockworks had grown old with some of its patrons, its thick wooden tables and chairs darkening over the years with the touch of countless hands, elbows, and rumps. The furniture's once-walnut skin-tones had become a mahogany, which reflected the pale light of glass-covered wall lamps.

The one hint of red in the room was in Frank's cheeks, an Irish coloring that he said he had worn for all of his 78 years. "Am I supposed to be wiser? Full of good advice? Well, I've certainly lived, but the longer I'm around, the more things come down—I hate to say it—to clichés. I hate to say it because *I find myself* using them." He pursed his lips and hmmmed. "Maybe there's wisdom in recognizing that. Yes—death and taxes."

This was one of Frank's voices, but when you listened to some of the others, they revealed, as he once claimed, that he was really "an incompleat fatalist." He sometimes spoke with genuine wonderment about how his life had twisted and turned after the rough-edged working-class upbringing in a New England mill town an hour west of Boston. "My father was an invalid by his 40s—spinal cancer—while my mother was fierce, independent. Very bigoted. Dealing with her served me well with Army sergeants. I knew how to take orders and then go my own way." When Frank announced his desire to go to college, his mother gave him $20, his father a halfhearted blessing and a skeptical send-off: " 'Sure, if you want that,' he told me, 'but you'll have to do it yourself.' "

The year was 1936. Frank waited tables, delivered milk, took whatever work he could, and, despite the Depression, got the first university degree in his family. Trained as a chemist, he got a job monitoring hygiene in a cheese factory. He was living closer to Boston by then, having moved there just as war was approaching.

For a few months he had been seeing a young woman, Fiona, "suitably Irish. She seemed very sweet, quiet, a contrast to my 'gift of gab.' " But she was also like Frank in being somewhat out of touch, and out of step, with her family. "We both had education, and read too many books," he explained, sounding like a lawyer invoking the mitigating circumstance. "Impressed with our own sensitivity, we were. And lonely. So when the country finally got into the war, it just made two lonely people feel even lonelier."

They got married in a civil ceremony attended by some friends but no close relatives. "It was a mistake from the start. We both knew it. When I got drafted it was almost a relief. I read somewhere once that the war destroyed weak marriages. But it prolonged ours by keeping us apart. We did have two children, two sons, one coming while the war was on. The second was born after I came home from Europe. But that didn't help. They were nice boys, very sweet, like their mother. But she was a sad soul, and we barely knew one another. And what we got to know . . ."

This was the rare moment that Frank conceded to silence. His eyes shifted from mine to his cup. The same silence occurred when he got too close to other, more current forms of unease. There was his evident pain over his youngest son Eamon, a sensitive, promising scientist whose career crumbled when he saw a colleague's face burst with blood as a lab experiment blew up. Eamon now lived off odd jobs and welfare in Boston's gay community, with an occasional check and phone call from his dad.

Frank did not think "life itself was accidental," but he placed due weight on the accidents and coincidences that conspired to direct its course. He applied that perspective to both Eamon's past and his own. "In the war I wound up assigned to an engineering unit, which handled sanitation and health. Near the end I found myself in Germany, where they trained me to organize relief work. And my unit was rushed to Dachau when it was liberated. A buddy of mine and I stood up in a transport, watching the survivors walk to a dressing station, and he said, 'This is a ghost town.' But I thought to myself—no one said a lot out loud, we were in such a state of shock—I said to myself, 'No. Not ghosts. Not *their* ghosts, 'cause they're alive. But they are *our* ghosts. Europe's ghosts. The victors' ghosts.' "

His eyes stayed fixed on mine this time, undeterred by doubt. "There I was, trying to clean up some small part of a world that had been destroyed by the very people who were going to 'cleanse it,' wipe it clean of Jews and Gypsies and—God, we didn't even know the half of it then. I get angry at those who want to turn everything into a metaphor or symbol for something else. The Holocaust was not just some manifestation of the 'dark side' of the soul. It was not one more battlefield between God and Satan. It was real. Faith and ideals did not just die there. People did. Babies burned."

These final months of service robbed the peace of whatever peace of mind it might have brought Frank. Relieved to be "out of it, done with the war," he came home with some new skills and no sense of what to do with them or his life. He slipped back into his marriage as if it were "a robe I found hanging in the closet," and tried to "get used to being a father." Within a year, Fiona was pregnant again, and they had moved to Wisconsin, where Frank had taken a job in the dairy industry. "The more responsibility I was given for running things, the less enthusiastic I was for what I was responsible for. I was not a born leader or fired up with ideas. The war had shown me that I would have been a hell of a second lieutenant. I mean I could execute well, just not command. But I also discovered that I was good with people—good at listening, good at helping, good at getting them to work well together. Then I took some education courses, and a few in psychology and human relations at a state college. In hindsight, I feel I could have been, *should* have been a social worker. I should have pushed life, instead of letting it push me. But the idea in the Depression had been to study something practical, something you could make a living from, and I was still that way after the war. I was too timid then. I had a family to support, and felt I couldn't take risks changing my whole profession. Even when my wife and I separated I never once missed paying child support. I wasn't exactly a paragon of enlightenment, but I never failed in that."

The divorce, when it came, did finally free Frank, if not from responsibility then at least from a work pattern cast in the fears of prewar days. Though all he had to his name now was "$50, two suits, no car, and lots of debts," he still decided to leave industry and move to the public sector. His experiences in the army, the human behavior courses, and his role as supervisor at the plant had convinced him that he had the desire and skill to organize people, not just production. His love of talk didn't hurt.

Frank applied for and got a newly created job in a new organization. A consortium of communities in his part of Wisconsin had recently developed a commission to promote health education, and they hired Frank to create a campaign to raise public awareness of everyday measures—diet, exercise, hygiene, child immunization—to improve people's well-being and reduce the social costs of poor health. The position went well beyond the boundaries of what Frank himself had done in the past, but he recalled how confident he had felt then that this was what he wanted.

His claim of confidence was open to interpretation, however. When his second wife Netta joined us for coffee one morning, she edited his earlier account of that change in his life and career. "I didn't even know Frank at that time, but I *know* my Frank, and"—putting her hand on his shoulder, reassuring him for what was about to come—"he's a coward." She patted his sweater. "He's sweet, but he's *so* afraid of taking risks. So conservative. Even with all his skills. He was a real success at what he did, you know.

But he needed something extraordinary to take that kind of chance. Like his divorce."

The smile on Frank's face as Netta spoke was wonderfully ambiguous, a mix of sheepishness, embarrassment and pride. "She's right, she's right." He nodded to himself. "If I hadn't kept after him," Netta said, but then she stopped and backtracked. "When I first met him it was a few years later and he'd just begun working for the Red Cross in Buffalo. It was all right, but not all that he was capable of. After we got married, I started to tell him, Take all those credits you've collected, and start a real graduate program. Get a degree."

Taking Netta's advice, Frank had started his fifties with a new job, a new marriage, a new school. The doctorate in public health meant three and a half years of evenings and summers in class. After a sputtering start, he completed dissertation and degree just weeks shy of his fifth anniversary. He and Netta celebrated the double triumph in Italy.

Though there was no way to know it at the time, Frank returned from the Mediterranean with a dozen years of good work left to him as a community educator. He started on the staff of Taylor County's United Way, and was then asked to join a new state department for health promotion. For over a decade this unit grew, with Frank developing programs in adolescent drug and alcohol abuse. The division's directors gave him encouragement and good evaluations. But each time they reorganized the staff, they altered the unit's structure and changed its rules, and Frank's position never became a regular line in the budget.

Despite the politics that lay behind this, Frank loved what he was doing; there was an element of hopefulness in the work. He enjoyed the platform that classrooms and community centers gave him, the feeling of connection to the teenagers who sought him out in the privacy of his office. "What's life all about? You try to help people get the information they need so that they can make a better life for themselves." Charged with a sense of efficacy, Frank became active on local health boards, political committees, and church clubs. He began to take Spanish lessons, hoping one day to assist medical missionaries in Latin America.

But at work, as the years passed, Frank's desire outran his desirability. His enthusiasm for a profession he had seized on only in midlife was at the mercy of other people's priorities and prejudices. His director wanted a young staff hungry enough for opportunity to labor long hours at even less pay than Frank got. Frank himself had little leverage except for his loyalty and his desire to work at a job he had paid for by taking risks that ran against the grain of his character. But that currency bought little from his superiors. His fate was that of the Mesakin keeper of cattle. Whether "it was age or ageism," at 77 they forced him to retire.

In the next few months, though he never left Shelby, Frank was all over the place emotionally. Informed in February that his position would be terminated at the end of May, he lived out the interval in shock and in fear of what was to follow. He sorted through the notes and materials he had been using in his presentations, deciding he could at least hand them on to a younger colleague. "I couldn't face throwing them out, so I gave them to David, a youth worker. I felt if he decides to toss them all in the trash, at least I won't have to know about it. But the whole process was demeaning. It left me ruminating about my career, the path, what the point was of those fine evaluations I'd gotten. They didn't even give me a party. But the real disappointment was that I still wanted to work."

The Irish moralist in him came forward. "It reminded me of a story I heard from a friend of mine, who used to be a big name in chemistry up at the college. He was about 73, and they finally pushed him to retire. So at his farewell, his friends and the dean there made these long, flowery speeches about how he was still such a valued colleague and teacher, and what important ideas he still came up with. And when he stood up after their applause he asked: 'So why are you firing me?' "

For Frank it was a winter and spring of deep discontent. And depression. That, however, was not a truth he cared to show or tell about; the first time he spoke to me of that period he would only acknowledge being "upset" at how he had been treated, and how "bored" he'd been with his new freedom. But when he repeated that version over coffee with me and Netta, she rapped her knuckles on the Clockworks' thick wooden table, calling him to order. "It was not that simple or that tame," she said, clipping her words for emphasis. "He was a wild man! Joel, in an hour's time he could go from being furious to being practically silent with despair. This was not my Frankie. I told him he was right to feel misused, but he'd have to find a way to move on or it would kill him."

Talking to the two of them revealed how different their realities, or their chosen memories, were. Frank would own that it had not been an easy time to live through, but he always stopped short of acceding to Netta's characterization of his distress. She draped his conduct in terms he found too unbecoming. His problems had not been psychiatric ones, Frank protested, but a simple lack of meaningful work.

Though Frank and Netta went their separate ways on diagnosis, they spoke as one on Frank's prognosis. Work would redeem him. The worry was whether it would come before the reversals of retirement became a downward spiral, and mind sucked body into its wake. Redemption, when it came, was delivered through Frank's church—not by divine intervention but through the medium of Mark Swanberg, another parishioner. Mark's work as a lawyer brought him into almost daily contact with regulars at the Taylor County courthouse. Knowing not only all the judges, DAs, attorneys, and police there, he was also acquainted with other levels of staff, from janitors to clerks. He had heard that Gunther Manfield, a court attendant, was going to be stepping down, vacating the part-time position he had held there for the last two years.

"Gunny was the third older man to hold that post since they expanded the court in '88," Frank said. "Mark came up to me after a parish council meeting and said, 'you should apply for it. It's perfect: part-time, easy, flexible hours. You stay with witnesses and appellants, you show them where to go, deliver some files. Do errands for the judges. That kind of thing. I can put in a good word for you.' "

Head nodding, Frank told me, "I was really surprised that Mark had even thought of me. It was October, or maybe late fall by then, and I'd put in lots of applications—with social agencies, the hospital, two banks. Even the state employment office. Nothing. I think, with a doctorate, I must have been overqualified as well as overage. Anyway—lots of paper, just two interviews. Nothing. Whew. You start thinking about yourself. It's a moment of truth. What am I good for? Who'd want me? Will I ever get another paycheck? I wasn't ready for the Senior Center—Tuesday dance, Wednesday whist, Thursday day trip. Here I was, a health educator heading toward a bad state of health. Thinking *too* much—and not sleeping-enough."

On a Monday morning, three weeks after talking to Mark, Frank walked into court, a free man. Employed. Sleeping easier. Counting on the modest paycheck. Relieved and reassured. When he ran into Mark later that same week, just before a hearing, he took him aside in the court's main lobby and whispered a seriocomic prayer of gratitude: " 'Thank God for crime,' I joked. 'And conflict and misery. They're keeping *me* out of trouble and off the streets.' I told Mark that I really didn't wish such troubles on anyone, but the truth is, on that day they were more comforting than death and taxes."

For Frank, the best thing about his retirement was "unretiring." Life without work was not the type of life he felt fit for—at least not as a full-time commitment. A year and a half after his first court appearance he confessed to me, "I've lived my whole life as a Catholic, but I'm really straight out of the Protestant work ethic; I never prepared myself to retire. You know, the state's laws on retirement changed about seven, eight months after they let me go, and the new rule would have kept me on. Despite my age. If my parents, who probably didn't do it often, had only had sex a year later, I could have stayed! What was the rush?"

He said he had seen a lot of his friends get caught in their own second thoughts about leaving work. "First they love lollygagging around for a few months, and then they start getting restless. Some end up working in the chain stores, behind the counter three or four hours a day, especially in the winter. Then they're free in the summer for golf. So they have a little extra money, which is what we're all after, because when you're on a fixed income, inflation starts to creep up on you."

The money Frank made was a help. He and Netta used it to pay for health coverage—"I think of the court job as uninsurance employment"—and for traveling. By his second year of retirement they had gone to Mexico and were hoping, again, for Italy. The extra income also went to cover the medicines Frank used for hypertension. "Without some cash like that coming in, you'd be living on wind soup and air pudding for part of the week."

Having work was not all about finances, however. "The thing is to feel useful, and feel alive, and be a person others can respect and care about, someone they'll listen to." This was Frank's version of Freud's prescription: that life is basically about *lieben und arbeiten*, about love and work.[1]

Being open to and engaged in the world, for Frank, meant being employed in it. Then he could give of himself in both action and word.

But he also lived his retirement with a consciousness of others' diminished lives. Frank mentioned one friend, "a real Lothario," who had been in the Air Force and then worked as a pilot. "A good-looking guy, he went through a number of wives. Always had a woman on his arm. Now he has emphysema, and carries an oxygen tank instead. He's a different person." A few months later, when Frank came back from his sixtieth high school reunion, he told me the tale of that trip by the numbers: 95 out of 132 classmates were dead; 13 couldn't be found; four or five were in nursing homes. "Some who were there wouldn't talk straight, using 'C' or 'CA' for 'cancer.' As a crowd, they were a textbook picture, all the illnesses of Western civilization: heart disease, stroke, cancer, diabetes. It was depressing."

What dismayed Frank on some days made him anxious on others. "Every time something seems to be wrong with your body—you wake up, say, and your stomach doesn't feel right—it makes you scared. Is this the start of something serious? Do others worry about death this much? Too much of that thinking, it saps your energy." But Frank also tried to keep his distance from such frailty, and took pride in the sharpness of his mind. "Some of my friends, who suffer from memory loss—what they call CRS, 'Can't Remember Shit'—when they ask me what advice I can offer for their problem, I tell them, 'Don't worry. Just forget it.' "

By the age of 80, in his third year after leaving full-time work, Frank remarked how his own levels of enthusiasm and drive had dampened down. He didn't meet with his "old fart cronies" as often at the Clockworks because too many were sick or in the hospital. Yet he had decided "to combat the fear of it all" by training to be a Hospice volunteer. "I think it will be a good reality check for me. Instead of being on the outside looking in, I'll be on the inside looking out."

And when Frank could not hold court at the Clockworks, he did it at the courthouse. Both the money and the sense of purpose paid him well for his efforts. The work itself was not hard, and for Frank—like Sophie, Carl, Les, Inez, and the part-timers at the chain stores—going back to work after retiring was not the same as it had been before. Just as they had once worked at play, they now played at work.

The very nature of his job, however, also brought out the dark, ghostly side that Frank had once seen at Dachau. As was true with the health of his aging friends, some of what Frank witnessed in court troubled his heart. In the waiting and hearing rooms, it was "civilization which seemed to be in decline," its "veneer even thinner than I thought. The drugs, the crime, these kids who go in and out of jail, or Family Court, with kids of their own in tow." He took one deep breath. "So much of what's wrong with people's lives, and health, is preventable. To me, in medicine and law we should be *preventing* the fires, not just putting them out. Where's our common sense? It's too much like a soap opera in there. But these are real people's lives. It's so sad! But what do they say? What does Tennyson say? 'No language but a cry.'[2] At Hospice at least, I ease some of what's painful to others and fearful to me. It's like I told you before. In the end what we know for a sure thing is death and taxes. And in uncertain times it's nice to have something sure to hold on to."

CHAPTER 6

DEATH AND TAXES

DEALING WITH HEALTH, FINANCES, AND
FATE IN RETIREMENT

Even the most thoughtful and critical of people can get caught up in the clichés of their culture. Though embarrassed when they catch themselves voicing ideas that seem hackneyed from overuse, they also realize that there is usually a ring of truth in them. That was why Frank Ryan was not apologetic about offering up "death and taxes" in this way. Frank had found something important below the surface of American optimism. More than mere rhetoric, the worrisomeness of mortality and money, of death and taxes, could not be avoided.

Beyond the inevitability of these two matters, however, lies a fundamental issue of control. For individuals at all stages of life, a sense of mastery, control, or "self-efficacy" allows them to deal more competently with the challenges they face.[1] Many people did try to master their retirement by planning for it in the way Harriet and Ed Trayvor did. And even those who did not prepare an agenda, like Sandra Golecki and Alan Freudenberg, had usually planned their finances. They had Social Security, savings, investments, or pensions. Though these individuals had not decided in advance what they would be doing in their later years, they had at least figured out how they would be able to afford it. Sophie Malounek once phrased this as a kind of categorical imperative: "If you want to have the time of your life in what's left of your life, you'd better be able to pay for it."

But there are always some who have been less attentive or less successful at this. In certain cases they have not been able to put much away or have simply not thought their finances through. Others have been misled by their own assumptions, or by the misinformation given them by bosses, co-workers, or friends. And some have been overtaken by circumstances they could not foresee; Frank's loss of his job and Alice's divorce illustrate the impact of the unexpected.

The same mix of prudence, improvidence, and chance that affects people's fiscal status also affects their physical well-being. By the time Frank, Donna, Les, Zoe, and their peers retired, older people in the diet- and health-conscious culture of the United States had lived through decades of warnings about the impact of nutrition, weight, alcohol, smoking, stress, and exercise on their longevity. Several of the retirees had taken this to heart by altering their lives to maintain good health. Nonny danced, Felix dieted, Ed and Stefan jogged, Johanna walked, and Zoe did *tai chi*. But some had been far less assiduous about this, and still others found themselves burdened by or worried about ailments that could not have been forecast or forestalled.

Rita and Tom Ellman, for example, began their retirements with financial and health concerns that their prudent lives could hardly be faulted for. As librarian and caregiver, salesman and minister, they had worked hard for decades. They owned a modest home and had modest pensions from the country library system and Feldman's. Rita's benefits were the more munificent, and included medical coverage. But what she and Tom could afford—house repairs, dinners out, a trip—was limited. And they frequently wondered,—reaching for reassurance like Bruce Palanos—how well other retirees were doing in comparison.

For the Ellmans, even with their well-intentioned lives, the start of retirement was not propitious. Rita took early retirement to care for her mother, who then died earlier than expected. This was soon followed by full-time attendance on Tom as he healed from his heart attack. For her husband, recently returned to the pulpit after a decade's absence, the dream of resuming pastoral work was part of what sustained him through a slow recovery—along with the conviction that his near-death experience would make him a more understanding counselor to the sick.

Tom's other source of sustenance was, of course, Rita, though *her* retirement so far had had less singing, sewing and swimming than she had hoped for because of all the caregiving. Tom never failed to appreciate Rita, but saw her sacrifice from his own perspective. The signs of fatigue and the slowness in her moves that Tom detected were to him the wages of sciatica, and of being overworked and overweight. He watched Rita's efforts in some frustration, wanting to help, feeling embarrassed at being their recipient. She sensed his judgment and moods but kept her peace. Privately she told me it was not her tasks that exhausted or tired her; it was her sense that her life was not living up to its promise. For now, she'd just settle for "ministering to the minister."

Time had taken its toll on many of Tom and Rita's peers in Shelby. Age was evident in Alice's excited, arthritic hands holding a paintbrush up to the light. It was there too in Donna's back and Sandra's arthritis, in Martin's prostate and Glen's angioplasty, in Les's coronary, in Felix's and Zoe's worries about their weight, in Frank's depression and hypertension, in Alice's forgetfulness, Sophie's diabetes, and Nonny's left knee. The health problems of relatives had also laid a hand on the retirees' lives, including mothers, husbands, and sons. No generation was exempt, and even the healthy elders bore some of the weight of others' frailty.

In the three stories that follow, one woman and two men show how some retirees have dealt with their health and finances. This trio of tales considers two questions: How do differences in medical and monetary circumstances develop in later life, and what are their consequences for the quality of people's retirements? A variety of answers emerge in the lives of:

- Nate Rumsfeld, a former postman, who took early retirement only to discover that neither his finances nor his mental state were sufficient to cope with the new life he found;
- Petra van Osten, a pediatrician, whose material security allowed her to respond to a medical crisis in her own family; and
- John Sant'angelo, a highway engineer, whose career was cut short by a disability, and who now spent time landscaping his backyard instead of creating safe roads for the state.

In concert with Frank Ryan's reflections and the Ellmans' experiences, these stories carry a half dozen lessons. First, *how much time and information people had at their disposal to make a retirement decision could be as critical as the literal amount of material resources they had to retire on.* Second, *family matters and money matters were as closely connected in retirement as in earlier stages of life.* Third, *retirees' sense of well-being could be a matter not only of financial security but of the capacity to earn income, the chance to be employed, and the cultural privilege of carrying a socially respected title as part of their identity.* Fourth, *retiring by choice was profoundly different from leaving work involuntarily.* Fifth, *that the perceptions of caregivers could be quite distinct from those of the people receiving care.* And sixth, *having one's retirement affected by one's own health carried a different weight from having it shaped by the health of someone else.*

Worried to Death about Money

Alarmists and pundits often take a great deal of pleasure telling us what we already know: Smoking Causes Cancer. Diets Don't Work. Politicians Lie. One of their other favorite themes is to rehash studies which show that most people do not put away sufficient funds for their retirement. Nate Rumsfeld's problem was different: he did not have enough time to figure out whether he had enough money to retire on. "It happened too quickly. They came around the post office and said there was this new program where older workers could walk out of there with a nice package. But we had only a month to decide. Geez, I thought that would've been a few years away for me. But the supervisors said, 'This is the deal. This is your chance.' So I had to think quick. And I did it, and here I am now: short on cash, long on regret."

We were sitting in a booth at Dave's Lake Street Cafe. The cold air outside made the moisture inside the diner condense, and a curtain of beaded water had formed on our side of the window. Droplets would merge and snake down behind the ketchup bottle and sugar jar, and every few minutes Nate would carefully wipe some of them off with a napkin. At the counter, men talked and joked about contracts, engine parts, and problems with wood, and wives, that got bent out of shape. The steamy air was filled with strong laughter and cigarette smoke. Nate knew two of the men from the American Legion, another from serving with him on the board of the Volunteer Ambulance Corps. When a few of the workers got off their stools to leave, Nate called out to them, and their caps turned almost in unison: Mack Truck, Plumbers and Pipefitters Union, Moose Lodge, Tioga Rod and Gun Club.

He introduced me to Jack—Moose Lodge—while the others paid Dave's wife Kate at the cash register. "Nate, how've you been keeping?" Jack asked. "This guy," he told me, "beat us to it," but then he looked back at his friend. "You getting into it—the retirement?" Nate answered "Sure," waving a hand over his cup as if stroking his new life.

"I bet you don't miss walking your route in this weather." Jack was urging Nate to show some enthusiasm. Nate agreed how nice it was "to wake up to days that are my own." But he seemed embarrassed. It was too easy to say "yes," he told me later. It was what people seemed to want to hear. At the cafe he had said a few other things to Jack: about the garden he was planning for the spring; a trip he and Charlotte were thinking of for the summer; the grandchildren he helped get off to school most mornings. Jack joked about Nate's "life of leisure," but his tone was warm rather than resentful. He said, "When the rest of us get there, you'll have it all figured out for us." And Nate responded, "Okay, I'm getting the hang of it."

The cash register crowd waved good-bye. Nate turned back to me and then to the curtain of water beads. "That's a bunch of bull," he said to the window. "But how can I tell a bunch of guys who're going to work that I don't like *not* going to work because I could really use the money? 'Hey,' they'd say, 'but you're retired, old man, you earned it. You've got it made.' What I *made* was a mistake." He wiped away part of the curtain. "But no one wants to hear that. And I don't want to hear myself say it."

Nate's laugh was short, uneasy. He was the proverbial man of few words, and the phrases in his mouth put thoughts in his mind, as if talking it out was thinking it through for the first time. But then he got apologetic. "I don't mean to put you on the spot. It's funny; I don't want them to know, and yet one of the reasons I'm glad to help you is so others *can* know. I guess," he nodded and laughed again, "I guess I'd rather they just hear it from *you*."

What Nate wanted others to know, the moral of his personal tale, was a twist on a saying he remembered from back in his childhood: "Decide in haste and repent in leisure." He rephrased it as "Retire in haste and you won't *be able to* repent in leisure." Seven months ago, at 59, leaving his job at the post office was as far from Nate's mind as some of the countries that printed the stamps in his mail sack. He had walked the streets of Shelby for over 35 years, delivering "letters, bills, bad news, junk and joy." Except for two brief periods—one on a rural route with a mail truck, the second a desk job scheduling carriers—he had, at one time or another, covered most of the town's neighborhoods and its main business district. Other than an army tour in Korea just after the war there ended, the post office had been Nate's only full-time work since high school.

For over three decades his life had been remarkably stable. In a century whose finale had been marked by a surfeit of divorce, social dislocation, and corporate downsizing, Nate had so far escaped all three upheavals. Married to Charlotte, his high school sweetheart, since the early Eisenhower years, he had raised two sons, one of whom lived across town, the other across the road. He saw two of his grandchildren nearly every day. He had kept the same house and employer for almost all of his adulthood. Even Nate's chosen role as citizen, serving as a volunteer driver and ambulance corps commissioner, had been built into his weekly routine for 24 years.

When the first word of an early retirement program was broached at work, Nate barely heard it. The very idea seemed clearly directed at other people. He had just turned 56, and in a detached way he wondered what those who were "senior" to him would think of it. "I thought of them as a different generation. I didn't realize until later that those guys, and a few women, were not my father's age; they were only four or five years older than me. It's funny when you think about how you see other people sometimes."

Only a few of Nate's "seniors" took that first program, which was called, by its promoters, an "incentive package." The deadline for signing on passed, and those who had signed it passed on to other things with little fanfare. But there was something new in the air even after they all left. Nate and his age-mates would get teased by younger colleagues about "being next." The first time this was said to him, the reference was obscure. Nate simply did not get it. But the second time, the point was unambiguous, and the news of the day helped him understand.

It was the summer of 1992 and the Democrats had just finished their nominating convention. In his acceptance speech for the vice presidency, Senator Albert Gore Jr. had hit on a popular refrain when targeting George Bush, the Republican incumbent. Gore led the delegates in a call-and-response rhythm that opened with a jab at Bush's age, energy, or ideas, cueing the convention floor to answer, in chorus, "It's time for him to go!" At the post office the joke was nonpartisan but no less pointed; for Nate and his fellows, the joke around the locker room was that "it's time for them to go."

There was even less subtlety from supervisors, who asked Nate how he would respond to a future "package" and what ingredients it needed to be attractive to him. He answered evasively but honestly: he really did not know how he felt or what he would want. He had never given it much thought. Then they changed his job, taking away one of his regular street routes and replacing it with part-time desk duty. That was boring and, by design, he felt, demoralizing. Nate had always loved walking the streets, being with people, following their lives and being a part of them. He knew practically everyone he delivered to, and what they feared or looked forward to in their mail.

Then *his* mail came, in two installments. The first was from the post office brass. A year and a half after the initial package had expired, a letter "from the guys upstairs" announced that a new one was being offered. In the description there was a formula for figuring out the size of a one-time lump departure payment—based on rank and years of service—and details about medical coverage and pension eligibility. A time frame for accepting the plan was also outlined. A few days later a second letter came. This one was from the union. It touted the package but also carried a thinly veiled moral message: older workers should think not just about their well-earned rewards but about the families and futures of their younger colleagues, about making way for others, "just as others, in their time, have made room for you."

Nate was caught in a classic squeeze between the right to retire and enjoy its benefits and the duty to retire and make room for those coming behind.[2] For Nate, the mixed message was also filled with uncertainty. The package sounded good; the taunts of co-workers didn't. The half-days at the desk dragged on. The union was long on encouragement, and the decision-making process short on time. Beneath it all ran an undercurrent of judgment, about older employees blocking the well-being of others. Nate talked it over with his wife and sons. "I only knew a few other men who were eligible, but they kept to themselves about what they were going to do."

Twice Nate went to the union, "and they gave me numbers, dollar amounts, but they told me it wasn't for them to say how well that would hold up in the future—you know, inflation, cost of living, that kind of thing. The half year's pay was the prime incentive. And my accountant told me I could survive. Then the union man said: 'Hey, you can still get a part-time job if you want, and collect all of this. So it looks like a pretty good deal for a guy your age.' "

Nate bought the package. It took him about six months to realize what was—and was not—in it. That was how long the novelty of pure leisure lasted, the excitement of making plans for gardens and trips. That was how long it took for the first few sets of bills to come in and for the bottom line of his finances to reveal itself. "My checks were coming in steady then, and so were those 'love notes' from the gas-and-electric company and the phone company, and I could see what inflation was going to do. We'd probably have enough to live on, but nothing left over. Vacations? Presents for the grandkids? What if the car went?"

It was clear that even with Charlotte's job as a receptionist, Nate would need to find some part-time work. When that settled itself in his mind, it surprised him by *not* bothering him that much. With hindsight, he later told me, he was able to grasp that he had really not been ready for full retirement. At the time, though, the decision to "un-retire" surprised him because he thought, so far, he was following in the footsteps of a man "who'd gotten retirement right," his own father-in-law. "Charlie bought a lake cottage, fixed it up, and was always busy doing things. I learned from him because we resemble one another: plan something for each day, even if it's only for a couple of hours. So I had a list of jobs for each morning."

Those first months Nate took up watercolors, cooked, remodeled the kitchen, and helped with Jody and Matt, his grandchildren. Most days he would give them breakfast and walk them to school. "It seems when my sons were growing up, I was always working at the post office, or these part-time jobs I had roofing or painting. It's like I never saw them grow up. But I enjoy my grandchildren tremendously."

It wasn't long, however, before Nate discovered a reversal of both his fortunes and feelings. By the half-year mark he found that "planning and making dinner, the house repairs, getting Matt and Jody off to school didn't amount to much. Someone needed to do all these things, sure, but most of the day was still left, which was too much time to think about the bills and taxes I wasn't making money for. So when I figured I needed to work to make some extra money, that was okay. I guess it was a relief to think of myself as not being so totally retired."

The relief, however, like the "honeymoon" of retirement, was short-lived. It ended almost as soon as Nate began to look for a job. "I put in to be a parking enforcer up at the college. No high-tech skills in that. But then I didn't hear anything from them for weeks. So I called. 'Oh,' they said, 'we don't need you! What the . . . !" He shrugged and tilted his head, trying to reproduce the disbelief he had felt. "Then I saw in the paper they were hiring security guards at the mall. I'm pretty fit and alert. And here's my army and ambulance experience—you know, being good in a crisis. But again, the same story! 'Geez,' I said to myself, 'what's going on?' Finally I went to the state employment office. Joel, I'll tell you, what a shock: the lines, the interviews, all those forms. I hadn't looked for a job since leaving the army and landing at the post office. 'Work history?' I had just that one job to put down." He pulled out a clean napkin, holding it up to read as if it were one of the forms. "References? Career goals? Computer skills?!"

The morning we sat in Dave's Cafe was the ninth month of Nate's retirement, the third in his serious search for work. He wore a pressed shirt and a worried look. Though he had never tried imagining all of what it would be like to be retired, he had never dreamed of it this way— to be fretting over money, looking for a job, dealing with rejection, and asking— and being asked—too many undreamed-of questions. Had he been fooled? Had he fooled, or failed, himself? And his family?

"Leaving the post office itself was pretty disappointing," he recalled. "There was no real party or celebration. The last day they gave me a certificate saying I'd worked there for 35 years, and we shook hands all around. That morning my wife and son gave me a card. But up in my office there, I really felt alone, just waiting for 4:30 so I could go home. I was at the top of my pay grade, full benefits. And here I'm going to give it away. Had I made a big mistake? I brought home a box with coats and hats and a few other things I'd kept there. But I shoved the box in a closet, and it's still sitting there. It seems I keep forgetting to unpack it."

On several occasions, when asked about the hardest part of retirement, Nate gave me different answers, variously focusing on disappearing people or broken promises. When he was a few months into it he said he was most affected by "losing contact with people. You become isolated real fast. The men from work who said they'd call never did." He admitted, though, he had never called them either. He told the union he'd be interested in helping them. They said fine, but never got back to him. "So I guess once you're out the door, you're out."

Other people either misled or confused Nate. His family had contradictory things to say when he was trying to decide about retiring. His oldest son told him to "get out and enjoy life." Charlotte, on the other hand, was very hesitant, feeling he was making good money and that they could use the salary. Nate's brother, an electrician, told him not to worry—he could easily get him work to do. A friend who painted houses said the same. But Nate's mother warned him: Be careful; you'll get bored; stay with what you have. Over at the Ambulance Corps, the men gave him lots of encouragement.

Nate summed up the impact of all the input in a careful reflection. "In retirement, it's not the watches that get broken, it's the promises. No one who talked to me about a job came through. I came to feel you can't rely on anyone, and I'd never felt that way before." His next words had the ring of a Mesakin herder, unwillingly put out to pasture. "Society tells you if you want to be an adult, then be productive. Then at work they say, Hey, make way for these others, and be happy about it and don't complain. You're told retirement's going to be great, but then the money's not there, or the jobs." Not having applied for work, literally, for over three decades, Nate compared retirement to some of the worst features of being a teenager: "It's like starting all over again after high school. Having to make your way, learn everything from scratch. You're grown up, but you've gone backwards, not forwards."

For Nate, the meaning of life had always been to "make the best of what you have. Living life as it's given to you. I'd always thought, get married, have a nice home and family, do my yard work, help the community and the grandchildren. I had no big desires and didn't expect to be a millionaire. So I can accept what I am and what I have. But it's hard to 'make the best' of it when you've gone into 'retirement shock' and your wife is on your case."

One year and two breakfast meetings after our morning at Dave's, Nate and I got together for coffee at the Clockworks. It would have to be brief, he explained. On Tuesdays he only took a half hour for lunch so that he could be home early to drive Matt to soccer practice.

Nate worked three days a week now at the Evergreen Savings and Loan, the same bank Johanna had been "merged" out of, where he delivered parcels, paperwork, and files to various departments and branch offices. He joked that his skills had been "privatized," but that he was glad to still be a postman. Yet it was too ironic an outcome to pass without further comment. "All that work and worry," he said before we got up, "and I'm back doing pretty much what I did before. I went from re-tired to re-hired."

At home, he reported, "things have been better and they've been worse." Like Frank, he had gone through a period of depression. He wondered if others had suffered that too, but he had kept it from most people, while inflicting it on his wife. He suggested I ask her for a "second opinion." Charlotte once described Nate after the "honeymoon" to me in terms that echoed those used by Netta: although he tried to stay busy with house projects and a bit of jury duty, he had been "irritable" and "withdrawn." Yet, she added, "he denied it. Wouldn't put a name to it."

Once he was back at work, Nate at least found it easier to talk about the other ways his marriage had been affected. "We're out of sync with one another. I'm a new hire and don't get the kinds of time off Charlotte does, or the choices she has about when to go. So it upsets her that it's hard to follow through on plans we'd made. Once in a while the wife says what I did was not fair, that I took advantage of her. She doesn't usually come right out with it, but it's like letting me know how much she looks for bargains. Or 'We can't go out tonight. It'll cost $20. Maybe we'll go next week.' "

Working, however, did make it easier for Nate to account for himself to others, and that was a great weight off his mind. "Now when someone asks 'What are you doing?' I can say 'I'm working at Evergreen Savings,' and they say, 'That's good, that's good.' " The need to have an answer was, perhaps, at least as important to him as the answer itself.

That left one question still unanswered. "Well, now I don't worry so much, but I don't know if it was worth it, or if I'm really even retired. So what am I? Semiretired? Semiworried? It's okay, I guess, but I wouldn't know what to call it." He picked up his pouch from the Clockworks' floor and smiled, laying a finger on my forearm. "That's for you to figure out."

The Doctor's Prescription

Nate's challenge was a reminder of how language has not caught up with life style. There is no standard phrase to describe the transitions he and Frank Ryan were going through, though their preoccupations could be subsumed under the words "work" and "worry." For both, the need and the desire to have a job did not end with retirement. And though Nate had retired willingly, and Frank involuntarily, financial insecurity troubled each man. For Petra van Osten, however, those concerns had long ceased to be an issue—well before retirement began, even before work began.

As a physician, Petra claimed, she had been given "a doctor's prescription" for her life, and for her retirement, back when she was an adolescent. At that age, though she was a child of the Depression, her physician father had urged her to follow in his footsteps. Neither her gender nor the economic climate of the times was seen as a barrier by either of them. And Petra was an ambitious and dutiful daughter who was easily drawn to medicine. Her admiration for her father extended to the profession and the kind of life he had chosen. "My one rebellious act," she once told me over tea, "came at the end of high school. I refused, absolutely, to follow my parents' wish that I go to Bryn Mawr. And I insisted I had to go to Wellesley." She laughed at that piece of her own history, mocking her adolescent self with the question, "Lord, how principled can you get? One generation's rebellion is the next generation's joke."

Tea that day was in the solarium of Petra's home, where she lived with Elliot, her husband, who was also a doctor. A particular medical detail to the afternoon was the sling that supported Petra's left arm. It kept the weight off her shoulder, which had been operated on two weeks before. Muscle problems there had caused several separations, and had troubled

Petra for the last four of her 63 years. But these had been only a minor factor in her decision to retire. A pediatrician, she had shared a family practice for close to three decades. Petra still loved medicine but was tired of full-time work, especially the business of managing a practice in the face of managed care. "For one thing, I don't have the energy I used to. It isn't that you're too tired to do your work. It's that you're too tired to do anything else. Also, the amount of hostility toward doctors—from the government, the public, insurance companies, HMOs—it's demoralizing. We're not all angels, but by and large, we're the good guys. Even Benjamin Spock; I didn't always agree with him, but I admired his activism. But the way the media seized on him, and on the physicans who've ripped off Medicaid, all make it easier for people to blame doctors for immorality and meddling where the public thinks we have no business."

Listening to Petra list the symptoms of the medical profession made it clear why, with increasing age, she and her shoulders could only support so much. For about 18 months before her surgery she had wavered over retiring, and then acceded to Elliot's wish that they do it at the same time. She gave her partners a year's notice, found a young doctor to buy her share of the practice, and began making her peace with letting go.

Petra had grown up in privilege, but she had worked hard her entire adult life. Her large, tasteful home, with its gardens and ornamental grasses, had not been bought with "old money." Her father had been able to spare his daughters the harshness of the Depression, and he had given them an education still rare among women of their generation. But he had not bestowed a large dowry or inheritance on either of them. Petra's main assets in early adulthood had been her father's example and his gift of medical school tuition.

During her residency in Cleveland, Petra had met Elliot at her hospital, and they had both stayed on in Ohio after marriage. One year ahead of Petra in getting his certification, Elliot, a urologist, worked as an emergency room physician until Petra finished out the second of two fellowships. They were then ready to take their next professional steps together—a stress on synchrony which was still operative, three decades later, when their retirements approached. "Elliot argued with me two Christmases ago that I should cut my plans short and retire when he did—because I still owed him a year."

She shifted slightly and sat up taller in the cushioned wicker chair. "But you'll never guess what I did! I made sure I retired about six weeks *after* he stopped. Why? Because then he would have to be home alone for a while, and learn to do the laundry, the vacuuming, the marketing—sort of a residency in domesticity—the things he'd assumed only I should do. I didn't want to get into that Tarzan and Jane routine. If he sees it's not child's play, I figure he'll be more willing to participate. I have to train him, otherwise we'd be into a pattern I'd have to fight to get out of."

Besides gender wars on the homefront, the prospect of retirement brought adolescence to mind for Petra. To her way of thinking, the resonance between these two stages of life was that in entering both periods, "you have to invent yourself. You make up your own vocabulary to describe what's happening. I see my teenage years as a time of great change. You're getting in touch with yourself, all kinds of talents and skills, and disasters. There are tasks of adolescence, and I guess there are tasks of retirement too. When you're young you're preparing for a career. Retirement's the reverse, giving it up and choosing something else to take its place. You may not have that much money in either period, or in retiring you learn to make do with less. The big difference, maybe, is how 'more and less' change places. Adolescents look forward to more power, privileges, new responsibilities. In later life what a lot of us look toward is what we are going to get rid of!"

Three decades before Elliot's "residency in domesticity," the van Ostens had faced another passage in life when they moved to upstate New York. Though new terrain to each of them, it was a return to the small towns they had both grown up in, and midway between their families in Connecticut and Pennsylvania. Shelby offered Petra a practice that she could work her way into and Elliot a staff position at Taylor County Hospital. They came, they stayed, they raised two children. Petra treated two generations of other people's offspring, including Alice Armani's sons, Sophie Malounek's youngest daughter, Stefan Nokalsky's son Ken, Becky and Ben Ulanoff, Rosa Pintero, and Matt and Jody Rumsfeld. When she had hung out her shingle at the age of 31 and begun to examine patients, Petra did not imagine that some of the first children she saw would become the parents of some of the last children she would treat.

When her own offspring came along—first a daughter, Megan, then a son, Paul—Petra was able to scale back her hours and her patient load rather than stop work entirely. With time, as her practice and her children grew, life got more established. She came to feel a stake in the community, and helped to found a day care commission. Later she got embroiled in sexual politics, serving on a task force for a new high school curriculum on reproductive health. It was one of the issues that later almost unhinged Stefan Nokalsky on the school board. Petra remembered "some of the frightened, know-nothing forces we were up against! These people wanted their kids to believe that Easter eggs were laid by the Easter bunny! But it wasn't funny. I'd never been called a subversive before. Me!"

Like the onset of adolescence for her own children, Petra's ventures as a volunteer marked the end of her innocence. "Forget politics and religion as 'taboo topics.' Try parenting and sex to see how thin people's skins and tolerance are. I lost it once at a public meeting. I shouted at another member of this panel, 'What are we trying to teach these young people: fairy tales or responsibility?!' " Petra's view of her community altered, shifting a few shades darker. "It was good, I guess, to see all that. I was less naive and more effective, but I know I was less happy with the world."

Staring into her cup as if reading the leaves, Petra remembered the past. For a second she bit her lower lip. "You hunker down more when you realize how much ignorance and evil is out there in the world. Doctors see some sides of it that others don't. It was sometime around then that Elliot began to talk for the first time about retirement. It was still maybe ten years away. But we'd both worked very hard, and our children were no longer kids. So when I'd get really tired from mothering, going to the office, running to the hospital, and suddenly remembering I had a meeting to get ready for, I'd allow myself to dream of what it would be like without all that. It was a nice fantasy in my forties. It was the great one of my fifties."

Individually, and as a couple, the van Ostens started putting into pension plans and retirement funds early. Besides those and Social Security, Petra's share of her practice was an asset she knew they would be able to cash in when the time came. As retirement approached, then, her feeling was that with the exception of her shoulder, her health was good, and her finances even better. One of her most emphatic pieces of advice was "save, save, save!" but she was quick to add that, as a person, "you should think about developing yourself. Your job can't be your whole life, because then who are you when you retire?" In her own case, she had a closet full of fabrics and a love of sewing, and she also toyed with the idea of volunteering for a stint in a clinic or a developing country. She hedged her bets by renewing her subscription to *The New England Journal of Medicine* because she could not believe "the day will ever come when I won't be reading it." She also saw her last year of work as an important time to "create continuity." In selling her part of the practice, she found "a worthy successor," a woman with a strong commitment to prevention, someone who she was optimistic might carry on her community work too. "At least I can hope. I just can't guarantee it."

Petra and Elliot mixed practicality and sentiment in another process, the critical one of drawing up new wills. There was a lot to take into account—not so much in terms of their assets, which in her view were "modest and straightforward"—but in terms of children and grand-children. They had two grandchildren from their daughter Megan, and two step-grandchildren from her husband Hector's first marriage. And there was a new baby on the way now from Paul and his wife Arlene. "Do we leave what we have to each of our children equally, or to each of their offspring—including the step-children? My daughter and son's spouses are of a different religion from me. Megan's husband Hector is Hispanic. There is a blended family there, the possibility she might adopt the step-kids. All the social trends of modern times. Plus revocable trusts, powers of attorney, executors. Writing out these terms and arrangements is not exactly like making a wedding. We'll provide and protect as best as we can, but these are wills for the '90s!"

What Petra's prudence could not protect against, however, was that part of life and health controlled by fate, by the genes. The cruelty of that lesson came home just a few months before the van Ostens were set to retire. Arlene had given birth to a baby boy, Daniel, who had been diagnosed, soon after delivery, with hemophilia.

Petra and Elliot were no less vulnerable to shock, dismay, and disbelief because they were doctors. Petra remembered how "your knees buckle, you reach for a chair, you collapse in tears. And suddenly the only word you have is 'no, no, no.' " The shock of Daniel's illness, though deeply troubling and life-changing for his parents, did not alter any plans that Petra herself had been making, mainly because her plans for retirement had themselves only been sketched out in the broadest strokes. The van Ostens already knew they would not stay on in Shelby permanently. But when they would leave, and where they would go to, were undecided. What they had agreed on, well in advance of the end of work that summer, was a framework for making a decision.

In the solarium over tea, six months before Daniel's birth, Petra had told me: "We know we want to be some place warm. Mostly, though, we'd like to be near our children—at least one of them. Unfortunately it can't be both: Megan lives in Tucson, and Paul's in Richmond. But that's the American family nowadays, right?" Unsuspecting of what Daniel would bring with him into the world, Petra had said, "Right now we've set up our next vacations to take a better look at both Arizona and Virginia. With a real eye to what it would be like to live in each place. We've visited them before, but never looked at housing, and culture, and what there might be if Elliot or I wanted to work or volunteer part-time. You don't think of any of those things if you're just visiting your kids."

So they had spent parts of December in Tucson and February in Richmond, giving each place close to two weeks. When Petra and I met again for tea at her home in March, she summed up the visits by saying that "both places seemed possible, but so different. Megan's new family, Hector's, is Mexican-American, and they are incredibly warm and so child-oriented. We could learn a lot from them. But Virginia," she took a deep breath before going on. "What keeps popping out of my mouth when people ask about it are 'green' and 'gracious.' It's the kind of beauty we've always loved. Maybe because we're such Easterners, and the South just seems to take what we have and make it even richer. The homes, too, are so comforting. And the people are more polite, and I don't care if some think those are clichés." She shrugged her good shoulder. "I'm not sure *how* we'll know. I'm just glad we don't have to rush. There are so many houses, so little time."

Then in late April Daniel was born, and life's pre-ordained progression seemed to collapse. The moral order that young and old count on, the idea that elders will be outlived by their children and grandchildren, was threatened with violation. As a pediatrician, Petra knew how basic and how frail such hope could be, how much her "own profession had elevated it almost to an American assumption."[3]

We met again in mid-June. Petra invited me to her office, and took me outside to a stone bench on the lawn behind the medical building. It was her next-to-last day at work, the seventh week of Daniel's fragile life. As she spoke, Petra's teeth came down hard on her lower lip. She was torn between those parts of her that were parent and doctor. The mother love and compassion were easy to feel, to express. But how much to suggest and inquire about as physician? "How much to be the advocate, the expert? I have never felt so careful, so tempted, so unsure. I know my medicine, Joel, and I tend to act quickly and decisively. But here I know I could so easily step over the line. I said to Paul and Arlene, 'Look, you must, you *must* let me know how and where I can help, and tell me to back off if I'm out of line. I don't want to make things any harder for you.' "

Amid all the fear and uncertainty, at least one thing had been made easier. Petra felt, and Elliot concurred, that they should move to Virginia. The reasoning was more convoluted, however, than necessity or parental obligation would suggest. They discussed the idea with Paul and Arlene. They did not want to impose or intrude, to make a difficult situation worse by adding another generation's worried presence to a crisis with a surfeit of drama. Petra reviewed the various conversations the two couples had had, reminding me of how drawn to Virginia she and Elliot had been even before the birth. But eventually she admitted, "I told them, and I realized it only as I was saying it, that I could not feel good about myself, decent as a person, if I was so far away, and that it would actually be easier for me to keep a proper distance if I could be closer to them."

In a large sense, the move for Petra meant not only a change in venue but, as had been true of housekeeping, a need to reinvent her life without reinventing herself. The challenge lay in how to incorporate "work" as well as "homework" into that sense of self. She told me, shortly after settling into her new home near Richmond, that she did "not want to trade 'Dr.' for 'Mrs.' van Osten." But though she was clear about not being recast as a housewife, Petra's ambivalence about returning to work had not really dissipated. Her daughter-in-law Arlene had given her the name of someone who could help her locate a position, "but I keep losing the phone number. So what am I telling myself?" Yet six months later, Petra had settled the matter the other way by becoming a paid clinical consultant for the local Planned Parenthood—a post that was sufficient but also part-time enough for her to keep both her title and her freedom.

Petra had found moving to a new community to be a bit like the excitement of "the first day of school. Finding out where everything is. How to do things all over again. A new setting, strange people, meeting your neighbors, even finding a new dentist and church." She and Elliot had made some new friends, and they both had cousins in the area whom they were getting closer to. After two years in Virginia, Petra described those ties now as "seamless. Intervals don't matter. We pick up exactly where we left off."

In other parts of life the edges were more visible. Daniel had gotten through his first 29 months, but there were repeated crises and constant worry. The van Ostens' marriage had reverted to some of its old patterns, though without the Tarzan costumes and the commands. Elliot was doing occasional shifts in an emergency room, which was a relief to each of them, and Petra had picked up her sewing again. They had both let most of their ties to Shelby drop, and rarely went back to visit. "It's that quaint American ritual," she observed. "It's down to Christmas cards."

The decision by Petra to begin her retirement by leaving Shelby was not at heart, or at first, a response to a family crisis. The likelihood that she and Elliot would change their residence—to be in the warmth, and near one of their children—had been laid out well before the baby.

In the end, in fact, the van Ostens' life was essentially as it had been at the beginning: house, marriage, and medicine all still part of it, with minor variations.

But what no doctor could have prescribed or predicted was the nature of what they had to remedy in retirement: how to be available to family without being invasive, how to stay engaged in life without letting work become intrusive. What Petra's career in particular had given her was not just the technical skill but the emotional intelligence she needed to handle these tasks. And what medicine had also bestowed on her was the money and the means to make her commitments not just a hope, but a comfortable and comforting reality. Like teaching sex to teenagers, the lesson she had in mind was about responsibility, not fairy tales.

The Sculptor of Water

The town that Petra left behind may have lacked the warmth of Virginia, but it had, for others, a richness in its own cold history, for Shelby sits in a region of upstate New York whose features were carved by the fingers of the Ice Age. The town's geography is a local instance of North America's larger antiquity—one in which water has been a sculptor on a continental scale. Time has brought it the knife and trowel of glaciers, the snaking of snow and rain-fed streams carving out mountains and filling lakes, the run of rivers that drain and feed and flood the land.

Few of Shelby's residents saw and felt time's imprint the way John Sant'angelo did. From his kitchen table you could look out a large picture window to a one-acre pond bordered by woods and backed by hills. There was a small dock, a beached canoe, and in the early spring, ducks and other wild fowl feeding near its shallow edge. Depending on weather and season, one could also see deer, raccoons, hedgehogs, squirrels and muskrats. Inside the home hung John's own watercolors of birds and leaves, and below these, leaning against the wall, his pair of walnut canes.

The pond, the paintings, and the canes each bore John's own mark. He had designed the pond while he was still working and reasonably well. A civil engineer, employed for 22 years by the state, he had "worked with what time did to the landscape," creating highways and bridges and rebuilding parts of the Erie Canal. The latter project had been the "pride and joy" of his mature years on the job. That assignment had involved reconfiguring the Erie's locks, integrating the water flow with the region's drainage system of lakes and rivers, and researching the history of the canal's construction and its economic significance.

To John, who loved both the planet's landscape and the human impulse to toy with and reimagine it, his role on the canal and pond was akin to that of an artist, "a sculptor with water." As an engineer, he saw earth, fire, and water as his media. He used to argue this view of his profession with Martin Karler, especially after his friend took up welding and sculpture in retirement. Martin, who lived on a lake, was never convinced by John's logic, saying he preferred "nature unmarked." But John challenged him to find "anything left in the state" that merited such words, and he would point out the dirt road and wooden boardwalk to the Karlers' own house, the posted woods and low stone walls in the nearby hills, and the steel figures and geometries that Martin made in his studio to put on his land.

As a sculptor, Martin explained his creations as "just an extension of his art and hands," not a part of or "a comment on nature." For John, however, what he did in his own backyard bore a kinship to what he himself had done on the canal. He had taken special pleasure in bringing his professional skill to the pond—"domesticating it, you might say"—by carrying his craft right into the heart of the space he lived in.

With John, whether talking about bridges, the elements, hunting, or his own tendency to argue and procrastinate, there was a painstaking intelligence at work, one that kept curving back on itself, forcing a reconsideration of already well-considered points. At age 54 now, he described decades-old highway projects in great detail, recounting the "endless, sometimes ridiculous politics" of trying to get county and town officials and local property owners to work with the Department of Transportation. Having negotiated so many agreements whose ultimate goal was to protect others from the vagaries of weather, machines, and human error, John was not insensitive to the fact that, in his adulthood, he could not protect himself from accidents that were bred in his own bones.

It happened early to John, too early to be fair, the result, he mused, "of a design flaw": arthritis at the age of 22. He was in his third year of engineering school when the symptoms first appeared, and a senior before a probable diagnosis could be made. Depressed for the first few months, he then turned with a fury to his studies, graduated, and took a job with a major construction company. By the time he was married to Fae at the age of 26, he had been asymptomatic for almost two years. John gave himself over to hope and denial until his knees and hips said no.

"I went to the company doctor, who couldn't cure me, but who saved my life, you could say, in another way. 'I'm not going to put this down as arthritis,' he told me. 'Rheumatoid arthritis? There's enough room for doubt—the hell with it.' He was a nice old guy, retired, filling in for someone on vacation. 'If a condition like that went on your record,' he said, 'you might never get another job, at least not with medical coverage.' I don't know why he offered to do that. He just did. He was pretty sympathetic obviously. He understood the consequences better than I did. Maybe he had some arthritis himself."

The good doctor had a long-term view that John would need several years to appreciate. This only dawned on him when he was filling out some papers about ten years later. John had left the construction company to take a job with the state, and on his first day at his new post, sitting with a stack of insurance forms in the personnel office, he realized he was bringing two intangible assets with him: for the job itself, his years of experience; and for his health coverage and family, the official lack of any preexisting condition.

To have a good civil service job with good benefits was no small triumph to a young man with a young family and an uncertain future. John had married before changing positions, and then decided to work for the state because it promised more security. He reasoned that if later on he could not travel or move easily, there was always administration. He thought it out like chess, or an engineering problem. And he was neither disappointed or defeated except by the one force even engineers can never command, which was nature itself.

John's second child was born five years before he needed his first hip replacement. Thirty-eight at the time, he now had a daughter as well as a son, neither of whom he could easily bend over to pick up. "When my children were little, I expected to worry about *them*, not fret about myself. I guess that's what I thought being a parent was all about, because when I was a kid, I was always troublesome. It must be biblical," he joked, reaching for irony. "Too much Sunday school, right? After all, Adam and Eve's first act was one of disobedience, the one thing that God told them *not* to do. Not an auspicious beginning," he summed up. "We've been disobeying our parents ever since."

The childhoods of John's son and daughter were not like his own. The kids were good and *he* was the worrisome one. His doctors tried physical therapy, experimental drugs, different pain killers and dosage levels. Periods of remission came and went. Nothing was stable. His moods moved more easily than his joints did, and his marriage, taking the strain, bent out of shape. But it didn't break. In the better times he began new projects and hobbies, some of which were manic at heart—he dug the pond, carved dozens of beautiful duck decoys that still awaited his paint brush, took up skeat shooting, and began writing a book on the history of canals. The pond was one of the few undertakings he finished. At work, he managed to keep his projects on track even though he had to spend more time at his desk now than in the field.

"It meant engineering people, something that twenty-plus years of schooling had not trained me for. And it's really the hardest part of building anything big. And of course, it's the stuff your teachers never talk about. People way below you in the hierarchy have more power than you ever dreamed of. Some crew foreman who just doesn't like the look of your face can be more trouble than some incompetent geologist or some messed-up calculations. That's another book I should write—the one on social engineering!"

By the age of 54, John was several years past his fourth hip replacement, and his back was in chronic pain. He had been using anti-inflammatories, on and off, since 24. Sixty percent of his spine was fused. Medication and physical therapy now seemed to have exhausted their potential. He had tried every doctor and treatment in town. He had gone to an arthritis support group but stopped after a few months "because all they ever did was hold fund-raisers." Joining a swimming club had been "much more real"—it was the same one, in fact, that Rita Ellman went to for her sciatica.

John's humor helped, but it couldn't heal him. By his mid-50s he was going to a pain clinic in a nearby city and seeing a local psychiatrist to keep his mood swings in check. Totally reliant on his canes to get around, he was less and less capable of doing his job well. "What I was looking at was disability, SSI, early retirement. It was a bureaucratic dream," he huffed, taking another tilt at irony. "No. It was actually a nightmare, all wrapped up in a neat little safety net. I couldn't believe it was happening to me. I thought I was going to retire when I wanted to, on my terms. I really felt I had it beat, because I'd made it to 55, speed limit, more than twice the age I was when I got out of college."

He raised a cane for emphasis. "They gave me a wonderful party at the end. A lot of people showed up—more than I'd ever seen at one of those events, including some who I thought for sure must have disliked me. They said kind things, lots of detail, so it seemed like they had really thought about it. I hardly recognized the person they were talking about! Maybe it just seemed that way because of the medication—theirs or mine!"

There were enough people around to worry about John, and some to worry him in return. His married son Billy now lived "just a thousand yards away," and he had a 96-year-old aunt and a mother, 88, in the area, both of whom had health problems that went "on and off in sequence." Then there was misplaced worry: as soon as John stopped working, his wife got anxious about their finances. "I explained to her that with disability, and the stock market, and my pension, we've actually got as much money as before. Fae knows it in her mind, but she can't quite fathom it. Our generation was probably the last one to look for security in a job and long-term benefits. I told her that possibly, I could have worked a bit longer, but if anything had happened to me when I was off the job, I might not have been able to get disability. Then we really would have been in deep . . . trouble. Is that polite enough?"

In earlier years, being honest about his health was more problematic for John than talking about his character. When his children were little, he had decided to keep his true condition a secret from them. Though both his son and daughter now criticized him for this, John still felt it was a good choice; it helped give them "a more normal childhood because they felt they had a normal father." The cost to him now, however, was that "they are less likely to console me. There's no history of compassion. Still, I know I look a lot worse. When I'm on the street I'm noticed because I use two canes, not one. People can absorb one without thinking. Two is a bit of a spectacle."

By the third year of his retirement, John had added some other aids to his mobility. He had bought a new van with a specially designed door and hand controls that made it easier for him to get in and out and drive. Retirement had made him both more self-conscious and more self-reflective.

Once, when we ran into one another at the farmers' market, he remembered visiting his mother, in his late 40s, at her senior housing complex. One of the other residents there had asked John how much he got from his pension, mistakenly assuming he was disabled, retired, and living there. John felt insulted, taking the question as implication: that he was unproductive and living on "found money." Yet a mere seven years later he had become what he had only seemed to be a short time before. "Retirement really did add insult to injury."

John's feelings were complex, and they varied with each of our visits. At the market he confessed that "the toughest, or the most perilous thing about retirement, is that you have time to slow down and reflect. If you view your life negatively, that's pretty serious. I run hot and cold on that; the thermostat keeps flipping over. You certainly can't change the past, or who you are. I've been lucky and I've been cursed. I never thought I'd make it this far, and still there's an underlying dissatisfaction with what I've done. It comes with being a Type A—the kind who's never satisfied. I went into this world adventurous, outgoing, and I was cut down. People will tell you, Oh John, he can handle it, he's held up well. But I don't know that I have. I could have been happier. I'm the kind of guy who built the pyramids, ran railroads right across continents. When I do things, I want to do them right. Now I see my unfinished projects all around me."

Another time, near the start of his fourth year of retirement, John gave a somewhat different cast to his enthusiasms. "I've literally seen guys die within 12 months of retiring because they had no interests. My problem is I have too many—so maybe retirement is as tough on me as on people who aren't doing anything. I'll never be content because I always want to try what I haven't done before." He told me his decoys and canal book had been inching along, but that they had been eclipsed, recently, when he got involved with the Lake District Land Trust. "Their struggles there keep my baffle going up and down."

John was amused when describing how his entry into that organization had puzzled some of those he knew there. "Martin teased me. Teri Rogers was surprised. Al Freudenberg, who I used to lock horns with at work, when he heard about it, he joked (I think it was a joke), 'Watch out—he's an infiltrator.' But engineers aren't all destroyers. Of course we change things, because we all have to live on this earth and use it. The whole point of life is to create and improve—leave the world a better place for our efforts. That's why I'll always be an engineer. But I respect the land, and what's natural on it. That's why I love to hunt and fish, and make a small world with this pond. People see this as contradictory, but it's not. To me it's really so simple: it's live and let live, and recognize what needs to be used and what's meant to die."

The figures of speech John favored—life as an engineering project, the metaphors of baffle and thermostat—came up in other contexts. "Up and down," "on and off," characterized the way he saw his retirement's first three years, their intimations of mortality. "The first 18 months had moments of euphoria because I hadn't been sure I'd make it to my 50s, and be able to take care of my family. So my responsibility was sort of over—but then I realized I had this responsibility to myself. And I saw that when my mother and aunt died I would be the oldest member of my family. Now my aunt's gone, and I'm not sure how I'm going to handle the next one when it happens. I need to know there's some relative older than me and that I'm judging my life by theirs. Who will I compare myself to?"

A few months later, back in John's living room, he picked up the thread of his retirement's early days and the years just before it. "I'd always told myself, well, if something like this happens, if I have to stop work, it'll happen later, when I'm old and ready for it. I'll say goodbye to my work not the other way around." He looked through the window. "So I have this pond, which I'm still playing with. I want to get enough depth and flow to keep bass in it. I'd love to draw some beaver in here too, but with all the birch wiped out I don't know. Fae thinks I'm crazy, but doesn't care so long as I take my pills and don't mess up the lawn. And the canal book's fun to think about, but maybe too monumental." His voice trailed away, and came back as a soft cough.

"Hey," he said, "how did I get here? I figured back then, when I was playing with the locks—the biggest toys I'd ever been given—I've got time. Now I have all the time, and I still don't have enough of it. It's not part of a man's thinking at 30 or 40, or even 50, to imagine that day when time's not on your side. When you discover it's not, you can't figure out how the two of you ended up on different sides of the fence. You just look across at it, as if you're going to say, Didn't I love you enough?"

Meaning, Money, and Mortality

In Genesis, said Rita Ellman, she could not fathom "why work was punishment," the lifelong charge that Adam carried out of Eden for the first sin. To her work was a gift, a form of service, a path *to* grace. That Rita and John Sant'angelo had both referred to the original Fall *from* grace surprised me, but it became less of a puzzle when I realized the different emphases these two gave to that story. Was the loss of Paradise a tragedy or an opportunity? Did it turn on curiosity or sin? Was the road from Eden an exile or a journey, and did its steps lead us to mere labor—or responsibility? John and Rita, as retirees weighed down by the burden of illness, brought their personal histories to that primal scene: John, his love of trouble and knowledge; Rita, her respect for work and its rewards. They each indulged themselves with a bit of interpretation, perhaps a bit of heresy.

Their biblical remarks were more than just a play on words, though. They highlighted the realization that the meaning of retirement is open to question, and that there is a significant difference between asking about the meaning *of* retirement and about the search for meaning *in* retirement. People's well-being in this life stage embraced a number of cultural concepts and contradictions, including those of security and risk, voluntary and involuntary statuses, the work ethic and the play ethic, mortality and morality, and the pressures to be productive and to step aside. As John's experiences, and those of Tom, Rita, Nate, Frank, Netta, and Petra also demonstrate, health and finances could play very distinct roles in the lives of people, leaving some relatively free of care and others worrying about themselves or those around them.

The weight of worry and the luxury of freedom are not strangers to the elders of other cultures, but their significance varies from one society to another. Older Bahamians, their lives centered on the care of grandchildren, get financial aid from their sons and daughters and help with health from their own knowledge of bush medicine. The African Korongo look for company to the peers in their age-grade, and for security in the transfer of cattle to their younger kin. The neighboring Mesakin do the same, but defer that succession for as long as possible, living in fear that age and witchcraft will catch up with them. Abkhasian seniors are burdened with neither of these concerns, enjoying good health and substantial support well into advanced age.

Chinese and Inuit elders depend on their offspring for a home and security, whereas retired Irish couples reserve a room of their own and a plot of land for their own sustenance. A good Irish death means dying in your own bed, alert, surrounded by kin, and celebrated with a wake; for the Chinese it means knowing that heirs will carry on the family line; for the Inuit, that reincarnation will animate them anew in the name, spirit, and body of a newborn child. For aged Indians too, reincarnation is a promise beyond this life, but they can also seek to transcend rebirth by walking the *sannyasin*'s path.

But the elders of Shelby were much more concerned with the here-and-now than the hereafter. To Frank, an involuntary retirement constituted a blow not only to his self-esteem but to his wallet and his physical well-being. A midlife career change, a risk occasioned by his regrets, had brought him great satisfaction at the cost of long-term security. His wife Netta realized that behind Frank's penchant for denial and jokes was a vulnerability of spirit and body. In reviewing his life, he judged not only his own morality but that of friends, fellow soldiers, the Germans, the Allies. What saved him from further despair were good fortune and friendship, the fruits of which were a new job, enhanced income, and a reborn sense of engagement with life.

Unlike Frank, both Nate and Petra had had stable marriages and work histories throughout their adult lives, but there the similarities ended. The most fundamental divide was economics—the gap between the monetary rewards of delivering mail versus those of delivering health care. Petra had worked hard, but felt she could still contribute to a society grown less enchanted with her profession. Nate believed he had followed the rules and led a decent, dutiful life, but that the promises of others and his own culture had misled him. And both these people worried, but about different things: for Petra, and her husband Elliot, it was a matter of where to live; for Nate and Charlotte it was how to live.

The situations that John Sant'angelo and the Ellmans found themselves in differed in yet another regard. In both their cases, health displaced money at center stage, but it did so in distinct guises. John's on-and-off chronic arthritis had troubled him for decades before forcing an early, sometimes angry retirement—one in which he dwelt, alternately, on his strengths and his works, his flaws and his fears. And though he had left work involuntarily like Nate and Frank, in John's case there were no obvious villains—bosses, co-workers, or indifferent unions—just an unlikely hero or two: a part-time company doctor and, perhaps, John himself.

Amidst the diversity of 26 lives, a few commonalities stood out in retirees' views of living well. When asked what advice they would give to younger people, virtually everyone said to save and invest for retirement, and start doing it early. "Begin with your first job," urged Zoe Leven. "Watch out for inflation," warned Nate. "Get new appliances before you retire," said Inez Karler. "Maybe new teeth, too" added Martin. "Live below your means," cautioned Ed Trayvor, "buy the cheapest house in the most expensive neighborhood you can afford—or your pride will come back to haunt you."

Several, like Frank and Stefan, took warning from having lived through the Depression; to not work was too scary to be seriously considered. Men such as Frank and Nate also came out of blue-collar families, and so the desire to resume some job in retirement had deep and multiple roots; their gender, self-image, present needs, and past experiences all conspired to make it hard to live without labor. Others, whether they worked or not, held on fiercely to their professional identity; Petra, would always be a doctor, and John an engineer.

But there were also cautions against unrewarding effort, such as Alan Freudenberg's warning about "working for nothing" if new income were offset by higher taxes and lower Social Security payments. Still others, like Alice, were more anxious about outliving their assets—a legitimate worry, especially for older women who brought to retirement not just passion but a fragmented work history, the lack of a pension, and unexpected insecurity. In sentiment, however, almost all the retirees, regardless of gender, disagreed with Thoreau, who a century and a half ago, before pension checks, railed against "spending the better part of one's life earning money in order to enjoy a questionable liberty during the least valuable part of it."[4] For the older people of Shelby, the value of neither their lives or their liberties were in question.

The second most common caveat voiced by Shelby's elders was to take good care of your health. They variously jogged, swam, dieted, gardened, golfed, walked, hiked, danced, and practiced *tai chi*. Only John felt he was living on borrowed time, but there was no denying the toll time took on everyone's body. They all suffered from something: arthritis, asthma, diabetes, hypertension, sciatica, depression, weight gain, memory loss, blocked vessels, creaky joints, bent backs, enlarged prostates. Many talked of less energy, of needing more time to do things. Frank felt it "almost too ironic; at the very stage of life when time has suddenly grown short, you must give up more of it to accomplish less."

Not everyone possessed Frank's sense of irony, but most were with him in seeing health and finances as interlocking pieces of the puzzle of later life. People worried whether they'd would have enough money to pay for medical coverage, and whether they'd have enough health to enjoy the retired life they had saved for. They fretted over how much money or help to give children and grandchildren, a dilemma solved in different ways by the Palanos' sublet to their son, the Freudenbergs' allowances, Alice's loans, Les's gifts, and the van Ostens' new wills. Marriages as well as bones creaked under fiscal uncertainty, a truth to which Nate, Frank, John, and their spouses could all attest. And perhaps Frank himself did not know how much he had borrowed from Benjamin Franklin, who had beat him, by some two centuries, to the observation that "in this world, nothing is certain but death and taxes."[5]

How did people make sense of their own frailties, and those of the others they saw around them? Tom felt his brush with death would make him a better minister to those in failing health. Some, such as Sandra, Les, Ursula, and Rita, found fulfillment in caring for their mothers. But in Rita's less guarded moments with Tom, one could also see how caregivers sometimes put on a false face for the world to hide the resentment that is such an understandable but unseemly companion to self-sacrifice. And in coping with decline, there was also a generous allowance of humor, regardless of how often it served to bolster people's defenses and denials—Les anticipating himself in the lake; Frank advising CRS sufferers and the forgetful to "just forget it"; Alan's political spin that "dying is democratic" because "everyone gets to do it"; Zoe putting down the PC police for calling the aged "chronologically gifted." And behind it all was a skeptical tone that questioned the mythic magazine cover image of a free, secure, and healthy late life. Though people's dissatisfactions had less to do with the impact of retirement than with the inevitable effects of aging itself, there were some, such as Nate, for whom the broken watch was really a broken promise.

Death lies deep down in the Latin roots of European sensibilities in the concept of *memento mori,* the small daily experiences that remind us of our mortality. Depending on what we are personally attuned to, the mementos may be found in the sound of bells or songs, in old family photographs, in a sudden shortness of breath, or in meeting a person with a lost loved one's name. To some scholars, life from middle age onward is lived in the shadow of death.[6] In retirement, each experience of loss can make death more a familiar, more capable of taking on the shape of each person's own self. That was what inspired Sophie, Felix, the Karlers, and others to retire as early as they could, while they still had the health to enjoy it fully.

Retirees were generally not reluctant to talk about the deaths of others or their own mortality, and they were often quite critical of friends and family, including their own children, who continued to deny, avoid, or taboo the whole subject. Thus Sandra Golecki took her sons and daughter to task for failing to thank her for the Living Wills that she and her husband had sent them. Frank was more irritated than amused by friends who insisted on saying "C" or "CA" instead of "cancer."

People also made a kind of sensory sense out of mortality. Touch, sight, sounds, and even smell could play a part. Alan held some piece of his life in his hands with each paper or project he chose to keep or discard. Felix and Teri once told me how the temporary experience of sleeping apart— the absence of the other's touch and odor when Felix had the flu—was like "being" alone; it was, for each, a small, nightly taste of the other's death. For Felix, the quiet terror he felt at the prospect of completing his writing project perplexed him until he realized that his "fear of finishing" was rooted in his emotional equation of completion with death. Teri, on the other hand, was led at 60 to the prospect of her mortality by the colored light and sculpted clouds of an October sunset; how many such autumn moments would be left to her, she wondered, in a hopeful allowance of 20 more years of life?

Other people's frailties or deaths were both *memento mori* and a stone against which to sharpen the keenness of appreciation for the life one had left. That was part of what made retirement a liberation for Alan, Alice, Zoe, and Sandra. When Donna Younger felt the full weight of her father's demise and her strange sense of being orphaned at 63, that was the moment when, finally, she took on the mantle of being an elder in her own right. Along with her whole generation, she had graduated. Yet that was the very rite of passage that John feared most. And for Sandra, having cared long and devotedly for her dying mother, it was the sound of the zipper closing the body bag that resonated, mantra-like, in later years. When they zip up the bag on me, she asked herself, what kind of accounting would I be able to give for my life? That imagined moment became her question for the present: What can I offer others in the here-and-now that will give my hour of death a note of grace?

In questioning themselves and retirement, Shelby's retirees turned to a very basic vocabulary of what and when, where and who, why and how. Lacking consensus but not curiosity, their answers turned on some of the central and endlessly discussable facts of life. Though they enjoyed different outlooks and degrees of health and wealth, their experiences included some shared dilemmas and lessons. Seven of these deserve special mention.

- *Getting help and finding time.* To make good decisions about retirement, people need access to sufficient information and informed, sympathetic help in order to choose among options. They also require adequate time to sort through those choices in the light of their values, their dreams, and their fears.
- *Family matters.* Although it is individual women and men who retire, they rarely do so in a social vacuum. Money matters, like health matters, are also family matters. When and how a person retires will thus affect—and be affected by—the well-being of significant others. These relationships will help determine how fulfilling and responsible a retirement can be.
- *Voluntary and involuntary retirement.* People's feelings about retirement are shaped by whether it was imposed or chosen. Voluntary retirement

in Shelby and elsewhere is tied to better physical and mental health and a more positive attitude. This can be equally important regardless of whether the critical forces contributing to this decision were acts of personal will or the dictates of bosses or health.[7]

- *Self and others.* Most people enter retirement with at least minor if not major health problems of their own, though few retire specifically because of a medical condition. On the other hand, older women and men may be very aware of how retirement affected the health of *their* elders and peers, just as caring for others may turn out to be a much more common feature of their own retirement than is usually recognized. Health as an issue in this life stage, then, comprises far more than just the well-being of the retirees themselves; it includes the statuses of those who have gone before and those who live around them.

- *Money and work.* Though retirement is often defined as withdrawal from work, many retirees continue to hold or seek part-time positions. Up to a third of women and men take up a job within a year of retiring.[8] For some, it is the nature of the work that is most meaningful; for others it is the reassurance that they are still employable and productive; in other instances it boils down to the need for the money itself; and for some who had once worked at play, it is now the ability to play at work.

- *Morality and emotion.* Even for people who do not consider themselves to be very philosophical or spiritual, retirement often becomes a time of reflection. It brings into play a broad palette of morals and emotions. These can include a sense of responsibility, altruism, commitment, obligation, and reciprocity; and feelings of anger, depression, mortality, worry, hope, enthusiasm, gratitude, regret, and resentment. People will differ in how keenly these are felt, and in how they choose or choose not to act on them. But along with medicine and money, these sentiments loom large in older people's mental and moral well-being.

- *Perspective and perception.* A single life may be seen from a multitude of perspectives. The accounts that retirees themselves give of their lives and feelings may alter over time, and also differ significantly from those offered by their friends, partners, and relatives. To discover what retirement is "really" like thus requires taking into account not only the stories of many people's lives, but the accounts that different people give of those lives at different moments in time.

In retirement, we can usually draw on six or more decades of experience to address these issues. Whether or not we choose to do that, our own mortality is near, as is that of some whom we know and love. The security we have wished for is tested daily by governments, markets, policies, and employment patterns that most people have limited control over. And the dreams we have had for ourselves call out to be questioned or realized.

Whether our attention turns to our fiscal health, our physical well-being, or the intangibles that form the substance of our hopes and our relationships, many of us—like Nate, Rita, Petra, Frank, and John—will continue to wonder how we got here, and what it all means. Retirement presents us with the opportunity, and sometimes the necessity, to confront those questions. For individuals who take these issues on, a key part of the meaning of retirement, then, is the search for meaning itself.

CHAPTER 7

CONCLUSIONS

LESSONS AND CAUTIONS

The young sometimes resent the old for their visible reminders of decline. But then they envy their elders the freedom, wisdom, and serenity they are presumed to possess. Older people are often puzzled by both aspects of this contradictory image that others foist on them. After all, they do not consciously go around as living signboards proclaiming, "The end is near." Nor do most assume or advertise that they are blessed with a lifetime of insights. Others may have assigned them to a state of grace, but elders themselves have not claimed it.

These paradoxes in the relations and perceptions between the generations underlie several important questions. What can our elders, and their retirement experiences, really teach us? Who do they look to as role models in making *their* decisions about the years after work? What forces shape their relationships to family and community? What do they need to know and what lessons do their lives convey about the larger society?

The people of Shelby described herein found answers that were diverse and ambiguous, and that shifted as their lives progressed. These qualities—diversity, ambiguity, and fluidity—reflect the fact that retirement expresses some of the deep contradictions that aging evokes in our culture, and that retirement itself constitutes an unfolding process rather than a single event. These features of maturity have implications for policy makers and social planners, and are given almost daily voice in our ongoing public debates about the appropriate ages for mandatory retirement and Social Security, about Medicare eligibility, and about generational equity.

The variety of older people's lifestyles is itself one of the fundamental lessons that Shelby's elders can teach us about this stage of maturity. Just as individuals pass through and come out of childhood, adolescence, and adulthood in different ways, these women and men show that the experience of retirement cannot be reduced to one scenario or stereotype, even among a group of white and largely middle-class individuals. Their diversity confirms what other studies of the life course have shown, which is that the lives of older people are far more varied than those of children and young adults. Unlike adolescents, who are mired in a conformity of clothes and music, retirees are considerably more individuated.[1] Thematically, several other issues also emerge from their stories, including insights about ritual, control, creativity, home, community, work, passion, friendship, family, gender, morality, mortality, meaning, health, responsibility, aging, and the very process of studying retirement. These themes, and the highlights that ended earlier chapters, point to a concluding set of lessons and cautions.

Lessons

• *Know thyself.* Other than saving and investing for financial security, there is no one way to retire. How people approach retirement needs to fit their personality, their circumstances, and their values. Several of Shelby's retirees expressed this idea of being honest and "true to yourself" in the form of rhetorical questions. Are you, as one put it, a "Zen master" who likes to leave things open to chance and novelty and does not want your retirement to be guided by the past? Or a "master planner," who wishes to work out an agenda of goals and purposes and achieve some of what you have dreamed of in the past but have had to defer? Are your possessions, a key part of your identity that you do not want to part with, or can the process of sorting out and giving some away help to clarify your life and your own feelings about mortality? Are you a "settler" or a "cowboy"? Is your primary attachment to a home and community that you feel deep roots in, leading you to want to "age in place"; or is your fulfillment to be found in journeys and a life in new places? In essence, these questions imply, a fruitful way to approach retirement is to follow the ancient Greek advice to "know thyself." That wisdom underlies the commitment of many older people to transcend America's "waged and staged" way of life, to define their retirements instead of letting "retirement" define them.[2] Those who can do this are able to turn retirement from a cultural "construction" into a personal creation open to many meanings.

• *Leave on a good note.* The way people end their full-time work can set the tone for how their retirements will begin. Individuals who retire by choice tend to do better than those who leave their jobs involuntarily, regardless of whether that exit happens because of uncooperative bosses or poor health. A meaningful retirement celebration is also important—one with guests who matter, a thoughtful gift, and an opportunity for the person being honored to reflect openly on his or her work, its legacy, and hopes for the future. The collective experience of Shelby's retirees indicates that it is best not to place too much stock in highly formal events that feature polite supervisors, canned speeches, clichéd presents, and formulaic food. These ceremonies may be a necessary but are rarely a sufficient way to mark a person's entry into a new phase of life.

• *Come to terms with letting go.* People do not retire just from a job but from a long adulthood of employment. The stories they tell of their labors and careers thus constitute an important way for them to make sense of how they have lived, and of their contributions to a company, an agency, a personal agenda, or a community. Their sense of accomplishment often proves more lasting than workplace friendships, which often do not endure into retirement.[3] It is important, then, for retirees to find a way to review their history and to come to terms with its fulfillments and disappointments. The opportunity to do this satisfies their psychological and moral need to be able to give a good account of themselves *to* themselves, as well as to others. The pride and self-respect expressed in such stories echo the satisfaction that businesspeople and motivated employees find in "staying the course"at work.[4] Doing such a "life review" is not just a retrospective project, however, an effort to sustain "ego integrity" or one's sense of a "continuous" or "ageless self"; it is part of people's active engagement with the problems and promises of the present, and connects the lives they have so far lived with the ones they are leading now.[5]

Being at peace with retirement can also be a matter of coming to terms with succession. Some men and women are deeply concerned that their legacy of programs and accomplishments from work will be carried on by those who succeed them; others have little investment in this. There are also retirees who feel the need to compare how well they are doing in life—how much fun they are having, how much money they have, how good their medical reports and spirits are—with peers who have made different choices about retirement. Such individuals like to compare themselves to those with poorer health, fewer resources, and less freedom, or they may contrast their current lives with how they lived in the less fortunate periods of their own past. They thus come out well in comparison, illustrating what one gerontologist calls "the relative meaning of relative deprivation."[6] Retirement then becomes another way that some Americans have of competing with one another, and with themselves, for success in life. And, finally, the very notion of "successful aging" can itself be a burden to those individuals whose health, finances, or lifestyle have moved beyond their control, despite their best efforts to be prudent. They feel that this idea over emphasizes the image of fit elders, patronizes others, and overlooks the fact that an old age free of worry and illness is ideal, not real. After all, there are still death and taxes.[7]

• *Take time.* When asked what retirement *is*, people commonly answer by talking about what it *is like*. That is, they turn to metaphor. Retirement is like "a month of Sundays," "an endless weekend," or "a long vacation" say some, focusing on the *quantity of time*. Others, by comparing it to the excitement of adolescence or the freedom of drifting or bicycling, instead stress a *quality of life*. But the responses of still other retirees contradict or caution us about such images, and carry the implicit warning: beware of metaphors. They note, for example, that holidays and weekends are special because they are short. Take away the brevity, and what is unique becomes everyday—and so retirement can soon turn commonplace. Even adolescence, which means freedom to some, conveys insecurity and disadvantage to others.

People also differ in their perception of how time passes in retirement. Many argue that time feels short because they are "busier than ever," whereas others complain that the sudden "gift" of time disorients and embarrasses them, eroding the structure they require in their daily lives. That sense of "busy-ness" is more than just a new wrinkle in Parkinson's Law, the idea that work expands to fill the time available to do it in.[8] Rather, it suggests that retiring creates for people a reordered sense of time. The convenient figures of speech that women and men resort to, then, can obscure how ripe this stage of life is with both promise and threat. The use and misuse of such common expressions indicate that it is important for people to take the time to discover the *kind* of time they need and want to live their lives by.[9]

• *Invest in passion*. There is no age limit to enthusiasm, and retirement is a period in which individuals can discover or rediscover their passionate interests. These can take many forms, including creative production, public service, travel, or spiritual and personal growth—the kinds of involvements that many people once consigned to weekends, but which can now become the focus for a new way of being and a reason for living. Consider the changed lives in Shelby: the firefighting sociologist; the banker who found Buddhism; the Marine who took command of the school board; the social worker who fell in love with Rembrandt; the advertiser who went on an odyssey; the engineer who now sculpted water; the doctor turned moral historian; the technician turned teacher of *tai chi*; the teacher who became a trustee of the land; and the musician who now orchestrated archives.

Whether people move out more into the community or take "a turn towards interiority,"[10] this diversity is at odds with the words of Willa Cather, Donna's favorite midwestern novelist, who says through a character in *O Pioneers!*, "Isn't it queer. There are only two or three human stories, and they go on repeating themselves as fiercely as if they had never happened before."[11] Instead, Shelby's retirees illustrate the various influences of personality, history, and cultural values in shaping people's choices, regardless of whether men and women describe themselves as a Type A, a hermit, a good guy, a gray-haired nomad, a farmer's daughter, or a product of the Depression or the Protestant ethic. Such expressions reflect the kinds of cultural vocabularies people use to understand and advertise who they are. And the reflections of retirees urge us also to pay careful attention to the example of the negative role models—those whose retirements were a disappointment because they failed to plan or find purpose for them. We all need more positive and realistic models of how to negotiate this life stage—not just the idealized public figures who have done it to perfection, but the people who show us how *not* to retire, who can be as instructive as those who exemplify good ways to do it.

• *Expect the unexpected*. Retirement evolves in stages that can include a "honeymoon" of travel, unscheduled days, and indulgence; a time of exploration and reflection; and the development of a weekly routine that, for some, may involve a return to full-or part-time work. Being retired does not preclude being rehired; a meaningful life may lie in work *or* alternative pursuits. As in earlier phases of life, however, mature people also need to expect the unexpected—illness, divorce, financial changes, family crises, caregiving responsibilities, and unplanned opportunities and interests, all of which can alter the course of retirement as it unfolds. Setbacks to a person's own health or that of someone close can radically alter even the best-laid plans. Older men and women may have to let go, then, both of their delusions of indispensability and their illusions of control as their retired lives develop.[12]

• *Family matters—and so does gender.* Retirement is a time of life that can change all of a person's relationships. Only a few people exit from work at the same time as their partners, and such timing may be less critical for the health of their retirements than the basic quality of that intimate relationship. Furthermore, the partners themselves often perceive the changes wrought by retirement in very different ways.[13] And partners may need to renegotiate not only their household economy and roles but also how much support to give to grown children and how close or distant to be from them. Regardless of whether people enter this stage of life with or without a companion, retirement is not gender-blind; men are more likely to have difficulty leaving their work and career identities behind, and women are more prone to experience financial and social vulnerability.

• *Use freedom responsibly.* The popular image of retirement emphasizes its reward of freedom, but such a view is narrow and naive. It fails to consider two different kinds of freedom: the negative freedom *from constraint*, which does not always guarantee the positive freedom *to do* what you want.[14] Thus, many retirees discover that their freedom from work does not necessarily liberate them to engage in all the activities they had dreamed of. Retirement does, however, create the freedom to be responsible in different ways: to be involved with family and friends, to be a caregiver, to be of service to the community, to realize one's gifts and talents, and to take responsibility for one's own health, possessions, and finances so as not to be an undue burden on others.

In moving between these freedoms, retirees usually replace the "work ethic" with a "busy ethic" whose moral message is: Stay active, engaged, productive, and self-sufficient. To the extent that Shelby reflects the larger society, it is the rare person who is disengaged. The widespread pattern of unpaid work that retirees take on supports arguments that, socially and economically, we should count the efforts of such people as part of the productive contributions older individuals make to our world. Recognizing the value of what elders do would not only enhance the self-esteem of such people, but also acknowledge that our communities could not function without the services they provide.[15] Most retirees live their lives in concert with Thoreau's warning not to act "as if you could kill time without injuring eternity."[16] The myth that Americans now labor less and have more leisure thus seems as questionable in retirement as in earlier phases of life. But the emphases do shift. People who once worked hard at their play and their jobs are now likely to work hard at their retirements, their commitments, and their relationships—and to play, instead, at their work.

Cautions

Communities, like books, have their characters, and Shelby was no exception. It was small enough to be knowable, large enough to get lost in, diversified enough to be compelling. And in the lessons of its characters' lives lay the poetry and poignancy of the everyday. The 26 women and men I got to know—postman and secretary, engineer and minister, musician and teacher, designer and lawyer, librarian and doctor—were not a representative sample in terms of race and class. But I was not trying to "represent" the community so much as explore how some of its members dealt with aging, maturity, morality, and the new American life stage of retirement.

Writing a community's biography through the biographies of its people is an American literary tradition. It is the essence of Sherwood Anderson's *Winesburg, Ohio*, Edgar Lee Masters' *Spoon River Anthology*, and Thornton Wilder's *Our Town*.[17] But I could never have invented or imagined the lives of Shelby's elders, nor did I need to invent the means to study them. The anthropologist's classic techniques—participant-observation, interviewing, and eliciting life stories—proved to be very portable, as much at home in a rural American town as in Samoa, the Congo, the Andes, or the Arctic. There were some unexpected moments, however, and—in at least one regard—the methods were perhaps almost *too* close to home.

For one thing, people's participation in the research did affect them. There were times when I asked questions they had never thought of, and so by the end of certain conversations, not only had I learned something but so had they. Carl, for example, had thought a lot about his father during his own adulthood, but not as a model—especially a negative model—for retirement. "I hadn't pictured him in those terms until you asked who I did not want to emulate. Now I realize that's a big part of what he stands for to me."

Second, participants and I also came to realize that their own accounts of their lives and their retirements were not necessarily incontrovertible. There was Netta Ryan sitting down next to Frank and me in the Clockworks, telling him what he was "really" like in the early months after he stopped work. Or Nate, urging me to get a "second opinion" by interviewing his wife Charlotte about his state of mind in the first few months after he left the post office. From Felix himself there were quite divergent accounts of the "first" and the "second" time he retired. There were also the independent references to the end of Eden and the start of human labor by Rita and John, each of whom invoked Genesis to derive different morals from the tale of work. With Rita and Tom, there were distinct perspectives on what their marital and caregiving relations were like. Thus, getting different people to talk about the same lives, and asking each person to talk about his or her own life at different points in time, produced distinct versions and interpretations of the same stories.

Finally, the chance to keep rethinking peoples' experience of retirement was one of the dividends of time—the result of anthropology's emphasis on long-term involvement in community life, rather than hit-and-run survey research. Hanging out with people, rewalking the same paths and revisiting the same topics, sitting with them over teapots and coffee cups, listening to their words and reflections over weeks, months and years—this methodology revealed that retirement is more than just a last day at work, the signing of forms, a farewell party, or the first Monday at home. It is an ongoing process during which people have to get used to being retired, and to coping with it, to establishing a new life, creating a new identity, addressing their dreams and disappointments, developing a sense of purpose, adjusting their relationships, and learning how to look at their past and look into the mirror. Recognizing how the lives of such people overlap through work, local government, places of worship, and voluntary organizations also allows their community to become a character in its own story.

In the course of this research, my life and the life around me became richer and also socially and morally more complex. Doing research not just in my own culture but in a neighboring small community meant it was hard to leave the field because the field never really left me. This had happened to me before in Shelby when I had spent nearly a decade visiting Elmwood Grove Nursing Home, and found that residents wanted me to advise their children or contact their lawyer; or that their families needed an advocate, a fellow mourner, or a witness; or that their nurses and aides wanted comfort or absolution. Years later I was still running into kin and caregivers whose history and conversation I continued to share.[18]

Now, with the community's retirees, I was once again among individuals whose lives were part of mine, not just people in far away places whom I would see, perhaps, once every few years or, maybe, never again. So a few months after my study presumably ended I walked into a concert and met Stefan, who wanted to know whether I could write a letter to the editor in support of his slate for the next school board election. I strolled through the farmers' market and ended up having tea with Johanna, hearing about the "retreat" she and Malvina had just returned from. Would I, by the way, like to donate to their study group's clothing drive for Tibetan refugees? Another day, at a nursery, I met Sophie, who was almost in tears about her son. His back was not responding to treatment, and he might have to go on disability; did I know a doctor who would be more sympathetic than his physician to supporting such a claim? And then one afternoon, crossing the street to get my car, I ran into Frank Ryan as he was entering the Clockworks. . . .

A FINAL CUP

THE BROKEN WATCH

We pushed our trays and cups along the rail at the counter, picked up two kaiser rolls, some packets of cream and sugar and, at the cash register, we played out our usual little scene. "Frank," I said, reaching into my pocket, "this time I'll. . . ." He never let me finish or pay. "I'll take care of this," he cut in on cue, speaking straight to Jimmy at the register. Frank liked to treat. He needed to; it was the kind of gesture that mattered, an act of graciousness that earned him far more merit than money alone could buy.

Most of the tables were empty, and so the sounds of our spoons, cups, saucers, and voices seemed to bounce off the walls as we settled in. Frank was usually pleased with the sound of his own words; he liked to tease as much as he could out of language, and laughed at his own jokes with the pure delight that only pun-makers really know. But this day, after we sat down, he was soon subdued, as if the quiet around us had made him self-conscious.

"Are you okay?" I asked. "Is Netta?" "Yes," he answered with a low tone and a quick lift of his hand that said their health, of course, was not the issue. He started to speak, and then stopped. He put his index finger through the handle of his cup, and used it to rotate his drink a full 360 degrees on the saucer. The gesture seemed to have the effect of moving a dial to "start" for him. He took in a breath.

"Remember my friend Mark? The lawyer from my church who helped me get the courthouse job? Well, I just came from there"—Frank's voice was inching up to its normal speed and volume now—"well, they canceled today's court calendar because the judge got sick, but I saw Maria Kovich, who's an attendant there like me, and she told me Mark had a heart attack last night." He shook his head and went on. "They called an ambulance and rushed him to the hospital, but it was no use, or too late. Maria said he'd died by the time they got to the emergency room." Frank's shoulders rose and fell in one quick punctuation.

I traced the rim of my own cup with a finger and told him I was sorry to hear. "How long did you and Mark know one another?" But Frank was well along the path of his own thoughts and did not hear my question. Instead, he pursed his lips, looked up at me, and continued.

"Sometimes, in your mind at least, you know how you make elaborate plans, full of details, about how to live—or how to die? Because your time is your own now, and then 'Time' takes over and makes a fool of you." He paused. "You start making bargains with God. Like me. Recently it's been: okay, give me just a few more years. I'd like to have until 2000—not for the end of the century, but to see my grandson graduate high school. What's behind all the bargaining? None of us are ever really ready to let go, not if we have decent health. We'd all like a little bit more time—and then a bit more again. It's foolish, but human I guess. I don't know where I'll be next year. Really, if I let myself think about it, I don't know where I'll be tonight. Did Mark know the answer to that yesterday morning?"

The question was not asked with an answer expected. So where did we go next? I pushed at memory's door. "The first time you spoke about Mark to me, you described him as—what? a happy, a hopeful person." Frank liked that. "Yes, yes. Both those things. He felt blessed. A very successful career. A good marriage. Nice kids. Grandchildren . . ." Frank went on, describing Mark personally, professionally, choosing words that might have been used for Carl, Petra, Ed, Harriet, Alan, and some of the others I had gotten to know, men and women who had had long-term careers and long-term marriages. But Frank wanted to be clear that, for him, Mark did not just stand for a "type" of person or lifestyle. There was a moral quality too. Mark going out of his way, for example, unasked, to help Frank find a job. "He paid attention to the people around him. Mark didn't just take refuge in his comfort, you could say."

Frank elaborated, drawing up images from the past and the present. "I appreciated that quality of his, the reaching out, because I know what a tendency I have to pull back; sometimes I think it's more because I'm in shock than that I'm indifferent to what I see around me." He cited the teen pregnancies he'd known at work, the divorce cases in court.

"At Dachau, after the liberation, some of us were numb, silenced, beyond words—or action. Mark would not have been that way, I think. I once told him some of the heroic things I saw then." His eyes widened, inviting me to see them with him. "One living skeleton offering bread to another. Inmates comforting each other. Can tears be heroic? Some of the guys in my unit were too terrified, too bereft, to ever speak of it. Ever. Once in a while I think of that time when I'm in the court looking at the faces: broken families, young lives being torn open. But here it's usually tragedies people create for themselves."

I asked Frank if he had lost many friends. "Quite a few," he said, "but not that many this year. A lot of the people we know now are Netta's age, so being eight or ten years younger than me makes that difference. I guess that's a blessing, not putting all your eggs in one generation." He laughed. "Not that I can take credit for having planned it that way. The truth is, like most people, I take my life and my good fortune for granted most of the time. I have to get up to pee two, sometimes three times a night now. So? What's worse? That, or never getting up again? Let's face it: everyday life only gets precious when you're far away from it, like in the war, or when some part of it gets destroyed, like with Mark gone. Then, when *we're* gone, we all become just photographs, or something colorful in someone else's stories. We rarely see what's close, or look at ourselves that way."

Frank went back to another moment. "Last year, before Mark got me this job, I was filling out my income tax, and on the front sheet it asks occupation. So—what do I put? Once it was 'chemist,' then 'health educator.' Now? I wanted to write 'bum.' " He paused for breath.

Though Frank's everyday speech often had long *aaa*'s and other New England sounds, he sometimes slipped into a bit of a brogue—an echo? an imitation of his long-dead father's voice?—which is when he spoke in capitals: "I HAVE A WEAKNESS," he resumed, "which is looking back, wondering what I could have done, might have been. See, we all age at the same rate, one day at a time, but when you're my age, and every day could be the last, counting and measuring don't count. And you don't have to be Catholic to live with a tragic sense of life—you look too close and see the gap between what you've dreamed and what you've been. No. Whatever your background, that thinking is what you drink in each day with your morning coffee."

Outside, back on the street, Frank shrugged and smiled, a bit surprised, perhaps embarrassed, at how confessional he had been. I thanked him for the coffee. He thanked me for listening. "It's okay," he said, trying to reassure us both. I gave him a hug, and he returned it. Suddenly I remembered something that Alice had told me once in her studio. "Wait," I said, taking Frank by the elbow.

"What you said about looking and seeing. A woman I know, retired, an artist, she said to me that if something is rounded and you shine light on it, you not only show what's there on the surface, you also create areas of darkness. It's what can't be seen that helps you to appreciate what's visible. Light and dark, she'd said, shading, the shadowy parts. . . ." I was trying too hard for the words, and getting lost in language. "Am I making sense?"

"Sure," Frank answered, reassuring us both again, this time that I was not so obscure, or he so dense. "It's contrast," he offered. "Depth. What the Italians call *chiaroscuro*. It's artistry. It's what it takes to bring out a face or a figure—or a life. I realize that. Hey, I realize *all* of that. It's just that what *I* want is for *mine* to be the life that shows up."

He winked—a *sannyasin*? a hungry ghost?—and patted the hand I still had on his elbow. "Let the *others* be the darkness. I want to be the one in the light." He stopped, and fixed me with his eyes. "I'd like to be the light itself."

APPENDIX

Characteristics of Study Participants at the Time of Retirement

	Age	Main Occupation	Family/Living Situation[a]
Males			
John Sant'angelo	54	Engineer	Married
Nate Rumsfeld	57	Postman	Married
Felix Davis	57	Professor	Married
Stefan Nokalsky	59	Hotelier	Married (2d time)
Martin Karler	62	Industrial designer	Married
Bruce Palanos	61	Media consultant	Married
Tom Ellman	61	Salesman and minister	Married
Lester Ulanoff	62	Accountant	Divorced, living with a married daughter
Alan Freudenberg	63	High school teacher	Married
Carl Withen	64	Lawyer	Married
Ed Trayvor	64	Fund-raiser	Married
Glen McReedy	71	Doctor	Married (2d time)
Frank Ryan	77	Health educator	Married (2d time)
Females			
Teri Rogers	57	High school teacher	Married
Sandra Golecki	58	Musician	Married
Zoe Leven	59	Lab technician	Married
Rita Ellman	61	Librarian	Married
Inez Karler	62	Bookkeeper	Married
Sophie Malounek	62	Secretary	Married
Petra van Osten	63	Doctor	Married
Harriet Trayvor	63	Hospital administrator	Married
Ursula Chalfin	63	Biologist	Single, living with a partner
Johanna Alexander	64	Administrative assistant	Married
Donna Younger	63	College administrator	Single, living alone
Nonnie Schein	65	Elementary school teacher	Divorced twice, living with a partner
Alice Armani	67	Human service specialist	Divorced, living alone

Note: Average age: 62.3. The national average for retirement age at the time of the study's start was 62. (See Vinick and Ekerdt [1991].)

[a] All currently and formerly married participants have children and grandchildren, although only one of these individual resides in a grown child's household.

NOTES

Introduction

1. The concept of "the definition of the situation" was introduced by sociologist W. I. Thomas. "If men define situations as real, they are real in their consequences" (Thomas 1928, 572).

2. On changes in life expectancy, see Brontë 1994, xvi and Rowe and Kahn 1998, 4. For "the demographic transition" and its effects on the American population and labor force, see Moen 1996, and Laabs 1997.

3. The varying treatment of the elderly in tribal societies is discussed in N. Foner 1984, Glascock 1997, Simmons 1945, and Sokolovsky 1987.

4. The material from traditional European and non-Western cultures in the following section draws on several sources: Ireland (Arensberg 1937), Abkhasia (Benet 1974), Korongo and Mesakin (Nadel 1952), Inuit (Guemple 1987), China (Harrell 1981; Olson 1990), the Bahamas (Savishinsky 1991b), and India (Eck 1985; Tilak 1989; Turnbull 1983). The concept of "kinwork," applied to Cat Island, is taken from Stack (1996, 105), who notes the same pattern of grandparental care for grandchildren among extended black families in the American South.

In considering these cross-cultural materials, some caveats are in order. Earlier claims that Abkhasian life expectancy commonly exceeds 120 years have been shown to be greatly exaggerated (Medvedev 1974). Also, the forces of modernization have significantly altered the status of older people in many of these societies. The erosion of the power of Irish elders, for example, has been analyzed by Scheper-Hughes (1982). The older Irish system echoes a traditional European pattern of "contractual" family retirement and the transmission of resources from the old to the young (Cole 1992, 11–12). Furthermore, older Inuit women and men are now among the most economically valued members of their families because of the pensions they receive (A. Foner 1986, 140). For global treatments of aging and social change in cross-cultural perspective, including material on China and Ireland, see J. Keith et al. 1994 and Sokolovsky 1997.

5. For the modern history of retirement, I have drawn on Achenbaum 1986, Cole 1992, Costa 1998, Graebner 1980, Haber and Gratton 1993, and Quadagno and Hardy 1996.

6. On the outmoded stereotypes of older workers, see Barth, McNaught, and Rizzi 1995. The arguments that retirement decisions are increasingly due to "new economic and cultural opportunities," and that people have been choosing to leave work because retirement itself has become so "attractive," are from Troyansky (1999, 624–25), who reviews and summarizes Costa 1998. For discussions of recent labor market factors, see Quadagno 1999, 241–47 and Quadagno and Hardy 1996.

7. The retirement "boom" after the Second World War is noted by A. Foner (1986, 39), and the figure on American men's shifting labor force participation is from Moen 1996, 239. The rise in the working rate of older men and women since 1985 is noted by the Bureau of Labor Statistics (cited in Johnston 1999).

8. On the illusions about American leisure time, see De Grazia 1994 and Schor 1991. Concerning the inadequate amounts of money that Americans have saved and invested for retirement and people's widespread anxiety over whether they can afford this stage of life, see Uchitelle 1995a, 1995b, Wayne 1994, and Willette 1995. Journalists have also been writing about the problems retirees face in collecting their pensions because of miscalculations, changed rules, or devious efforts by employers (e.g., Drew 1996, Oppel 1999). Some individuals have even hired "bounty hunters" to help them collect what is due them (Rowland 1995). Though an increasing percentage of American workers are now saving for retirement, relatively few have carefully planned for it, and 75 percent do not know how much they will need to support themselves (Employee Benefit Research Institute et al. 1997; see also Ekerdt 1989, 327–28).

9. Prentis 1992 contains over 40 brief case histories of women and men from Michigan dealing with various phases of retirement. Brontë (1994) studied 150 Americans over 65 who continued working by choice, not necessity. She regards these people as "a startling departure from the concept of retirement" (11).

10. For studies of retirement communities, both planned and unplanned, see Francis 1984, Hochschild 1973, Jacobs 1974, Johnson 1971, J. Keith 1982, Myerhoff 1978, Stokes 1990, and Vesperi 1986.

11. On NORCs, see Lewin 1991 and Barrow 1996, 211–12.

12. The formal development of Disengagement Theory was by Cumming and Henry (1961). The concept of Differential Disengagement comes from the work of Streib and Schneider (1971). For Activity Theory, derived from Burgess 1950, 1960, Havighurst 1963 and Rosow 1967, and for critical responses both to it and to the idea of disengagement, see Achenbaum and Bengtson 1994, Barrow 1996, 69–71, Chambré 1984, Guttman 1976, Hazan 1980, and Sokolovsky 1987. The concepts of "Crisis," "Consolidation," and "Continuity" are discussed by Atchley (1989, 1999, 2000) and Quadagno (1999, 253–54).

13. On the percentage of people who plan to retire and those who take "bridge jobs," see Atchley 2000, 239 and Ruhm 1990. Most people go from full-time employment to "full-time leisure" (Moen 1996, 240). The observation that the "working retired" are from the economic extremes is made by Palmore et al. (1985, 82). The value for some retirees of working at least part-time is discussed in many studies (e.g., Barrow 1996, 164–72; Brooke 1986; Palmore et al. 1985, 169–70). By the mid-1990s, about one-third of retirees were returning to work within a year (Mergenhagen 1994). On the minimal effects of changes in mandatory retirement laws, see Noble 1986 and Ruhm 1989. The tie between the work attachment and retirement attitude of professionals is considered by Newman, Sherman, and Higgins (1982, 114). For a study of 80 middle-class New England men, aged 35 to 55, who stressed "staying the course" in successful jobs, see Weiss 1990. The coexistence of high job commitment and positive retirement orientation is noted by Jewson (1982, 173) and Price-Bonham and John-

son (1982, 125), and the minimal loss to identity occasioned by retirement is observed by Kelly (1983: 83). The widespread support for, predictability of, and normative nature of retirement are discussed by Atchley (2000, 242–44), Ekerdt (1989, 323–25), and Palmore et al. (1985, 167).

14. The decline in the role of health and finances in twentieth-century retirement decisions and the increased salience of "work commitment and work history" are discussed by Belgrave and Haug (1995, 60–61), as well as Costa (1998), Quadagno (1999, 251), and Troyansky (1999). Numerous studies have found that when retirees are compared to their working peers, health declines are generally associated with age, not retirement (Belgrave and Haug 1995; Crowley 1985; Ekerdt, Bossé, and Locastro 1983). The quote on "deterioration in health" is from Hooyman and Kiyak 1999, 324. The myth that retirement damages health nevertheless persists because retirement is such a vivid event that, for many people, "it simplifies the interpretation of subsequent changes in physical or emotional well-being" (Ekerdt et al. 1983, 9; see also Ekerdt 1987). The lack of connections between stress, depression, and retirement is noted by Bossé et al. (1991), Palmore et al. (1985, 44–49), and Reitzes, Mutran, and Fernandez (1996), though there is also contradictory evidence on how retirement affects life satisfaction and mental health (e.g., Bossé et al. 1987). The 60-percent and 75-percent estimates for retirement income are from McConnel and Deljavan (1983) and Palmore et al. (1985, 167) respectively. Materials on the retirement savings and financial anxieties of American workers are cited above in note 8.

15. The economic vulnerability of older women and minorities, including the current generation of elders and baby boomers, is examined by Barrow (1996), Belgrave (1988), Dailey (1998), Quadagno (1988, 1991, 1999), and Rogers (1985). The 60-percent pension figure is from Belgrave 1989, 51. Women's career patterns and their risk for widowhood are discussed by Barer (1994), Depner and Ingersoll (1982, 74–75), Hayward and Liu (1992, 50), and Szinovacz (1982a, 13–21). The economic impact of retirement on blacks and the working poor is analyzed by Palmore et al. (1985, 144–45, 171–72) and Parnes (1985). The differences in attitude and adjustment between blue-collar and white-collar workers and between professionals and managers are examined by Barrow (1996, 163–64), Mergenhagen (1994, 32), and Quadagno (1999, 235–58).

16. On good adjustment despite low levels of formal planning for retirement, see Atchley 1982, Campione 1988, and Ekerdt 1989, 350. On the positive morale, self-image, and life satisfaction of retirees, see Atchley 1982, 160–66; 2000, 244–45; A. Foner 1986, 39, 70–71; McGoldrick 1989; Palmore et al. 1985, 168; and Young 1989.

17. This summary of the phases and paths of retirement is taken from Atchley 1976, 63–73; 2000, 253–55. The concept of "anticipatory socialization" was introduced by Rosow (1974); see also A. Foner 1986, 108–11. The idea of "conducting mental dress rehearsals" for retirement is from Evans, Ekerdt, and Bossé 1985, 369. Ekerdt, Bossé, and Levkoff, studying shifts in the level of retirees' satisfaction, found that "the immediate postretirement period is marked by more enthusiasm and that some degree of temporary letdown or dysphoria is likely during the second year of retirement" (1985, 95).

18. The ideas of "normless" or "roleless" roles in retirement were proposed by Burgess (1960, 20) and Rosow (1962, 1967, 1974). The countervailing argument that retirement is a role with rights and duties is summarized by Atchley (2000, 251–52) and Palmore et al. (1985, 2–3).

19. The contrast between the "work ethic" and the "busy ethic" is from Ekerdt 1986. The connection between volunteering and health comes from a study of upstate New York retirees done by Phyllis Moen (see Szegedy-Maszak 1999, 11).

20. On aging in place, the myth of migration, and the reasons why some retirees do relocate, see Cuba 1992, Henretta 1986, Litwak and Longino 1987, Merrill and Hunt 1990, Mutschler 1992, and Speare and Meyer 1988.

21. Factors influencing good cognitive and intellectual functioning are summarized by Schaie (1996), who draws on a number of other studies: see, for example, Miller, Slomczynski and Kohn 1987, Schooler 1987, 1990, and Rowe and Kahn 1998, 125–42.

22. The relationship between levels of leisure activities and retirees' responsibilities is discussed by Atchley (2000, 257–58). The qualities of leisure in later life are examined by Kelly, Steinkamp, and Kelly (1986), who studied how older people "play in Peoria." Prospective retirees have been found to overestimate their future involvement in leisure pursuits (Bossé and Ekerdt 1981), and such activities do not "contribute to life satisfaction of retirees merely by substituting for their previous work activity" (Parnes and Less 1985, 224).

23. The effect of caregiving responsibilities on retirees is considered by Dailey (1998), O'Grady-LeShane and Williamson (1992, 75–76), O'Rand, Henretta, and Krecker (1992, 86), Stone, Cafferata, and Sangl (1987), and Szinovacz, Ekerdt, and Vinick (1992, 5). The percentages on women caregivers are from Brubaker and Brubaker (1992, 223–24).

24. On planning and entering retirement as a couple, see Atchley 1992, 145, Hayward and Liu 1992, 37, 47, and Szinovacz 1982, 19. For the statement that retirement is increasingly a "couple experience," and the impact of men's early retirement wishes on their wives' occupational goals, see Szinovacz, Ekerdt, and Vinick 1992, 4. On the effect of retirement timing on couples, see Atchley and Miller 1983. For data showing that the transition to retirement is not a crisis for most couples, see Szinovacz 1980 and Vinick and Ekerdt 1991. The levels of work identification and regret among professional women are examined by Prentis (1980), Price-Bonham and Johnson (1982, 124–25), and Szinovacz (1982a, 18–19). The effect of husbands' pensions on women's retirement attitudes is discussed by Price-Bonham and Johnson (1982, 133).

25. See Savishinsky 1990, 1991a, 1991b, 1994a.

26. In what follows, the ideas of "consolidation" and the "continuity" of personality are from Atchley 1989; 1999; 2000, 119–21, 165–66. "Old-age style" is discussed by Clark (1972) and Feldman (1992). Theories of "age heterogeneity" and "age stratification" are summarized by Campbell, Abolafia, and Maddox (1985) and A. Foner (1986), while the idea of "ego integrity" is explained by Erikson (1963), and the "ageless self" by Kaufman (1987). Philosophers who have worked with the concept of "moral agency" include Riker (1997) and Schmidtz (1997).

27. The use of life-course theory in gerontology is discussed by Kohli (1986), Fry (1990), and Hagestad (1990).

28. On female labor force participation, and the insufficient attention to women in earlier retirement studies, see Belgrave 1989, Szinovacz 1982a, and Szinovacz, Ekerdt, and Vinick 1992.

29. See Alinsky 1971, Berry 1988, Cather 1918, and Puller 1993.

30. The lines are from Agee and Evans 1941, xxvii, xlvi.

A First Cup

1. The writer Carl Klaus speaks of a similar set of frustrations and fears as he faced retirement from his university position: the "charade" of the annual salary review; the tedium of grading essays; and the loss of an office and a title (Klaus 1999).

2. Felix barely refrained from singing this line from the Eagles' song "Hotel California." He actually had the words wrong but their spirit right (see Henley, Frey, and Felder 1976).

Chapter 1. The Unbearable Lightness of Retirement

1. Important studies of rites of passage include the works of Myerhoff (1978), Turner (1969), and van Gennep (1908).
2. The quote on the "unceremonious" nature of retirement is from Maddox 1968, 357. The historical lack of retirement and old age rituals in Europe is noted by Cole (1992, 11). The "rite of passage we haven't figured out" is a point made by Manheimer (1994, 44).
3. On our lack of knowledge about retirement ceremonies, and their lack of standardization, see Atchley 1976, 53–59; 2000, 251.
4. Parallels between adolescence and old age are noted by Keith and Kertzer (1984, 39).
5. On the ritual role of marginal figures, and the importance of liminality in the ritual process, see Turner 1969, 110, 125 and Myerhoff 1984, 310–11.
6. See Berry 1988.
7. The quote on journeys is from Durrell 1957, 1.
8. On the travels of mythic heroes, see J. Campbell 1968. In a more modern vein, Klaus (1999, 189–234) writes with insight of his post-retirement trip to the Rockies—a reprise of a journey he had taken with his wife on their 25th anniversary.
9. Turner (1969, 94–130) considers the meaning of being "betwixt and between" life's stages. Atchley (1976, 64) notes the stress on "separation" in retirement's significance.
10. De Grazia (1994) and Schor (1991) discuss work as a source of personal meaning. The modern origins of the weekend are traced by Rybczynski (1991).
11. On the loss of identity with retirement, see Barrow 1996, 165, Chambré 1984, and Hazan 1994, 66. The disjunctures between culture and biology, and functional and chronological age, are explored in Keith and Kertzer 1984.
12. See Kundera 1985 and Sartre 1956.
13. Hobsbawm (1983) examines the "invention of tradition." For the role of "definitional ceremonies," see Myerhoff 1978; 1984, 312. The six arts recognized by the Chinese were calligraphy, charioteering, ritual, arithmetic, music, and archery (Tu 1983, 72).

A Second Cup

1. See Lennon's "Beautiful Boy (Darling Boy)," recorded on the album *Double Fantasy* (Lennon 1981, 133). Sam Meyer, host of Ithaca College radio station WICB's "Breakfast with the Beatles," identified the source of the lyric for me.
2. The symbolic meaning of the first pension or Social Security check was mentioned to me by other retirees; see also Atchley 1976, 58.

Chapter 2. Zen Masters and Master Planners

1. Kuhn (1905–95), a social activist and advocate for older people's rights, was founder and head of the Gray Panthers. For her impact on social policy, see Hessel 1977.

2. See Alinsky 1971.

3. John Cage explains the aesthetic ideas that Sandra refers to in his book *Silence* (1961).

4. This need for visibility is true for other high-powered, achievement-oriented people. In her biography of President Lyndon Johnson, Doris Goodwin wrote: "So dominant had politics been, consuming all his energies, constricting his horizons in every sphere, that once the realm of high power was taken from him he was drained of all vitality. Retirement became for him a form of little death" (1991, xviii). A number of the participants in Lydia Brontë's study of men and women over 65 with long, prominent careers were unhappy "retirers" who then became "returners" to work (1994, 238–63).

5. The final years and death of Fritz Reiner (1888–1963) are summarized in Hart 1994, 224–35.

6. The late career boredom and lack of challenge that Sandra complained of are not uncommon experiences among professionals after age 50 (see Karp 1989).

7. The stories told here show how people struggled to construct both a life and an account of that life as they were living it. Kohli (1986) writes of the way retirees wrestle with different kinds of time as they develop their subjective biographies. Concerning the emphasis on "play" in the way some people in Shelby spoke of this process, see De Grazia (1994, 16), whose distinction between play and leisure draws on Aristotle's *Politics*. It is ironic, given the career Sandra left behind, that Aristotle cited only two activities worthy to be called true leisure: namely, contemplation and music (Aristotle 336–322 B.C.: 335–52).

8. Inkeles 1979, 413.

9. The importance of role models for people's occupational and retirement attitudes is noted by Kimmel (1974) and Prentis (1992, 11). The focus in these sources on models for elders, however, is on those persons who present positive examples for emulation.

Chapter 3. At Work, at Home, at Large

1. The emotional and symbolic importance of personal possessions for older people has been examined by Rubinstein (1987).

2. "To see a world in a grain of sand" is from William Blake's poem "Auguries of Innocence" (Blake 1800–1810).

3. Pioneering studies of gifts, trade, and exchange in non-Western cultures include those of Malinowski (1922) and Mauss (1925).

4. SSI refers to Supplemental Security Income, a federal program begun in 1974 that provides minimum incomes for the elderly and support for the blind and the permanently and totally disabled.

5. See Counts and Counts 1996, 73, 75, 130.

6. Bruce was referring to Jack Kerouac's classic "beat generation" novel *On the Road* (1958).

7. On the pattern of "serial retirement," in which older people make a series of moves before settling down, see Collins 1991. Simone de Beauvoir once observed that older people often make mistaken decisions by moving closer to children who do not want them, shifting to a climate that turns out to be bad for their health, or relocating to a place where they have no friends or interests (de Beauvoir 1972, 265).

8. The references are to Payne and Bishop's song "There's No Place Like Home" (1823, 143–45); Thoreau's *Walden* (1854, 80); and Voltaire's *Candide* (1759, 87).

A Fourth Cup

1. See Bateson 1990.
2. Alice's surmise about older women's money worries is well-founded. See Feldstein 1998, the study by the Older Women's League 1995, Quadagno 1988, 1991, and Szinovacz 1982b.
3. For "old-age style" or *altersstil*, see Introduction note 26.
4. Alice's emphasis on the spiritual side of retirement, coupled with her artistic search for the light, suggests a Quaker emphasis on an "inner light" within each person. She did have Quaker friends, but was herself a Unitarian.

Chapter 4. Looking for the Light

1. Nonny was quite elated, during the time we worked together, that a number of currently popular films centered on dance; she mentioned *Strictly Ballroom, Shall We Dance?* and *The Tango Lesson*—noting, with regret, that none of these had an American setting. The first was Australian, the second Japanese, and the third primarily Argentinian.
2. Lewis Puller Jr. committed suicide two years after his book won the Pulitzer Prize (*New York Times* 1994).
3. The phrase is attributed to Clemenceau (see Eiseley 1973, 82–83).
4. Carl's experience echoes an observation made by a retiree in Prentis's study, a man who looked forward to visiting other places because, he said, he had "traveled extensively as part of my career, but never really had the time to see anything" (1992, 62).
5. The idea derives from the aphorisms in Francis Bacon's *Novum Organum* (1620, 43), where he states that "human knowledge and human power come to the same thing, for where the cause is not known the effect cannot be produced." Elsewhere Bacon wrote that "the true ends of knowledge" are "a restitution and reinvesting of man to the sovereignty and power which he had in the first state of creation" (from Eiseley 1973, 84–85).
6. Flanders is a coastal region covering parts of Belgium and northwestern France, where large numbers of soldiers were killed in the First World War. Glen was probably referring to the Allied cemeteries there, and to the poem "In Flanders Fields" (McCrae 1919, 1235–36), which commemorates those buried in that region. The poem's opening lines, which many of Glen's generation had learned in school, read:

> In Flanders fields the poppies blow
> Between the crosses, row on row
> That mark our place; and in the sky
> The larks, still bravely singing, fly
> Scarce heard amid the guns below.

7. In Hegel's *Lectures on the Philosophy of World History* (1840), the main historical trend, the thrust of universal history, is toward the development of the spirit of freedom. The "cunning of reason" is that it sets people to fulfill this great purpose without their becoming conscious of the role they have in the process (xxv, xxviii, 89).
8. David Gaunt (1998) has shown that the virtues of the "busy ethic" (Ekerdt 1986) for people's moral and medical well-being are even reinforced by the contrasting images of active and slothful retirees featured on American and European greeting cards sent to individuals upon their retirement.

9. On the search for immortality by mythic heroes and artists, see Rank 1914, 1932 and Segal 1990; and on the heroic self-image and mission of retired American CEOs, see Sonnenfeld 1988. A number of psychoanalytic thinkers have pointed out the symbolic connection for artists between finishing creative projects and their own mortality (e.g., Rank 1932, 386).

10. See DuBois 1955, 1234. The psychologist Martha Wolfenstein described "the emergence of fun morality" in American child-rearing (1951).

11. Simone de Beauvoir comments on prominent thinkers' view of old age as passionless (1972, 275). The historian Thomas Cole notes that the philosophers of antiquity linked our passions with our animal nature, and so welcomed their passing as a blessing (1992, 8). The line from Thoreau is from *Walden* (1854, 6). Emphasis has been added to the quote from Pieper (1963, 55).

12. The psychological rewards of of this effort are discussed by Schaie (1996) and others; see Introduction, note 21.

13. On cultures that encourage elders just "to be," see Turnbull 1983, 223–62. For one of the more thoughtful of modern spiritual teachers who supports the same way of "being" in the world, see Chödrön (1997).

14. On the split between inner and outer images of the self in old age, see Hazan 1994, 84–85, 90–91 and several of the individual cases presented in Gubrium 1993, Kaufman 1987, Savishinsky 1991a, and Shield 1988. The quote about "passion in our hearts" is from Florida Scott-Maxwell's journal (1979, 129).

15. The company that uses this phrase is discussed by Hübler (1999, 12).

A Fifth Cup

1. Shakespeare's *Tragedy of King Lear* (1608) opens with the monarch deciding to retire, divide up his kingdom, and live out his life by breaking the year into alternating periods of residence with each of his three daughters. It was not a good plan.

2. Martin is referring to the popular film *On Golden Pond* (Thompson 1979). Set at a lakeside cottage, this drama is about an eccentric elderly couple, Norman and Ethel Thayer, and their relationship with their adult daughter. Norman is portrayed as an irascible cynic who is preoccupied with his death.

Chapter 5. The Kaleidoscope and the Conspirators

1. Whether they help to create or simply reflect this stereotype of marriages cast up on the rocks of retirement, newspaper advice columns frequently feature such situations (e.g., Landers 1998; Peterson 1995). In the past, women who have been housewives often viewed their husbands' retirement as a potential interference in household tasks (Darnley 1975; Fengler 1975; Hill and Dorfman 1982). We know less about the perceptions of this situation by presently employed or retired wives (Brubaker and Hennon 1982, 207). There has also been relatively little attention to how men are affected by their wives' retirement (Szinovacz 1982a, 19). Recent research indicates, however, that it is a myth that wives do not like having their husbands around (e.g., T. Anderson 1992; Atchley 1992; Vinick and Ekerdt 1991). This old image is based on the now outmoded picture of a man retiring to an unemployed housewife; by the 1990s, only some 25 percent of older couples fit this model. In most modern cases, both spouses have been employed (Atchley 2000, 259). In contrast to the image of tension, professional women claim high marital satisfaction because they and their spouses now have

more time together (Jewson 1982, 177). Several studies have nevertheless shown that traditional gender roles persist in the households of retirees (Dorfman 1992; Keating and Cole 1980; Szinovacz 1980, 1982a; Vinick and Ekerdt 1991).

2. The reference is to Woolf's classic essay *A Room of One's Own* (1929).

3. In the years preceding Johanna's retirement, President Reagan's wife Nancy had come up with the cheapest and simplest way to eliminate drugs as an American problem. She advised people faced with the pressure or temptation to use them to "just say no." This worked as well as King Lear's retirement plans.

4. The American writer Willa Cather (1873–1947), who spent much of her childhood in Nebraska, devoted a number of her major novels, including *O Pioneers!* (1913) and *My Ántonia* (1918), to an exploration of the lives of people in the American Midwest. Her central characters were usually women whose gifts and talents were at odds with the physical and social environments in which they found themselves.

5. See E. H. Carr's book *What Is History?* (1962, 14).

6. Retirees often report enjoying an increase in neighborhood contacts through helping and doing things both with and for the people around them. But this is usually noted by women, not men (see Jewson 1982, 176).

7. The Chinese maxim is quoted in Moody 1996, 21.

8. In identifying factors that enhance, or at least predict, good intellectual and cognitive functioning in adulthood and old age, Schaie 1996 highlights a lengthy marriage to a well-educated and intelligent spouse.

9. For analyses of the effect of work and retirement on social ties, see Bossé et al. 1990, 1993; on older women's friendships, see Block 1984, Depner and Ingersoll 1982, P. Keith 1982, and Szinovacz 1983. Bossé et al. 1990, 41 found that even when friendships were maintained, "retirees almost never discussed personal problems with former co-workers." For contrasting cases among women retirees—one group bound by a shared history of employment and union activism and another connected by a rural lifestyle—see Francis 1991 and Shenk 1998; both use the concept of "convoys" of social support (Kahn and Antonucci 1980). The phrase about the "desire to be missed" is from Klaus 1999, 91.

A Sixth Cup

1. The concept has been traced to a "cryptic phrase, reportedly uttered by Freud in his mature years, that the definition of maturity was to be found in the capacity to love and to work" (Smelser 1980, 4). This idea is expressed by Freud in *Civilization and Its Discontents* (1930, 48), where he states that love and work, "Eros and Ananke [Love and Necessity] have become the parents of human civilization." For Freud, it is the sublimation, the redirection of love energy into work through aim-inhibited libido, that makes the productive life of civilization possible. For an extended discussion of Freud's ideas on love and work, see Hale 1980.

2. The line Frank quoted is from Section 54 of Tennyson's book-length poem *In Memoriam* (1850, 34). In this section Tennyson places hope in the "trust that somehow good / Will be the final goal of ill." The last stanza reads:

So runs my dream: but what am I?
An infant crying in the night:
An infant crying for the light:
And with no language but a cry.

Kevin Murphy identified this source for me.

Chapter 6. Death and Taxes

1. There is a considerable body of evidence indicating the importance of a sense of self-confidence and mastery in people's ability to cope with crises and challenges. This is variously referred to by such terms as "control" or "self-efficacy." See, for example, Bandura 1997 and Rodin 1986.

2. On the tension between the right and the duty to retire, see Palmore et al. 1985, 2 and Brontë 1994, 318–19. As two students of the aging experience have put it, "In combination, both public and private policies urge older people to retire and we then blame them for doing so" (Rowe and Kahn 1998, 34).

3. Petra's view of death and generational succession was, as she recognized, a very modern one. In the mid-nineteenth century, by contrast, almost half of the deaths in the United States occurred among individuals under age 15, while less than 15 percent were people over 60. These figures from Spierer 1977, 39–40 are cited by Cole (1992, 80), who remarks of that earlier time that "death still visited children far more than old people."

4. See Thoreau 1854, 51.

5. The Franklin quote appears in Faber and Faber 1987, 122.

6. See, for example, Levinson 1979, 213–18.

7. On the better physical and mental health of voluntary retirees, see Barrow 1996, 163 and Herzog, House and Morgan 1991.

8. This percentage comes from Mergenhagen 1994, 30.

Chapter 7. Conclusions

1. This feature of the life course is examined in Campbell, Abolafia, and Maddox 1985.

2. The observation that Americans lead a "waged and staged" life is made in J. Keith et al. 1994, 193.

3. For a group with a different outcome, see Francis 1991.

4. The rewards of "staying the course" are stressed in the study of successful work by Weiss (1990, 252–53).

5. The "life review" is described and illustrated in Butler (1968); the concept of "ego integrity" is discussed by Erikson (1963); "Continuity Theory" is explained in Atchley 1989, 1999; and the idea of the "ageless self" is developed by Kaufman (1987).

6. This idea is from A. Foner 1986, 79–82.

7. For criticisms of the moralistic tone that some people have adopted when using concepts of "normal" or "successful" aging, see Cole 1992, 161–211 and Kidder 1993, 221–22. A more supportive approach is taken by Rowe and Kahn (1998). For an analytic approach from the behavioral sciences, see Baltes and Baltes 1990.

8. Some of the participants in Brontë's study (1994, 245) also felt that they had had more leisure time when they were working. Parkinson's Law was developed by C. Northcote Parkinson: "Work expands so as to fill the time available for its completion" (1962, 2). Parkinson, incidentally, has a final chapter devoted to strategies for forcing people to retire. His two main recommendations are: require them to travel by air to an endless number of international meetings, and also to fill out an endless number of forms before and after each trip. He feels this is a preferable solution to the method used by ancient and tribal societies, where leadership succession involved killing the king or chief priest before his powers waned and then replacing him with a young successor whose vigor would guarantee the society's prosperity. This latter

technique, in its ritual form, was the starting point for James G. Frazer's classic work *The Golden Bough* (1890–1915), as well as the subject of such modern novels of succession as Mary Renault's *The King Must Die* (1958), set in ancient Greece, and Saul Bellow's *Henderson The Rain King* (1959), set in twentieth-century Africa.

9. For suggestive examples of how people use metaphors to express and understand their lives, see Lakoff and Johnson 1980 and Luborsky 1990. For studies of how older people perceive and deal with time, see Barrow 1996, 165, Gubrium 1976, Hazan 1980, and Lawton, Moss, and Fulcomer 1987. Barrow summarizes work which argues that, compared to the young, older people are more content with the amount of time they have (1996, 165).

10. This phrase is from Kelly 1983, 86.

11. Spoken by the character Carl in *O Pioneers!* (1913, 46).

12. For additional material on the unexpected in retirement, see Anderson, Burkhauser, and Quinn 1986.

13. On the differences in how partners perceive domestic and family situations, see Bernard 1972, Larsen and Olson 1990, Szinovacz, Ekerdt, and Vinick 1992, 15, and Vinick and Ekerdt 1991.

14. Philosopher Isaiah Berlin (1958) has examined this distinction in political terms, arguing that a just society requires both a "negative" liberty from state interference, and a "positive" liberty derived from official limits on some freedoms so that all may enjoy a greater liberty as individuals.

15. For arguments that we should count the "unpaid work" of elders in the same way we calculate paid employment as a part of productivity, see Moen 1996, 257–58 and Rowe and Kahn 1998, 191–92.

16. Thoreau 1854, 6.

17. See Anderson 1919, Masters 1915, and Wilder 1938. The adaptability of this genre is borne out by the way these three authors employ, respectively, the media of the short story, poetry, and drama.

18. For some of the ethical and personal dilemmas of doing research in one's own culture, in a nursing home setting, and in a nearby community, see Savishinsky 1994b and the other essays in Henderson and Vesperi 1994.

REFERENCES

Achenbaum, W. Andrew. 1986. *Social Security: Visions and Revisions.* Cambridge: Cambridge University Press.

Achenbaum, W. Andrew, and Vern L. Bengtson. 1994. "Reengaging the Disengagement Theory of Aging." *The Gerontologist* 34(6): 756–63.

Agee, James, and Walker Evans. 1941. *Let Us Now Praise Famous Men.* Reprint, Boston: Houghton Mifflin, 1988.

Alinsky, Saul. 1971. *Rules for Radicals: A Pragmatic Primer for Realistic Radicals.* Reprint, New York: Random House, 1989.

Anderson, Kathryn, Richard V. Burkhauser, and Joseph F. Quinn. 1986. "Do Retirement Dreams Come True? The Effects of Unanticipated Events on Retirement Plans." *Industrial and Labor Relations Review* 39(4): 518–26.

Anderson, Sherwood. 1919. *Winesburg, Ohio: A Group of Tales of Ohio Small Town Life.* New York: B. W. Huebsch.

Anderson, Trudy B. 1992. "Conjugal Support among Working-Wife and Retired-Wife Couples." In *Families and Retirement,* edited by Maximiliane Szinovacz, David J. Ekerdt, and Barbara Vinick, 174–88. Newbury Park, Cal.: Sage.

Arensberg, Conrad. 1937. *The Irish Countryman: An Anthropological Study.* Reprint, Garden City, N.Y.: Natural History Press, 1968.

Aristotle. 335–322 B.C. *The Politics of Aristotle,* edited and translated by Ernest Barker. New York: Oxford University Press (1962 edition).

Atchley, Robert C. 1976. *The Sociology of Retirement.* Cambridge, Mass.: Schenkman.

———. 1982. "The Process of Retiring: Comparing Women and Men." In *Women's Retirement: Policy Implications of Recent Research,* edited by Maximiliane Szinovacz, 153–68. Beverly Hills: Sage.

———. 1989. "A Continuity Theory of Normal Aging." *Gerontologist* 29(2): 183–90.

———. 1992. "Retirement and Marital Satisfaction." In *Families and Retirement,* edited by Maximiliane Szinovacz, David J. Ekerdt, and Barbara Vinick, 145–58. Newbury Park, Cal.: Sage.

———. 1999. *Continuity and Adaptation in Aging: Creating Positive Experiences.* Baltimore: Johns Hopkins University Press.

———. 2000. *Social Forces and Aging: An Introduction to Social Gerontology.* 9th ed. Belmont, Cal.: Wadsworth.

Atchley, Robert, and Sheila Miller. 1983. "Types of Elderly Couples." In *Family Relationships in Later Life,* edited by Timothy Brubaker, 77–90. Beverly Hills: Sage.

Bacon, Francis. 1620. *Novum Organum, with Other Parts of the Great Instauration.* Edited and translated by Peter Urbach and John Gibson. Reprint, Chicago: Open Court, 1994.

Baltes, Paul B., and Margaret M. Baltes, eds. 1990. *Successful Aging: Perspectives from the Behavioral Sciences.* New York: Cambridge University Press.

Bandura, Albert. 1997. *Self-Efficacy: The Exercise of Control.* New York: W. H. Freeman.

Barer, Barbara M. 1994. "Men and Women Aging Differently." *International Journal of Aging and Human Development* 38(1): 29–40.

Barrow, Georgia M. 1996. *Aging, The Individual, and Society.* 6th ed. St. Paul, Minn.: West.

Barth, Michael, William McNaught, and Philip Rizzi. 1995. "Older Americans as Workers." In *Older and Active: How Americans over 55 Are Contributing to Society,* edited by S. A. Bass, 35–70. New Haven: Yale University Press.

Bateson, Mary Catherine. 1990. *Composing A Life.* New York: Penguin.

Beauvoir, Simone de. 1972. *The Coming of Age.* Translated by Patrick O'Brian. New York: Putnam's.

Belgrave, Linda L. 1988. "The Effect of Race Differences in Work History, Work Attitudes, Economic Resources, and Health in Women's Retirement." *Research on Aging* 10(3): 383–98.

———. 1989. "Understanding Women's Retirement: Progress and Pitfalls." *Generations* 13(2): 49–52.

Belgrave, Linda L., and Marie R. Haug. 1995. "Retirement Transition and Adaptation: Are Health and Finances Losing Their Effects?" *Journal of Clinical Geropsychology* 1(1): 43–66.

Bellow, Saul. 1959. *Henderson The Rain King.* New York: Viking.

Benet, Sula. 1974. *Abkhasians: The Long-living People of The Caucasus.* New York: Holt, Rinehart and Winston.

Berlin, Isaiah. 1958. *Two Concepts of Liberty.* Oxford: Clarendon.

Bernard, Jessie. 1972. *The Future of Marriage.* New York: World.

Berry, Thomas. 1988. *The Dream of the Earth.* San Francisco: Sierra Club.

Blake, William. 1800–1810. "Auguries of Innocence." In *The Portable Blake,* edited by Alfred Kazin, 150–54. New York: Penguin (1976 edition).

Block, Marilyn R. 1984. "Retirement Preparation Needs of Women." In *Retirement Preparation: What Retirement Specialists Need to Know,* edited by Helen Dennis, 129–40. Lexington, Mass.: Lexington Books.

Bossé, Raymond, and David J. Ekerdt. 1981. "Change in Self-perception of Leisure Activities with Retirement." *Gerontologist* 21(6): 650–54.

Bossé, Raymond, Carolyn M. Aldwin, Michael Levenson, and David J. Ekerdt. 1987. "Mental Health Differences among Retirees and Workers: Findings from the Normative Aging Study." *Psychology and Aging* 2(4): 383–89.

Bossé, Raymond, Carolyn Aldwin, Michael Levenson, Kathryn Workman-Daniels, and David J. Ekerdt. 1990. "Differences in Social Support among Retirees and Workers: Findings from the Normative Aging Study." *Psychology and Aging* 5(1): 41–47.

Bossé, Raymond, Carolyn Aldwin, Michael Levenson, Kathryn Workman-Daniels. 1991. "How Stressful Is Retirement? Findings from the Normative Aging Study." *Journal of Gerontology: Psychological Sciences* 46(1): P9–P14.

Bossé, Raymond, Carolyn Aldwin, Michael Levenson, Avron Spiro III, and Daniel Mroczek. 1993. "Change in Social Support after Retirement: Longitudinal Findings from the Normative Aging Study." *Journal of Gerontology: Psychological Sciences* 48(4): P210–P17.

Brontë, Lydia. 1994. *The Longevity Factor: The New Reality of Long Careers and How It Can Lead to Richer Lives.* New York: HarperCollins.

Brooke, James. 1986. "Retirees, Many Bored, Try 'Un-retirement.' " *New York Times,* 19 January 1, 26.

Brubaker, Ellie, and Timothy H. Brubaker. 1992. "The Context of Retired Women as Caregivers." In *Families and Retirement,* edited by Maximiliane Szinovacz, David J. Ekerdt, and Barbara Vinick, 222–35. Newbury Park, Cal.: Sage.

Brubaker, Timothy H., and Charles B. Hennon. 1982. "Responsibility for Household Tasks: Comparing Dual-Earner and Dual-Retired Marriages." In *Women's Retirement: Policy Implications of Recent Research,* edited by Maximiliane Szinovacz, 205–19. Beverly Hills: Sage.

Burgess, Ernest. 1950. "Personal and Social Adjustment in Old Age." In *The Aged in Society,* edited by Milton Derber, 138–56. Urbana: University of Illinois Press.

———. 1960. "Family Structure and Relationships." In *Aging in Western Societies,* edited by Ernest Burgess, 271–98. Chicago: University of Chicago Press.

Butler, Robert. 1968. "The Life Review: An Interpretation of Reminiscence in the Aged." In *Middle Age and Aging,* edited by Bernice Neugarten, 486–96. Chicago: University of Chicago Press.

Cage, John. 1961. *Silence.* Middletown, Conn.: Wesleyan University Press.

Campbell, Joseph. 1968. *The Hero with a Thousand Faces.* 2d edition. Princeton: Princeton University Press.

Campbell, Richard T., Jeffery Abolafia, and George L. Maddox. 1985. "Life-course Analysis in Social Gerontology: Using Replicated Social Surveys to Study Cohort Differences." In *Gender and the Life Course,* edited by Alice S. Rossi, 301–18. New York: Aldine.

Campione, Wendy. 1988. "Predicting Participation in Retirement Preparation Programs." *Journal of Gerontology: Social Sciences* 43(3): S91–S95.

Carr, Edward Hallett. 1962. *What Is History?* New York: Knopf.

Cather, Willa. 1913. *O Pioneers!* Reprint, New York: Dover, 1993.

———. 1918. *My Ántonia.* Reprint, New York: Dover, 1994.

Chambré, Susan Maizel. 1984. "Is Volunteering a Substitute for Role Loss in Old Age? An Empirical Test of Activity Theory." *Gerontologist* 24(3): 292–98.

Chödrön, Pema. 1997. *When Things Fall Apart: Heart Advice for Difficult Times.* Boston: Shambhala.

Clark, Kenneth. 1972. *The Artist Grows Old.* Cambridge: Cambridge University Press.

Cole, Thomas R. 1992. *The Journey of Life: A Cultural History of Aging in America.* Cambridge: Cambridge University Press.

Collins, Claire. 1991. "Retirees in Search of the Perfect Fit." *New York Times,* 8 August, C1, C10.

Costa, Dora L. 1998. *The Evolution of Retirement: An American Economic History, 1880–1990.* Chicago: University of Chicago Press.

Counts, Dorothy Ayers, and David R. Counts. 1996. *Over the Next Hill: An Ethnography of RVing Seniors in North America.* Peterborough, Ontario: Broadview.

Crowley, Joan E. 1985. "Longitudinal Effects of Retirement on Men's Psychological and Physical Well-being." In *Retirement among American Men,* edited by Herbert Parnes, 147–73. Lexington, Mass.: Lexington Books.

Cuba, Lee. 1992. "Family and Retirement in the Context of Elderly Migration." In

Families and Retirement, edited by Maximiliane Szinovacz, David J. Ekerdt, and Barbara Vinick, 205–21. Newbury Park, Cal.: Sage.

Cumming, Elaine, and William Henry. 1961. *Growing Old: The Process of Disengagement.* New York: Basic Books.

Dailey, Nancy. 1998. *When Baby Boom Women Retire.* Westport, Conn.: Praeger.

Darnley, Fred. 1975. "Adjustment to Retirement: Integrity or Despair." *Family Coordinator* 24(2): 217–26.

De Grazia, Sebastian. 1962. *Of Time, Work, and Leisure.* Reprint, New York: Random House, 1994.

Depner, Charlene, and Berit Ingersoll. 1982. "Employment Status and Social Support: The Experience of the Mature Women." In *Women's Retirement: Policy Implications of Recent Research,* edited by Maximiliane Szinovacz, 61–76. Beverly Hills: Sage.

Dorfman, Lorraine T. 1992. "Couples in Retirement: Division of Household Work." In *Families and Retirement,* edited by Maximiliane Szinovacz, David J. Ekerdt, and Barbara Vinick, 159–73. Newbury Park, Cal.: Sage.

Drew, Christopher. 1996. "Retiring? Check over the Boss's Arithmetic." *New York Times,* 18 February, 10F.

DuBois, Cora. 1955. "The Dominant Value Profile of American Culture." *American Anthropologist* 57(6, pt. 1): 1232–39.

Durrell, Lawrence. 1957. *Bitter Lemons.* New York: Dutton.

Eck, Diana L. 1985. *Daršan: Seeing the Divine Image in India.* 2d ed. Chambersburg, Penn.: Anima.

Eiseley, Loren. 1973. *The Man Who Saw through Time.* New York: Scribner's.

Ekerdt, David J. 1986. "The Busy Ethic: Moral Continuity between Work and Retirement." *Gerontologist* 26(3): 239–44.

———. 1987. "Why the Notion Persists That Retirement Harms Health." *Gerontologist* 27(4): 454–57.

———. 1989. "Retirement Preparation." In *Annual Review of Gerontology and Geriatrics,* vol. 9, edited by M. Powell Lawton, 321–56. New York: Springer.

Ekerdt, David J., Lynn Baden, Raymond Bossé, and Elaine Dibbs. 1983. "The Effect of Retirement on Physical Health." *American Journal of Public Health* 73(7): 779–83.

Ekerdt, David J., Raymond Bossé, and Joseph S. Locastro. 1983. "Claims That Retirement Improves Health." *Journal of Gerontology* 38(2): 231–36.

Ekerdt, David J., Raymond Bossé, and Sue Levkoff. 1985. "An Empirical Test for Phases of Retirement: Findings from the Normative Aging Study." *Journal of Gerontology* 40 (1): 95–101.

Employee Benefit Research Institute, American Savings Education Council, and Mathew Greenwald and Associates. 1997. *Retirement Confidence Survey 1997.* Washington, D.C.: Employee Benefit Research Institute, American Savings Education Council, and Mathew Greenwald and Associates.

Erikson, Erik H. 1963. *Childhood and Society.* 2d ed. New York: Norton.

Evans, Linda, David J. Ekerdt, and Raymond Bossé. 1985. "Proximity to Retirement and Anticipatory Involvement: Findings from the Normative Aging Study." *Journal of Gerontology* 40(3): 368–74.

Faber, Doris, and Harold Faber. 1987. *We the People: The Story of the United States Constitution since 1787.* New York: Scribner's.

Feldman, Frances. 1992. *"I Am Still Learning": Late Works by Masters.* Washington, D.C.: National Gallery of Art.

Feldstein, Kathleen. 1998. "Social Security's Gender Gap." *New York Times,* 13 April, A27.

Fengler, Alfred P. 1975. "Attitudinal Orientations of Wives toward Their Husbands' Retirement." *International Journal of Aging and Human Development* 6(2): 139–52.

Foner, Anne. 1986. *Aging and Old Age: New Perspectives*. Englewood Cliffs, N.J.: Prentice-Hall.

Foner, Nancy. 1984. *Ages in Conflict: A Cross-Cultural Perspective on Inequality between Old and Young*. New York: Columbia University Press.

Francis, Doris M. 1984. *Will You Still Need Me, Will You Still Feed Me, When I'm 84?* Bloomington: Indiana University Press.

———. 1991. "Friends from the Workplace." In *Growing Old in America*, 4th ed. edited by Beth B. Hess and Elizabeth W. Markson, 465–80. New Brunswick, N.J.: Transaction.

Frazer, James George. 1890–1915. *The Golden Bough: A Study in Comparative Religion*, 3d ed. 12 vols. London: Macmillan.

Freud, Sigmund. 1930. *Civilization and Its Discontents*. Translated by James Strachey. Reprint, New York: Norton, 1961.

Fry, Christine. 1990. "The Life Course in Context: Implications of Comparative Research." In *Anthropology and Aging: Comprehensive Review*, edited by Robert L. Rubinstein, 129–49. Boston: Kluwer Academic Publishers.

Gaunt, David. 1998. "Nature och Kultur, Människor och Djur: Moraliska Föreställningar om Pensionering i Populärkultur (Nature and Culture, Humans and Animals: Moral Representations of Retiring in Popular Culture)." In *Pigga Pensionärer Och Populärkultur*, edited by Owe Ronström, 197–228. Stockholm: Carlssons.

Glascock, Anthony P. 1997. "When Killing Is Acceptable: The Moral Dilemma Surrounding Assisted Suicide in America and Other Societies." In *The Cultural Context of Aging: Worldwide Perspectives*, 2d ed., edited by Jay Sokolovsky, 56–70. Westport, Conn.: Bergin and Garvey.

Goodwin, Doris Kearns. 1991. *Lyndon Johnson and the American Dream*. New York: St. Martin's.

Graebner, William. 1980. *A History of Retirement: The Meaning and Function of an American Institution*. New Haven: Yale University Press.

Gubrium, Jaber F., ed. 1976. *Time, Roles, and Self in Old Age*. New York: Human Sciences Press.

———. 1993. *Speaking of Life: Horizons of Meaning for Nursing Home Residents*. Chicago: Aldine de Gruyter.

Guemple, Lee. 1987. "Growing Old in Inuit Society." In *Growing Old in Different Societies: Cross-cultural Perspectives*, edited by Jay Sokolovsky, 24–28. Littleton, Mass.: Copley.

Guttman, David. 1976. "Alternatives to Disengagement among the Old Men of the Highland Druze." In *Time, Roles, and Self in Old Age*, edited by Jaber Gubrium, 88–108. New York: Human Sciences Press.

Haber, Carole, and Brian Gratton. 1993. *Old Age and the Search for Security: An American Social History*. Bloomington: Indiana University Press.

Hagestad, Gunhild O. 1990. "Social Perspectives on the Life Course." In *Handbook of Aging in the Social Sciences*, 3d ed., edited by Robert H. Binstock and Linda K. George, 151–68. New York: Van Nostrand Reinhold.

Hale, Nathan. 1980. "Freud's Reflections on Work and Love." In *Themes of Work and Love in Adulthood*, edited by Neil J. Smelser and Erik H. Erikson, 29–42. Cambridge: Harvard University Press.

Harrell, Stevan. 1981. "Growing Old in Rural Taiwan." In *Other Ways of Growing Old: Anthropological Perspectives*, edited by Pamela T. Amoss and Stevan Harrell, 193–210. Stanford: Stanford University Press.

Hart, Philip. 1994. *Fritz Reiner: A Biography.* Evanston, Ill.: Northwestern University Press.

Havighurst, Robert J. 1963. "Successful Aging." In *Processes of Aging: Social and Psychological Perspectives,* edited by Richard H. Williams, Clark Tibbits, and Wilma Donohue, 299–320. New York: Atherton.

Hayward, Mark D., and Mei-chun Liu. 1992. "Men and Women in Their Retirement Years: A Demographic Profile." In *Families and Retirement,* edited by Maximiliane Szinovacz, David J. Ekerdt, and Barbara Vinick, 23–50. Newbury Park, Cal.: Sage.

Hazan, Haim. 1980. *The Limbo People: A Study of the Time Universe among the Aged.* London: Routledge and Kegan Paul.

———. 1994. *Old Age: Constructions and Deconstructions.* Cambridge: Cambridge University Press.

Hegel, Georg Wilhelm Friedrich. 1840. *Lectures on The Philosophy of World History. Introduction: Reason in History.* Translated by H. B. Nisbet. Reprint, Cambridge: Cambridge University Press, 1975.

Henderson, J. Neil, and Maria D. Vesperi, eds. 1994. *The Culture of Long Term Care: Nursing Home Ethnography.* Westport, Conn.: Bergin and Garvey.

Henley, Don, Glenn Frey, and Don Felder. 1976. "Hotel California." Cass County Music, Red Cloud Music, and Fingers Music. *Cavalcade of Rock through The Years,* 244–50. New York: Warner Brothers Publications.

Henretta, John C. 1986. "Retirement and Residential Moves by Elderly Households." *Research on Aging* 8(1): 23–37.

Herzog, A. Regula, James S. House, and James N. Morgan. 1991. "Relation of Work and Retirement to Health and Well-being in Older Age." *Psychology and Aging* 6(2): 202–11.

Hessel, Dieter, ed. 1977. *Maggie Kuhn on Aging.* Philadelphia: Westminster.

Hill, Elizabeth A., and Lorraine T. Dorfman. 1982. "Reactions of Housewives to the Retirement of Their Husbands." *Family Relations* 3(2): 195–200.

Hobsbawm, Eric. 1983. "Introduction: Inventing Traditions." In *The Invention of Tradition,* edited by Eric Hobsbawm and Terence Ranger, 1–14. Cambridge: Cambridge University Press.

Hochschild, Arlie. 1973. *The Unexpected Community.* Englewood Cliffs, N.J.: Prentice-Hall.

Hooyman, Nancy, and H. Asuman Kiyak. 1999. *Social Gerontology: A Multidisciplinary Perspective.* 5th ed. Boston: Allyn and Bacon.

Hübler, Eric. 1999. "The New Faces of Retirement." *New York Times,* 3 January, section 3: 1,12.

Inkeles, Alex. 1979. "Continuity and Change in the American National Character." In *The Third Century: America as a Post-industrial Society,* edited by Seymour Martin Lipset, 389–416. Chicago: University of Chicago Press.

Jacobs, Jerry. 1974. *Fun City: An Ethnographic Study of a Retirement Community.* New York: Holt, Rinehart and Winston.

Jewson, Ruth Hathaway. 1982. "After Retirement: An Exploratory Study of the Professional Woman." In *Women's Retirement: Policy Implications of Recent Research,* edited by Maximiliane Szinovacz, 169–81. Beverly Hills: Sage.

Johnson, Sheila. 1971. *Idle Haven: Community Building among The Working-class Retired.* Berkeley: University of California Press.

Johnston, David Cay. 1999. "A Growing Gap between the Savers and the Save-nots." *New York Times* special section 15 on Retirement, 21 March, 12.

Kahn, Robert L., and Tony C. Antonucci. 1980. "Convoys over the Life Course: Attachment, Roles, and Social Support." In *Life-Span Development and Behavior,* vol. 3, edited by Paul Baltes and Orville Brim, 253–86. New York: Academic Press.

Karp, David A. 1989. "The Social Construction of Retirement among Professionals 50–60 Years Old." *Gerontologist* 29(6): 750–60.

Kaufman, Sharon R. 1987. *The Ageless Self: Sources of Meaning in Late Life.* New York: New American Library.

Keating, Norah C., and Phyllis Cole. 1980. "What Do I Do with Him 24 Hours a Day? Changes in the Housewife Role after Retirement." *Gerontologist* 20(1): 84–89.

Keith, Jennie. 1982. *Old People, New Lives: Community Creation in a Retirement Residence.* Chicago: University of Chicago Press.

Keith, Jennie, and David Kertzer. 1984. "Introduction." In *Age and Anthropological Theory,* edited by David Kertzer and Jennie Keith, 19–61. Ithaca: Cornell University Press.

Keith, Jennie, Christine Fry, Anthony Glascock, Charlotte Ikels, Jeanette Dickerson-Putman, Henry Harpending, and Patricia Draper. 1994. *The Aging Experience: Diversity and Commonality across Cultures.* Thousand Oaks, Cal.: Sage.

Keith, Pat M. 1982. "Working Women versus Homemakers: Retirement Resources and Correlates of Well-being." In *Women's Retirement: Policy Implications of Recent Research,* edited by Maximiliane Szinovacz, 77–91. Beverly Hills: Sage.

Kelly, John R. 1983. *Leisure Identities and Interactions.* London: Allen and Unwin.

Kelly, John R., Marjorie Steinkamp, and Janice R. Kelly. 1986. "Later Life Leisure: How They Play in Peoria." *Gerontologist* 26(5): 531–37.

Kerouac, Jack. 1958. *On the Road.* New York: New American Library.

Kidder, Tracy. 1993. *Old Friends.* Boston: Houghton Mifflin.

Kimmel, Douglas C. 1974. *Adulthood and Aging.* New York: Wiley.

Klaus, Carl. 1999. *Taking Retirement: A Beginner's Diary.* Boston: Beacon.

Kohli, Martin. 1986. "Social Organization and Subjective Construction of the Life Course." In *Human Development and the Life Course: Multidisciplinary Perspectives,* edited by Aage B. Sørensen, Franz E. Weinert, and Lonnie R. Sherrod, 271–92. Hillsdale, N.J.: Lawrence Erlbaum Associates.

Kundera, Milan. 1985. *The Unbearable Lightness of Being.* Translated by Michael Henry Heim. New York: Harper and Row.

Laabs, Jennifer J. 1997. "What If They Don't Retire?" *Workforce* 76(12): 54–60.

Lakoff, George, and Mark Johnson. 1980. *Metaphors We Live By.* Chicago: University of Chicago Press.

Landers, Ann. 1998. "Wife Baffled by Husband's Behavior after Retirement." *Ithaca Journal,* 20 January, 4C.

Larsen, Andrea, and David H. Olson. 1990. "Capturing the Complexity of Family Systems: Integrating Family Theory, Family Scores, and Family Analysis." In *Family Variables: Conceptualization, Measurement, and Use,* edited by Thomas W. Draper and Anastasios C. Marcos, 19–47. Newbury Park, Cal.: Sage.

Lawton, M. Powell, Miriam Moss, and Mark Fulcomer. 1987. "Objective and Subjective Uses of Time by Older People." *International Journal of Aging and Human Development* 24(3): 171–88.

Lennon, John. 1981. "Beautiful Boy (Darling Boy)." In *Lennon: The Solo Years,* 131–34. Winona, Minn.: Hal Leonard Publishing.

Levinson, Daniel J. 1979. *The Seasons of a Man's Life.* New York: Ballantine.

Lewin, Tamar. 1991. "Communities and Their Residents Age Gracefully." *New York Times,* 21 July, A1, A16.

Litwak, Eugene, and Charles F. Longino Jr. 1987. "The Migratory Patterns of the Elderly: A Developmental Perspective." *Gerontologist* 27(3): 266–72.

Luborsky, Mark. 1990. "Alchemists' Visions: Cultural Norms in Eliciting and Analyzing Life History Narratives." *Journal of Aging Studies* 4(1): 17–29.

Maddox, George L. 1968. "Retirement as a Social Event in the United States." In *Middle Age and Aging*, edited by Bernice Neugarten, 357–65. Chicago: University of Chicago Press.

Malinowski, Bronislaw. 1922. *Argonauts of the Western Pacific: An Account of Native Enterprise in the Archipelagoes of Melanesian New Guinea*. Reprint, New York: Dutton, 1961.

Manheimer, Ronald J. 1994. "The Changing Meaning of Retirement." *Creative Retirement* 1(1): 44–49.

Masters, Edgar Lee. 1915. *Spoon River Anthology*. New York: Macmillan.

Mauss, Marcel. 1925. *The Gift: Forms and Functions of Exchange in Archaic Societies*. Translated by Ian Cunnison. Reprint, New York: Norton, 1967.

McConnel, Charles E., and Firooz Deljavan. 1983. "Consumption Patterns of the Retired Household." *Journal of Gerontology* 38(4): 480–90.

McCrae, John. 1919. "In Flanders Fields." In *Great Poems of the English Language: An Anthology*, compiled by Wallace Alvin Briggs, 1235–36. Reprint, New York: Tudor, 1936.

McGoldrick, Ann E. 1989. "Stress, Early Retirement, and Health." In *Age, Stress, and Health*, edited by Kyriakos Markides and Cary L. Cooper, 91–118. New York: Wiley.

Medvedev, Zhores A. 1974. "Caucasus and Altay Longevity: A Biological or Social Problem?" *Gerontologist* 14(5): 381–87.

Mergenhagen, Paula. 1994. "Rethinking Retirement." *American Demographics* 16(6): 28–34.

Merrill, John, and Michael Hunt. 1990. "Aging in Place: A Dilemma for Retirement Housing Administrators." *Journal of Applied Gerontology* 9(1): 60–76.

Miller, Joanne, Kazimierz M. Slomczynski, and Melvin L. Kohn. 1987. "Continuity of Learning-generalization through the Life Span: The Effect of Job on Men's Intellectual Process in the United States and Poland." In *Cognitive Functioning and Social Structure over the Life Course*, edited by Carmi Schooler and K. Warner Schaie, 176–202. Norwood, N.J.: Ablex.

Moen, Phyllis. 1996. "Changing Age Trends: The Pyramid Upside Down?" In *The State of Americans: This Generation and the Next*, by Urie Bronfenbrenner, Peter McClelland, Elaine Wethington, Phyllis Moen, and Stephen Ceci, 208–58. New York: Free Press.

Moody, Harry R. 1996. *Ethics in an Aging Society*. Baltimore: Johns Hopkins University Press.

Mutschler, Phyllis H. 1992. "Where Elders Live." *Generations* 16(2): 7–14.

Myerhoff, Barbara. 1978. *Number Our Days*. New York: Simon and Schuster.

———. 1984. "Rites and Signs of Ripening: The Intertwining of Ritual, Time, and Growing Older." In *Age and Anthropological Theory*, edited by David Kertzer and Jennie Keith, 305–30. Ithaca: Cornell University Press.

Nadel, S. F. 1952. "Witchcraft in Four African Societies: An Essay in Comparison." *American Anthropologist* 54(1): 18–29.

Newman, Evelyn S., Susan R. Sherman, and Claire Higgins. 1982. "Retirement Expectations and Plans: A Comparison of Professional Men and Women." In *Women's Retirement: Policy Implications of Recent Research*, edited by Maximiliane Szinovacz, 113–22. Beverly Hills: Sage.

New York Times. 1994. "Lewis Fuller Jr., Vietnam Hero and Biographer, is Dead at 48." 12 May, B14.

Noble, Kenneth. 1986. "End of Forced Retirement Means a Lot—to a Few." *New York Times* 26 October, E5.

O'Grady-LeShane, Regina, and John B. Williamson. 1992. "Family Provisions in Old-age Pensions: Twenty Industrial Nations." In *Families and Retirement,* edited by Maximiliane Szinovacz, David J. Ekerdt, and Barbara Vinick, 64–77. Newbury Park, Cal.: Sage.

Older Women's League. 1995. *The Path to Poverty: An Analysis of Women's Retirement Income.* Washington, D.C.: Older Women's League.

Olson, Philip. 1990. "The Elderly in the People's Republic of China." In *The Cultural Context of Aging: Worldwide Perspectives,* edited by Jay Sokolovsky, 143–61. New York: Bergin and Garvey.

Oppel, Jr., Richard A. 1999. "Companies Cash in on New Pension Plan." *New York Times,* 20 August, C1, C16.

O'Rand, Angela M., John C. Henretta, and Margaret L. Krecker. 1992. "Family Pathways to Retirement." In *Families and Retirement,* edited by Maximiliane Szinovacz, David J. Ekerdt, and Barbara Vinick, 81–98. Newbury Park, Cal.: Sage.

Palmore, Erdman, Bruce Burchett, Gerda Fillenbaum, Linda George, and Laurence Wallman. 1985. *Retirement: Causes and Consequences.* New York: Springer.

Parkinson, C. Northcote. 1962. *Parkinson's Law: And Other Studies in Administration.* Boston: Houghton Mifflin.

Parnes, Herbert. 1985. "Conclusion." In *Retirement Among American Men,* edited by Herbert Parnes, 209–24. Lexington, Mass.: Heath.

Parnes, Herbert, and Lawrence Less. 1985. "Variation in Selected Forms of Leisure Activity among Elderly Males." In *Current Perspectives on Aging and the Life Cycle: Work, Retirement and Social Policy,* vol. 1, edited by Zena Smith Blau, 223–42. Greenwich, Conn.: JAI Press.

Payne, John Howard, and Henry Rowley Bishop. 1823. "Home, Sweet Home." In *Songs of the Civil War,* edited by Irwin Silber, 143–45. New York: Columbia University Press (1960 edition).

Peterson, Karen. 1995. "What to Do with a Bossy and Retired Husband." *Ithaca Journal,* 12 December, 10B.

Pieper, Josef. 1963. *Leisure: The Basis of Culture.* Translated by Alexander Dru. New York: New American Library.

Prentis, Richard S. 1980. "White-collar Working Women's Perception of Retirement." *Gerontologist* 20(1): 90–95.

——. 1992. *Passages of Retirement: Personal Histories of Struggle and Success.* Westport, Conn.: Greenwood.

Price-Bonham, Sharon, and Carolyn Kitchings Johnson. 1982. "Attitudes toward Retirement: A Comparison of Professional and Nonprofessional Married Women." In *Women's Retirement: Policy Implications of Recent Research,* edited by Maximiliane Szinovacz, 123–38. Beverly Hills: Sage.

Puller, Lewis B., Jr. 1993. *Fortunate Son: The Autobiography of Lewis B. Puller, Jr.* New York: Bantam.

Quadagno, Jill. 1988. "Women's Access to Pensions and the Structure of Eligibility Rules: Systems of Production and Reproduction." *Sociological Quarterly* 29(4): 541–58.

——. 1991. "Generational Equity and the Politics of the Welfare State." In *Growing Old In America,* 4th ed., edited by Beth B. Hess and Elizabeth W. Markson, 341–51. New Brunswick, N.J.: Transaction Books.

——. 1999. *Aging and the Life Course: An Introduction to Social Gerontology.* New York: McGraw-Hill.

Quadagno, Jill, and Melissa Hardy. 1996. "Work and Retirement." In *Handbook of Aging and the Social Sciences,* edited by Robert H. Binstock and Linda K. George, 325–45. San Diego: Academic Press.

Rank, Otto. 1914. *The Myth of the Birth of the Hero, and Other Writings,* edited by Philip Freund. Reprint, New York: Random House, 1964.

——. 1932. *Art and Artist: Creative Urge and Personality Development.* Translated by Charles Francis Atkinson. Reprint, New York: Norton 1989.

Reitzes, Donald C., Elizabeth J. Mutran, and Maria E. Fernandez. 1996. "Does Retirement Hurt Well-being? Factors Influencing Self-esteem and Depression among Retirees and Workers." *Gerontologist* 36(5): 649–56.

Renault, Mary. 1958. *The King Must Die.* New York: Pantheon.

Riker, John. 1997. *Ethics and the Discovery of the Unconscious.* Albany: State University of New York Press.

Rodin, Judith. 1986. "Aging and Health: Effects of the Sense of Control." *Science* 233(4770): 1271–76.

Rogers, Gayle Thompson. 1985. "Nonmarried Women Approaching Retirement: Who Are They and When Do They Retire?" In *Current Perspectives on Aging and the Life Cycle: Work, Retirement and Social Policy,* vol. 1, edited by Zena Smith Blau, 169–91. Greenwich, Conn.: JAI Press.

Rosow, Irving. 1962. "Old Age: One Moral Dilemma of an Affluent Society." *Gerontologist* 2(4):182–91.

——. 1967. *Social Integration of the Aged.* New York: Free Press.

——. 1974. *Socialization to Old Age.* Berkeley: University of California Press.

Rowe, John W., and Robert L. Kahn. 1998. *Successful Aging.* New York: Pantheon.

Rowland, Mary. 1995. "The Bounty Hunters of the Pension Business." *New York Times,* 4 June, 9F.

Rubinstein, Robert L. 1987. "The Significance of Personal Objects to Older People." *Journal of Aging Studies* 1(3): 225–38.

Ruhm, Christopher J. 1989. "Why Older Americans Stop Working." *Gerontologist* 29(3): 294–99.

——. 1990. "Career Jobs, Bridge Employment, and Retirement." In *Bridges to Retirement: Older Workers in a Changing Labor Market,* edited by Peter B. Doeringer, 92–107. Ithaca: ILR Press.

Rybczynski, Witold. 1991. *Waiting for the Weekend.* New York: Viking.

Sartre, Jean-Paul. 1956. *Being and Nothingness: An Essay on Phenomenological Ontology.* Translated by Hazel Barnes. New York: Philosophical Library.

Savishinsky, Joel S. 1990. *Dementia Sufferers and Their Carers: A Study of Family Experiences and Supportive Services in the London Borough of Islington.* London: PNL Press.

——. 1991a. *The Ends of Time: Life and Work in a Nursing Home.* Westport, Conn.: Bergin and Garvey.

——. 1991b. "A New Life for the Old: The Role of the Elderly in the Bahamas." *The World and I* 6(3): 617–29.

——. 1994a. *The Trail of the Hare: Environment and Stress in A Sub-arctic Community.* 2d ed. New York: Gordon and Breach.

——. 1994b. "In and Out of Bounds: The Ethics of Respect in Studying Nursing Homes." In *The Culture of Long Term Care: Nursing Home Ethnography,* edited by J. Neil Henderson and Maria D. Vesperi, 93–109. Westport, Conn.: Bergin and Garvey.

——. 1995. "The Unbearable Lightness of Retirement: Ritual and Support in a Modern Life Passage." *Research on Aging* 17(3): 243–59.

———. 1998a. "At Work, at Home, at Large: The Sense of Person and Place in Retirement." *North American Dialogue* 3(1): 16–18.

———. 1998b. "Mastering the Art of Retirement." *Anthropology Newsletter* 39(7): 15.

Schaie, K. Warner. 1996. "Intellectual Development in Adulthood." In *Handbook of the Psychology of Aging*, 4th ed., edited by James E. Birren and K. Warner Schaie, 266–86. San Diego: Academic Press.

Scheper-Hughes, Nancy. 1982. *Saints, Scholars and Schizophrenics: Mental Illness in Rural Ireland*. Berkeley: University of California Press.

Schmidtz, David. 1997. *Rational Choice and Moral Agency*. Princeton: Princeton University Press.

Schooler, Carmi. 1987. "Cognitive Effects of Complex Environments during The Life Span: A Review and Theory." In *Cognitive Functioning and Social Structure over the Life Course*, edited by Carmi Schooler and K. Warner Schaie, 24–29. New York: Ablex.

———. 1990. "Psychological Factors and Effective Cognitive Functioning in Adulthood." In *Handbook of the Psychology of Aging*, 3d ed., edited by James Birren and K. Warner Schaie, 347–58. San Diego: Academic Press.

Schor, Juliet B. 1991. *The Overworked American: The Unexpected Decline of Leisure*. New York: Basic Books.

Scott-Maxwell, Florida. 1979. *The Measure of My Days*. New York: Penguin.

Segal, Robert A., ed. 1990. *In Quest of the Hero*. Princeton: Princeton University Press.

Shakespeare, William. 1608. *The Tragedy of King Lear*. Edited by Alfred Harbage. Reprint, Baltimore: Penguin Books, 1958.

Shenk, Dena. 1998. *Someone to Lend a Helping Hand: Women Growing Old in Rural America*. Amsterdam: Gordon and Breach.

Shield, Renée Rose. 1988. *Uneasy Endings: Daily Life in an American Nursing Home*. Ithaca: Cornell University Press.

Simmons, Leo. 1945. *The Role of the Aged in Primitive Society*. New Haven: Yale University Press.

Smelser, Neil J. 1980. "Issues in the Study of Work and Love." In *Themes of Love and Work in Adulthood*, edited by Neil J. Smelser and Erik H. Erikson, 1–26. Cambridge: Harvard University Press.

Sokolovsky, Jay. 1987. "Culture, Society, and Aging." In *Growing Old in Different Societies: Cross-cultural Perspectives*, edited by Jay Sokolovsky, 9–13. Littleton, Mass.: Copley.

Sokolovsky, Jay, ed. 1997. *The Cultural Context of Aging: Worldwide Perspectives*. 2d ed. Westport, Conn.: Bergin and Garvey.

Sonnenfeld, Jeffrey. 1988. *The Hero's Farewell: What Happens When CEOs Retire*. New York: Oxford University Press.

Speare, Alden, Jr., and Judith W. Meyer. 1988. "Types of Elderly Residential Mobility and Their Determinants." *Journal of Gerontology* 43(3): 74–81.

Spierer, Howard. 1977. *Major Transitions in the Human Life Cycle*. New York: Academy for Educational Development.

Stack, Carol. 1996. *Call to Home: African Americans Reclaim the Rural South*. New York: Basic Books.

Stokes, Eleanore M. 1990. "Ethnography of a Social Border: The Case of an American Retirement Community in Mexico." *Journal of Cross-cultural Gerontology* 5(2): 169–82.

Stone, Robyn, Gail Lee Cafferata, and Judith Sangl. 1987. "Caregivers of the Frail Elderly: A National Profile." *Gerontologist* 27(5): 616–26.

Streib, Gordon F., and Clement J. Schneider. 1971. *Retirement in American Society: Impact and Process.* Ithaca: Cornell University Press.

Szegedy-Maszak, Marianne. 1999. "Done with Work, Volunteers Move on to Giving Back." *New York Times* special section 15 on Retirement, 21 March 11.

Szinovacz, Maximiliane. 1980. "Female Retirement: Effects on Spousal Roles and Marital Adjustment." *Journal of Family Issues* 1(3): 423–40.

———. 1982a. "Introduction: Research on Women's Retirement." In *Women's Retirement: Policy Implications of Recent Research,* edited by Maximiliane Szinovacz, 13–21. Beverly Hills: Sage Publications.

Szinovacz, Maximiliane, ed. 1982b. *Women's Retirement: Policy Implications of Recent Research.* Beverly Hills: Sage.

Szinovacz, Maximiliane. 1983. "Beyond the Hearth: Older Women and Retirement." In *Older Women: Issues and Prospects,* edited by Elizabeth Markson, 93–120. Lexington, Mass.: Lexington Books.

Szinovacz, Maximiliane, David J. Ekerdt, and Barbara Vinick. 1992. "Families and Retirement: Conceptual and Methodological Issues." In *Families and Retirement,* edited by Maximiliane Szinovacz, David J. Ekerdt, and Barbara Vinick, 1–19. Newbury Park, Cal.: Sage.

Tennyson, Alfred. 1850. *In Memoriam.* Edited by Robert H. Ross. New York: Norton (1973 edition).

Thomas, William I., with Dororthy Swaine Thomas. 1928. *The Child in America.* New York: Knopf.

Thompson, Ernest. 1979. "On Golden Pond." In *Best American Screenplays. First Series,* edited by Sam Thomas, 425–59. Reprint, New York: Crown Publishers, 1986.

Thoreau, Henry David. 1854. *Walden.* Reprint, New York: Time-Life Books, 1962.

Tilak, Shrinivas. 1989. *Religion and Aging in the Indian Tradition.* Albany: State University of New York Press.

Troyansky, David G. 1999. "Why Do People Retire? Some Historical Answers." *Gerontologist* 39(5): 624–26.

Tu, Wei-ming. 1983. "The Idea of the Human in Mencian Thought: An Approach to Chinese Aesthetics." In *Theories of the Arts in China,* edited by Susan Bush and Christian Murck, 57–73. Princeton: Princeton University Press.

Turnbull, Colin M. 1983. *The Human Cycle.* New York: Simon and Schuster.

Turner, Victor. 1969. *The Ritual Process: Structure and Anti-structure.* Chicago: Aldine.

Uchitelle, Louis. 1995a. "Another Day Older and Running Out of Time." *New York Times,* 26 March, sec. 3: 1, 4.

———. 1995b. "Retirement's Worried Face." *New York Times,* 30 July, sec. 3: 1, 4, 5.

van Gennep, Arnold. 1908. *The Rites of Passage.* Translated by Monica Vizedom and Gabrielle Caffee. Reprint, Chicago: University of Chicago Press, 1960.

Vesperi, Maria. 1986. *City of Green Benches: Growing Old in a New Downtown.* Ithaca: Cornell University Press.

Vinick, Barbara J., and David J. Ekerdt. 1991. "The Transition to Retirement: Responses of Husbands and Wives." In *Growing Old in America,* 4th ed., edited by Beth B. Hess and Elizabeth W. Markson, 305–17. New Brunswick, N.J.: Transaction Books.

Voltaire (Francois Marie Arouet). 1759. *Candide.* Edited by Stanley Appelbaum. Reprint, New York: Dover, 1991.

Wayne, Leslie. 1994. "Pension Changes Raising Concerns." *New York Times* 29 August, A1, D3.

Weiss, Robert. 1990. *Staying the Course: The Emotional and Social Lives of Men Who Do Well at Work.* New York: Free Press.

Wilder, Thornton. 1938. *Our Town: A Play in Three Acts.* New York: Coward McCann.
Willette, Anne. 1995. "Will Boomers Go Bust?" *Ithaca Journal,* 11 May, 12A.
Wolfenstein, Martha. 1951. "The Emergence of Fun Morality." *Journal of Social Issues* 7(4): 15–25.
Woolf, Virginia. 1929. *A Room of One's Own.* Reprint, New York: Harcourt, Brace and World, 1957.
Young, John B. 1989. "Effects of Retirement on Aspects of Self-perception." *Archives of Gerontology and Geriatrics* 9(1): 67–76.

INDEX